WHEN WOMEN RULE THE COURT

Critical Issues in Sport and Society

Michael Messner and Douglas Hartmann, Series Editors

Critical Issues in Sport and Society features scholarly books that help expand our understanding of the new and myriad ways in which sport is intertwined with social life in the contemporary world. Using the tools of various scholarly disciplines, including sociology, anthropology, history, media studies and others, books in this series investigate the growing impact of sport and sports-related activities on various aspects of social life as well as key developments and changes in the sporting world and emerging sporting practices. Series authors produce groundbreaking research that brings empirical and applied work together with cultural critique and historical perspectives written in an engaging, accessible format.

Jules Boykoff, *Activism and the Olympics: Dissent at the Games in Vancouver and London*

Diana T. Cohen, *Iron Dads: Managing Family, Work, and Endurance Sport Identities*

Jennifer Guiliano, *Indian Spectacle: College Mascots and the Anxiety of Modern America*

Kathryn Henne, *Testing for Athlete Citizenship: The Regulation of Doping and Sex in Sport*

Jeffrey L. Kidder, *Parkour and the City: Risk, Masculinity, and Meaning in a Postmodern Sport*

Michael A. Messner and Michela Musto, eds., *Child's Play: Sport in Kids' Worlds*

Jeffrey Montez de Oca, *Discipline and Indulgence: College Football, Media, and the American Way of Life during the Cold War*

Stephen C. Poulson, *Why Would Anyone Do That? Lifestyle Sport in the Twenty-First Century*

Nicole Willms, *When Women Rule the Court: Gender, Race, and Japanese American Basketball*

WHEN WOMEN RULE THE COURT

Gender, Race, and Japanese American Basketball

NICOLE WILLMS

RUTGERS UNIVERSITY PRESS

New Brunswick, Camden, and Newark, New Jersey, and London

978–0-8135–8415–7
978–0-8135–8416–4
978–0-8135–8417–1
978–0-8135–8418–8

Cataloging-in-Publication data is available from the Library of Congress.

A British Cataloging-in-Publication record for this book is available from the British Library.

♾ The paper used in this publication meets the requirements of the American National Standard for Information Sciences—Permanence of Paper for Printed Library Materials, ANSI Z39.48–1992.

www.rutgersuniversitypress.org

Manufactured in the United States of America

For my firstborn, Celia Tsutako Bingo

CONTENTS

WHEN WOMEN RULE THE COURT

Introduction

"This Is What We Do"

Entering the Japanese Cultural Institute Carnival in the summer of 2009, I smell teriyaki-style barbeque wafting through the hot June air. Looking for former University of California, Los Angeles (UCLA) and University of Southern California (USC) basketball players Natalie Nakase and Jamie Hagiya, I enter the main building—an elementary school—for refuge from the heat. In the upstairs library, several youngsters, mostly girls, hover around a nearby table waiting to surrender three dollars for a photo with the collegiate stars. It is a bit of a mad house: the cashier is being inundated with new photo requests, while also trying to handle printing the photos that were already taken. Slowing down the process, Nakase and Hagiya stop to talk to each of their fans and challenge them to a shooting contest at a play-size basketball hoop in the corner. The tallies are neatly recorded on the blackboard at the back of the room: USC versus UCLA, with USC currently leading. As each photo rolls off the printer, Nakase and Hagiya stop and sign it, writing special messages to their fans.

As community heroines, Nakase and Hagiya have been special invited guests at many similar events in Southern California. They represent an exceptional type of sport icon and role model, one who is not only remarkably talented and accomplished, but also accessible. As Japanese Americans—Nakase is third- and Hagiya fourth-generation—they engender a sense of ethnic identification and pride for many of their co-ethnic fans. More than that, many of the Japanese Americans at these events feel proud that their community helped create these star players. Nakase and Hagiya—along with a number of other Japanese American women who have played college-level basketball and beyond—are the fruition of a Japanese American community investment in women's basketball.

More accurately, Japanese American community basketball leagues and tournaments ("J-Leagues") have been an investment in basketball opportunities for *all* community members. However, on the tails of the successes of many female players, many J-League participants have expanded and developed new community resources that cultivate female talent. The institutionalization of early training and playing opportunities paired with an impressive Japanese American social network within the world of women's basketball have created many channels for talented women to find places on high school, club/Amateur Athletic Union (AAU), and university basketball rosters.

Hagiya exemplifies this trend and has emerged as a distinct athletic icon for Japanese Americans, particularly in the greater Los Angeles area. She is also the original inspiration for this study. It was in the late fall of 2003 that I began attending women's basketball games at the University of Southern California and noticed Hagiya, who was then a freshman point guard. When Hagiya enters the basketball game, there is no mistaking her. She's kinetic, whether she is bringing the ball up the court, playing dizzyingly distracting defense, or whisking off nothing-but-net three-pointers. Her hair, which at the time she tied up in a high, braided ponytail, tends to swing to the rhythm of her ever-moving feet. She is quick, penetrating and indefatigable. She is a joy to watch.

Fairly quickly, I realized that I was not Hagiya's only fan. In a fast-paced, entertainment-saturated city, a college women's basketball game in the middle of South-Central Los Angeles rarely draws a crowd. So, with audiences commonly of just a couple hundred fans, it stood out that many of them—around fifty on an average night—were of Asian descent. Furthermore, perhaps not surprisingly, many of them were obviously there for Hagiya, producing roaring cheers when she made a basket and holding up signs with her name.

Soon after, the sociological imagination took hold and I began to wonder about the circumstances that had created this top-level player and the subsequent fan base that seemed to revel in her every move. Admittedly, her Asian ancestry was one reason why I was curious about her since it seemed like very few Asian Americans played in the higher divisions of college basketball. Yet somehow, I was even more excited by the fans. As a women's basketball enthusiast, I have often lamented that many players and teams do not get the support they deserve. Therefore, I was intrigued not only by how this great basketball player had come to be, but also by how her fans had come to support her in this way.

Just by scratching the surface of Hagiya's experience, I would begin to learn the rich story of a community—a community united, in part, by the game of basketball. Japanese Americans throughout many regions of California have created highly organized and expansive basketball networks that serve to unite thousands of Japanese Americans. Although some spots on teams are saved for non–Japanese Americans, the J-Leagues are viewed as a basketball network created by and for the Japanese American community, and many of the leagues and tournaments have policies of racial/ethnic exclusion in order to protect that goal (Chin 2012; King 2002).

The act of playing basketball as a community endeavor represents a larger, ongoing commitment to ethnic solidarity among many Japanese Americans in California. Ancestral connections to Japan and the collective experience of incarceration during World War II have historically united Japanese Americans living in communities along the West Coast. However, these past experiences are becoming distant from the lived experiences of the current generations. Longtime sport enthusiasts, many Japanese Americans have turned to community basketball as their most universal practice of Japanese American culture. Particularly for youth, it is a comfortable, if not necessary, way of "doing" Japanese American. As one scholar put it, "The tradition of playing in the J-league is more than just a family custom or community expectation; it is a Japanese American community induction" (Hedani 2015).

The Japanese Americans involved in J-Leagues tend to be passionate about what they have created. Some of the more enthusiastic participants start their children in youth clinics at the age of four and play themselves until well into their fifties and sixties. Many families sign up their children because playing in the J-Leagues is a way to establish a connection with an increasingly dispersed ethnic community. For many, it has become their primary connection, placing a greater significance on participation. Basketball has become more than a fun pastime. There is now an imperative that the J-Leagues remain a vibrant part of community life and be passed along to the next generation.

Over the nearly hundred-year history of Japanese American community involvement in basketball, girls and women have always been co-participants. In the contemporary context, their involvement has become even more important to the vision of the J-Leagues as an inclusive, meaningful, community-driven endeavor. Particularly at the youth level, offering nearly egalitarian playing opportunities to boys and girls has been key to fostering widespread community involvement. It could be argued that the more tenuous the links among Japanese Americans, the more important it has become to build a gender-inclusive basketball network.

As Title IX opened up more opportunities and college scholarships for female athletes, Japanese American women trained in the J-Leagues stood ready to take advantage of these new prospects.[1] This marked the beginning of a trend that continues to this day: Japanese American women have been a relatively small, but consistent presence in California collegiate basketball. Hagiya and Nakase are the most accomplished examples of what has become a fairly steady stream of female basketball talent emerging from the J-Leagues. Check the rosters of many of the California State University women's basketball teams and you will likely see a Japanese surname. A few of the private colleges in Southern California, such as Chapman University and the University of La Verne, also consistently recruit from the J-League talent pool. Even the bigger women's basketball powerhouses—UCLA, USC, UC Berkeley— have had Japanese American women on their rosters. The sustained presence of J-League women in collegiate basketball is in part due to networks of J-League-affiliated coaches—who not only train and mentor talented players, but also use their connections to cultivate opportunities.

As basketball is an activity of such importance to J-League participants, it possesses its own icons. The most prominent icons in the post–Title IX era have been young women who have emerged from the leagues to find success in collegiate basketball and beyond. Many Japanese American women have enjoyed a small taste of subcultural celebrity: fans come to their games, and the Los Angeles Japanese American newspaper, *Rafu Shimpo*, eagerly covers the highlights of their careers.

Nakase and Hagiya took their subcultural celebrity to the next level, and on their own home turf. The greater Los Angeles area is the epicenter of the J-Leagues, and Nakase and Hagiya are both from Los Angeles suburbs and grew up playing in the leagues. Each became a standout point guard at the one of the largest universities in Southern California. Hagiya, a dominant point guard at USC (2003–2008), would later go on to play basketball professionally in Europe and is now making a huge splash in the competitive CrossFit scene. Natalie Nakase made waves as a successful guard at UCLA (1998–2003) and then went on to play in a U.S. semiprofessional league, as well as professionally in Europe. After retiring from playing, she went on to break barriers in the world of men's basketball: she coached a men's professional team in Japan, and is now on the coaching staff of the Los Angeles Clippers, an NBA team.

The celebrated athletes are an outgrowth of the Japanese American community investment in women's basketball, yet they themselves have become a widely dispersed symbolic resource, part of the dividends on this investment. After their playing careers, some of the well-known players have both given back to the community and simultaneously capitalized on their fame by running basketball camps, coaching youth teams, and training young athletes. Most stay close to the community—one might see them at J-League basketball tournaments, playing in the elite adult divisions or giving inspiring speeches during the opening ceremonies. However, the importance of their presence resonates beyond basketball environments: players also make featured appearances at community festivals, parades, carnivals, and fund-raisers, with a select few even receiving honors and keynote speaking engagements at prominent Japanese American organizations.

These successful players help to reinforce the practice of Japanese American basketball itself, but are also framed as heroines in ways that symbolize important elements of community identity. The success of Nakase and Hagiya, as well as that of all the other women whose names have been scattered across team rosters throughout California and beyond over the past forty-plus years, serves to confirm the purpose and potential of the J-Leagues as a community project. For many Japanese American participants in the J-Leagues, ethnic identity and solidarity are built not only in the practice of maintaining basketball leagues, but also through star players. These players become a source of pride and ethnic identification, as well as role models for youth. They are an attractive symbolic package—successful basketball players who embody idealized Japanese Americans citizenship, "good girls" who bring pride and esteem to the community.

Recently, Taiwanese American Jeremy Lin has been a major focus of attention as an Asian American basketball star. The 2012–2013 outpouring of media attention on Lin and a surge in scholarship on the surprise star (e.g., Combs and Wasserstrom 2013; Park 2015; Yep 2012) show that his success was momentous. However, in focusing on Lin, journalists and scholars are missing the predominant story since the passage of Title IX—that the majority of contemporary Asian American basketball stars have been women.

This book tells the story of women who became sport icons by looking specifically at the place of basketball in the Japanese American communities of California. As these communities created the institution of J-League basketball, they simultaneously reimagined the boundaries that define who is an expected or recognized "athlete," who counts as a basketball player. As a community project, basketball is a shared asset not limited to the fastest or the tallest and not created solely for boys and men. A unique space for female athletic empowerment emerged.

RACIAL/ETHNIC COMMUNITY AND SPORT

Japanese Americans are far from unique in their community attachments to sport. In the modern era, numerous marginalized groups have engaged in community-exclusive engagements with sport. It has been an especially popular practice among first- and second-generation immigrants to the United States, as these groups have often sought out the comfort and safety of the ethnic community while at the same time feeling an attraction to the sporting pursuits valued by the dominant society (Franks 2010; Levine 1992; Gems 2013). Ethnic-exclusive sport was even more widespread in the first half of the twentieth century when more formal policies of racial segregation meant that even play at the YMCA was primarily with co-ethnics. In California, recreational teams were often made up of co-ethnics, but played against teams of different racial/ethnic backgrounds (Culver 2010; Yep 2009).

It was in the early twentieth century that Japanese Americans first became involved in playing sports, with the nisei, or second generation, most interested in basketball and baseball (Franks 2010, 2016; Regalado 2013). Chinese Americans in this era also engaged with a variety of sports (Park 2000), including baseball (Wren 2016), basketball (Yep 2009), and volleyball (Liang 2014; Nakamura 2016), and continue to do so to this day. White ethnic groups, such as Jewish Americans (Kugelmass 2007; Levine 1992; Sclar 2008) and Italian Americans (Gems 2013), also pursued sport as a community. Early traveling professional "barnstorm" basketball teams were often composed of one ethnic or racial group, such as Irish American, African American, or Chinese American

(Yep 2009). Mexican Americans have also had notable historical community engagements with sport (Alamillo 2003; Balderrama and Santillan 2011; Innis-Jiménez 2009). Native Americans
have played both traditional games and, since the era of boarding
schools, been active participants in many American sports, often
in tribal or intertribal exclusive spaces (Davies 2012). In addition
to events such as the "All-Indian Rodeo" (Penrose 2003), several
Native American nations have maintained strong community ties
to basketball, which has helped them build intertribal connections.
Davies (2012, 275) argues that "basketball is a force that has helped
American Indians create a shared intertribal sporting identity."

Emerging out of World War II and into the civil rights era, formal segregation in sport began to disappear. However, one can still
find numerous examples of sports teams and leagues created by
and for recent immigrant groups. For example, in Southern California, first- and second-generation Mexican Americans play in
community leagues for teams composed of players from the same
region in Mexico (Pescador 2004), and migrant laborers from
Mexico set up their own soccer leagues in Salinas, California, in
which many of their children also play (Figueroa 2003).

The attractiveness of ethnic-exclusive sport is likely the result
of a push-pull phenomenon: the pull of shared culture—language,
food, customs—and the push of being ostracized by the mainstream culture. The popularity among more recent immigrant
groups is most comprehensible because of the strength of shared
culture. However, how can we make sense of multigenerational
Americans playing in ethnic sport leagues?

Asian American sport leagues and tournaments represent a
thriving part of the contemporary sport scene (Franks 2016). They
are at times panethnic, open to a wide range of players of Asian
descent, and at other times ethnic-exclusive. Chinese Americans
continue to hold annual national volleyball and basketball tournaments (Nakamura 2016). South Asian Americans play basketball
in Indo-Pak leagues in Atlanta and participate in regional Asian
American tournaments (Thangaraj 2015). Hmong Americans
hold both Hmong-only and Asian American sport tournaments

in the Midwest, where flag football and soccer are popular (Vang 2016). Although second-generation Americans seem to make up the majority of participants in many of these leagues and tournaments, this is not always the case. Particularly for Japanese and Chinese Americans, who are more likely to be third-, fourth-, or even fifth-generation Americans, the persistent desire to play on Asian American teams points to larger social contexts that create constraints on Asian American engagement with sport.

As I will discuss more fully later in this introduction, it is not a coincidence that it is groups of Asian Americans who are seeking out segregated sporting experiences. The dominant society often racializes Asian American bodies as *not* athletic, providing an incentive to play in environments where people do not carry these assumptions. It creates a safe space, away from the overt racism and microaggressions Asian Americans often face in mainstream sporting spaces (Chin 2015). It also allows the players to define themselves and their playing style in ways that feel good to them (Thangaraj 2015).

What is unique about contemporary Japanese American engagements with basketball? Although there are few other ethnic communities that match J-League basketball in terms of its longevity, scope, and size, what might most set this community most apart is the extent of its community investment in girls' and women's basketball.

Japanese Americans have been playing basketball as a community for nearly one hundred years, creating a feel of tradition, family bonding, and passing the torch to the next generation. Parents and their adult children sometimes play together. At times, the grandparents are still playing! The longevity of the community's involvement with basketball, and the multigenerational environment it creates, is rare in community sport, although it does exist in some Chinese American sports (Nakamura 2016; Park 2000; Yep 2009) and in the sporting traditions of some Native American nations (Davies 2012).

The size and scope of today's youth and adult J-Leagues are remarkable. How do the J-Leagues accommodate Lil Tigers (age four) up through the "dirt" or "legend" divisions (for players over fifty)? They do so by being large enough to facilitate multiple basketball-playing experiences—often divided by region, gender, age, and skill level. As a group with a higher than average median income (2006–2010 American Community Survey), Japanese participants are generally able to afford organization and tournament fees, helping to support the expansiveness of the playing opportunities. The scope may be unmatched, although the national network of Native American basketball tournaments may be a close second (Davies 2012).

How many are playing? When the Japanese American National Museum produced an exhibit on sport in the Japanese American community, they asked basketball community leaders to count the participants. The number for the Southern California region was estimated at ten thousand—and that is just Southern California! The more recent estimate is at fourteen thousand for the same region (King 2012). Fugita and O'Brien (1991) conducted a survey of Japanese American men in 1979–1980 in three major urban concentrations of Japanese Americans in California: Fresno, Gardena, and Sacramento. They found that 20.1 percent of Japanese American men were participating in a Japanese American sport league. This reflects only direct participation—the effects of the J-Leagues and their athletic icons reverberate throughout the Japanese American communities of California. The Little Tokyo Service Center produced a map (see image I.1) showing all of the contemporary organizations in Southern California that sponsor basketball teams for leagues and tournaments. The map illustrates the sheer number, as well as the wide geographical distribution, of J-League organizations in the greater Los Angeles area.

Because contemporary J-Leagues exist primarily in California, and most extensively in Southern California, they allow for larger networks of players and frequent, year-round competition. Most ethnic- or race-centered sport leagues are either smaller, based in one community, or hold only one or two regional or national tournaments a year. For examples, this is the model of the "Indo-Pak"

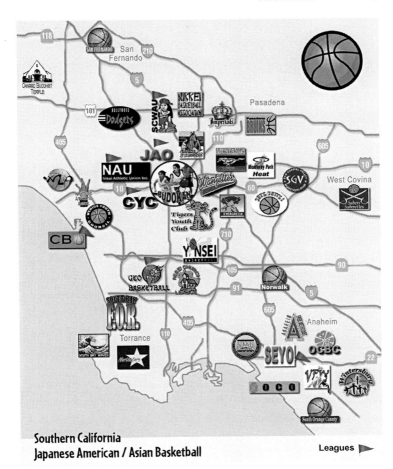

IMAGE I.1. The World of Japanese American Basketball. Each icon on the map represents an organization involved with the J-Leagues in Southern California. (Credit: Mike Murase.)

leagues in Atlanta (Thangaraj 2015) and also holds true for several Native American nations (Anderson 2006; Davies 2012).

Finally, not all ethnic leagues provide extensive opportunities for women. Indo-Pak and Hmong leagues and tournaments offer some limited playing opportunities for girls and women, but there is a clear gender hierarchy (Thangaraj 2015; Vang 2016). Women have had a long history of play in the Chinese Leagues of California (Yep 2009), but there just is not the community-wide support and infrastructure for a widespread engagement with sport—many Chinese American women interested in basketball migrate over to the J-Leagues. Many leagues officially reserve spots for their Chinese American counterparts.

For Japanese American women, timing has been everything. The first wave of Japanese American interest in basketball was in the 1920s, also a "golden age" for women's basketball in California (Emery and Toohey-Costa 1991). Japanese Americans continued to create playing opportunities for girls and women, even in times when mainstream interest waned. However, only in the post–Title IX era have high school, college, and professional standouts started to become community icons and inspire even more participants. Other social forces likely influenced the investment in girls' basketball in the contemporary era, as well. As organized youth sports became an increasingly important part of North American middle-class family life (Adler and Adler 1994, 1998; Coakley 2009; Messner 2009; Trussell and Shaw 2012), Japanese Americans kept up with the demand by creating more and more playing opportunities for boys *and* girls.

The historical and contemporary contexts of Japanese American engagement with sport have created an environment today where girls' participation is normalized and even perceived as mandatory for families who view basketball as their primary link to the Japanese American community. The social benefits that Japanese Americans describe receiving through J-League basketball are accessible only if one is actively participating, so parents often see the value in placing their children on J-League teams from an early age. If the parents are no longer playing, their child's participation is the parents' link to the community. Shuddering at the thought of the community investing in basketball only for boys, one participant exclaimed, "What if a family had only girls?"

The expansiveness of the leagues paired with an ethic of including all community members has led to gender-inclusiveness, broadly defined. Participants do not necessarily need to meet a particular standard of masculine embodiment; there is far less policing of

which bodies belong in sport. Important to recruitment and reten-
tion, less competitive-minded or less capable players can usually still
find a basketball team on which they can thrive. At the same time,
more physical and competitive play is also abundant, as well as teams
that embrace a little of both. This kind of inclusive engagement with
sport has meant a renegotiation of the traditional gendered meanings in sport. Gender-inclusive engagement with basketball has
become integral to the structure and culture of the J-Leagues and
productive of new ways of imagining female athleticism.

Cementing their unique support of women's basketball, the
J-Leagues have produced many successful female basketball players
who are beloved by the community. Admiring and identifying with
male sport stars from one's ethnic group is nothing new (Gems 2013,
2014; Kugelmass 2007), but female icons have been much rarer. The
J-Leagues are also relatively distinctive in that these heroines are
homegrown, trained within the community. The only other communities that might come close to this relationship with their female
basketball stars are a few of the North American First Nations and
Native Americans who offer playing opportunities to both girls and
boys and follow the successes of those athletes who do well in the
mainstream (Paraschak 1990; Paraschak and Forsyth 2010).

COMMUNITY CULTURAL WEALTH: BASKETBALL LEAGUES AND ICONS

Basketball has become a shared community endeavor for Japanese Americans and a source of community cultural wealth (Yosso
2005). Simply put, Japanese Americans invest in basketball, and
specifically women's basketball, because it pays off in community
dividends. Importantly, it may yield benefits in ways that are not
commonly recognized.

According to scholar Pierre Bourdieu, sport is made up of social
environments—"fields," he would say—where people are able to
distinguish themselves by possessing knowledge, networks, and
other resources that give them access to a particular sport and any

social benefits it conveys (1978, 1984). By developing a large net-work of community sport organizations and leagues, as well as links to mainstream sporting institutions, Japanese Americans could be interpreted as creating capital, or resources that have value in the larger society.

In Bourdieu's theory of distinction (1984), getting access to the most rewarded forms of capital is key to achieving a higher social status. He also lays out in detail why that is so difficult to achieve for those born into lower status groups—privileged groups have set the bar high and make sure that their group has the smoothest path to acquiring recognized and rewarded capital for high status fields. For example, if mainstream men's basketball is seen as high status, as a marginalized racial/ethnic group, Japanese Americans may face barriers to achieving in this field.

There are barriers for Japanese Americans who seek men's basketball-related capital. Japanese Americans have invested quite heavily in youth basketball, but in recent decades have had very few men from their community play at the college or professional level. The culture of contemporary men's basketball suggests that appropriate basketball bodies are tall and powerful—Asian bodies symbolize the opposite. Asian American players have a difficult time meeting the entry requirements because they possess bodies already marked as deficient. The theory suggests that these barriers will end up reproducing Japanese American marginalization in the mainstream sporting world.

The J-Leagues are able to provide a space for Asian American boys and men to play basketball, a work-around for the oftentimes limited access in the mainstream. However, the J-Leagues have also built an equally supportive girls' basketball program that *is* yielding success in the mainstream. Women's basketball capital may not carry the same level of mainstream status and rewards as men's, but it has become a huge source of pride and validation for the Japanese American community.

The community investment in women's basketball may be a rather intelligent adaptation to the contemporary context. Yosso (2005) argues that Bourdieu's theories about cultural resources are often applied in a way that creates a deficit view of communities of color. The focus is all too often on how marginalized groups lack the forms of capital that are recognized and rewarded by the dominant groups in society, inevitably painting the marginalized group as deficient. Instead, she suggests looking at the community cultural wealth produced by marginalized groups. Many of these groups have not only shared cultural resources, but also adaptive strategies for surviving as minorities in society.

The J-Leagues and their embedded investment in women's basketball represent community practices that are not necessarily aimed at assimilation or improving social status in a direct way. Yet, the J-Leagues are undoubtedly a part of Japanese American community cultural wealth. They help create forms of capital that are not always directly recognized or rewarded by the dominant culture. Nonetheless, they tend to produce positive effects for the group members. They help build community, an important source of support and solidarity. They provide a gender-inclusive sporting environment, defying the gender and racial stereotypes often present in mainstream sports. The J-Leagues have fostered impressive networks in mainstream women's basketball, a huge source of social capital for aspiring Japanese American athletes. Finally, the players who achieve in college and beyond are symbolic resources—the successful women evoke a sense of pride and are regarded as healthy role models for youth. Put together, the J-Leagues and the community investment in women's basketball are highly valuable, even if not in ways automatically recognized by the dominant culture.

Importantly, the community cultural wealth is not a wealth that can or should be measured against other communities' wealth. It does not serve as evidence that Japanese Americans are model minorities, able to achieve in spite of their marginalized status. J-League basketball is not a cultural wealth that helps Japanese Americans do well in sports, despite their perceived deficiencies. J-Leagues and the concurrent investment in women's sports are adaptive cultural practices—these practices have been influenced by racism and racist imagery, but they do not necessarily overcome these social forces, but paint around them.

The inventive projects of community cultural wealth form in response to the marginalization experienced by communities of color. In the following sections I discuss some of the historical and contemporary context for the investments in the J-Leagues and in women's basketball.

SOCIOHISTORICAL CONTEXT

Japanese Americans have had a history of state-sanctioned discrimination in the United States (Daniels 1974). Until after World War II, Japanese Americans were not permitted to become naturalized citizens, and Japanese Americans are the only US group to have experienced "wholesale incarceration because of their ethnic background" (Fugita and O'Brien 1991, 30). In addition, prior to World War II, Japanese Americans were excluded from employment in most occupations within the private and public sectors. In response, Japanese Americans formed "a parallel community" (Fugita and O'Brien 1991, 30), creating their own interconnected economy and social life. An important piece of this strategy involved establishing voluntary associations (often based on models in Japan) that helped to support their communities through the times of exclusion. The nisei, or second generation, more often formed organizations that mirrored those in mainstream society, such as basketball and baseball teams and leagues (Fugita and O'Brien 1991).

During World War II, the experience of the concentration camps affected every aspect of Japanese Americans' lives. Although evacuation irrevocably damaged many of their business and economic networks, in the postwar period many Japanese Americans sought each other out and attempted to rebuild aspects of the prewar community (Fugita and O'Brien 1991). In addition, the incarceration became a "unique shared event" (Fugita and O'Brien 1991, 31) providing an even deeper connection among Japanese Americans. Interwoven into these experiences were sports, a shared practice that helped Japanese Americans through the experience of incarceration and the postwar recovery.

UNEXPECTED ATHLETES,
UNEXPECTED COMMUNITY

That Japanese Americans have chosen basketball as a gender-inclusive, community-wide activity and women as their basketball icons may seem to outsiders as a bit of an unexpected path. Japanese Americans are considered part of the larger racial group known as Asian Americans. Asian Americans are stereotyped as too bookish, too foreign, or too physically slight to play such a physical, all-American game like basketball (King 2006, 2010; Thangaraj 2015). For further shock value, Japanese American women—often stereotyped as quiet, passive, and petite—are highly active in these leagues and make up the majority of successful players who venture out into the mainstream.

That Japanese American women's achievements in basketball are, to those outside the community, an unexpected phenomenon speaks to US cultural understandings of race, class, and gender and reveals a cultural production of hierarchy and exclusion. Expectation, according to Deloria (2004, 11), is how "popular culture works to produce—and sometimes to compromise—racism and misogyny." When we are caught by surprise, it reveals our expectations. In these feelings, Deloria argues, lies a story of power; it is the normalization of some groups and the othering of others. King (2010) applied Deloria's ideas to Asian Americans in sport, arguing that in the US imagination, the idea of an Asian athlete is viewed as an oxymoron—completely unexpected.

The intersection of identities associated with power relations—such as race and gender, as well as class, sexuality, nationality—informs the unexpected nature of the Asian American athlete and, in particular, the elite Japanese American female basketball player. Their participation is mediated by the gendered and racialized imagery that surrounds Japanese American and Asian American bodies and the sport of basketball. It has been argued that Asian Americans have been racialized in contrast to other groups—against the white normative and African American extremes (Kim 1999; Yep 2012). Basketball's connections to masculinity and African

American culture, not to mention its associations with height and athleticism, make Asian American women involved in competitive basketball particularly paradoxical figures.

Because of the perception of noninvolvement, media attention and academic scholarship on Asian Americans in sport have been limited, with a notable bump in the past couple of years focusing on Jeremy Lin and Asian American men in sport (Combs and Wasserstrom 2013; Park 2015; Thangaraj 2015; Yep 2012). Even more limited is the attention to Asian American women in sport, again with some notable exceptions (Hanson 2005; Yep 2009).

Asian American Bodies

The racialization of Asian Americans is a topic under constant debate, but I outline the theories of racialization that seem to have the most bearing on how Asian Americans are perceived in the sport context. Racialization, according to Omi and Winant (2014), signifies "the extension of racial meaning to a previously unclassified relationship, social practice or group" (14). Omi and Winant emphasize that this is a process that is another constant revision in response to political pressures from various groups, making the concept of race "an unstable and 'decentered' complex of social meanings" (15).

Although care must be taken in theorizing racialization in comparative ways, Kim (1999) has several compelling insights embedded in her theory of racial triangulation that help us to understand how Asian Americans have been interpreted in US society. Kim argues that Asian and African Americans have often been imagined in contrasting ways, triangulated against white Americans who occupy an invisible "normal" category. In cultural terms, for example, African Americans are often portrayed as culturally inferior to other groups, while Asian Americans are often portrayed as culturally superior. However, Asian Americans are also marked as cultural and political outsiders—they may be perceived as successful, but only due to their foreignness. Yep saw this trend in coverage of NBA player Jeremy Lin (2012). He was portrayed as a novelty and an outsider, even as his supposed cultural superiority was touted.

I think there is a strong case to be made that a similar type of comparative racialization is highly influential in the sport context. Building on the ideas of Kim (1999) and Yep (2012), I would like to introduce the idea of an embodied racial triangulation, a comparative racialization of the physical bodies of athletes. Particularly in sports that are perceived as aggressive and physical, such as basketball, essentialized racial categories are salient and racial comparisons are often overt or thinly veiled. This is very evident in college and professional men's basketball. The game is strongly associated with African American players and culture. More than that, it is commonly assumed that African Americans are genetically gifted athletes (Hoberman 1997; Miller 1998). Common stereotypes are that they are faster and jump higher than men of other races. Asian Americans, in contrast, have essentially the opposite stereotypes associated with their athleticism. They are seen as small and weak. If accorded any acknowledgment of athletic talent, they may be perceived to be good at the fine-motor-skill sports with strong connections to East Asian societies, such as ping-pong, badminton, and martial arts. African Americans are imagined as genetically gifted, superior, "natural" athletes, whereas Asian American are imagined as the deficient, inferior, "unnatural" athletes. White Americans are assumed to be the normal athletes, the normal bodies. White athletes might occasionally be tall, but most of white athletic talent is attributed to hard work or intelligence on the court, giving credit to the players' personal moral character. It is these moral qualities that are often seen as enabling whites to transcend normalcy and achieve greatness.

In recent years, these same attributions of character-built success have been applied to an Asian American, Jeremy Lin, but they have had an Asian American twist. His personal qualities have been seen as enabling him to overcome a supposedly unnatural, highly unexpected rise to NBA success. As Yep (2012) argues, however, he has also been seen as a novelty. Precisely because he is such an anomaly he has ended up confirming both the cultural and the physical racial triangulation. The unexpected nature of his success has been key to his portrayal as a popular news story.

Gender also plays a role in how athletes are racialized. Stereotypes and other imagery surrounding Asian Americans can be described as "controlling images" (Collins 2002). These images influence the way that groups are understood and act to other members of these groups. In this way they act as ideological assaults (Le Espiritu 2008). Although symbolic, these images are powerful and influence interactions and self-perceptions (Collins 2002; Le Espiritu 2008; Pyke and Johnson 2003). Gendered controlling images tend to exclude Asian Americans from most characteristics associated with masculinity. Because of the common association between masculinity and sport, Asian Americans become symbolically excluded from many sport contexts.

Controlling images of Asian American women paint them as an even more unlikely athlete. Le Espiritu (2008) argues that gender and sexuality play a key part in constructing racist images. Asian American women tend to be exoticized in strongly feminine archetypes, such as "Lotus Blossom" or "China Doll," in which they are imagined as demure and subservient, or as "Dragon Lady," in which they are imagined as hypersexual and seductively dangerous (Le Espiritu 2008). They are seen as a "petite and exotic beauty" (Paek and Shah 2003, 236). Nearly all of these stereotypical images of Asian American women, when juxtaposed against images of an athlete in a physical sport such as basketball, create a paradoxical picture.

Forever Foreigners, American Sport

The dominant conception of Asian Americans as foreigners or as possessing a foreign culture also places them at odds with the image of an athlete in an all-American sport. Research has shown that Asian American athletes can still be perceived as "foreign" or as possessing a foreign culture, even when the athlete is a multigenerational American (Creef 2004; Tuan 1999).

Japanese Americans have long had to fight the battle of being perceived as foreigners, and the consequences of this perception have not been limited to isolated instances of interpersonal discrimination. Specifically, holding Japanese Americans in US concentration camps during World War II represented a full-scale denial of the rights of citizenship based on a perception of foreign allegiance. Then, post-1965, an influx of Asian American immigrants caused Japanese to be "reracialized as foreigners" (Lim 2006, 189). Japanese Americans, along with other Asian Americans, still experience microaggressions that communicate that they must be new to America, even though their grandparent or great-grandparent may have immigrated here (Sue et al. 2007).

Model Minorities?

In the famous article that first articulated the model minority myth (Petersen 1966), Japanese Americans were described as having an essentialized Japanese culture, despite being majority US-born, that allowed them to thrive in the face of discrimination, while African Americans, possessing a supposed inferior culture, did not possess this cultural resilience. The myth positioned Japanese Americans, as well as other Asian Americans, as superior to African Americans and other marginalized groups with high levels of poverty, but foreign to whites. Their valorization is still linked to civic ostracism, to not quite belonging (Kim 1999). The perceived cultural traits that allegedly make the group culturally superior to "not-so-model minorities" are also seen as out of sync with mainstream (white) culture due to their foreignness. An example of this type of racialization is in how mainstream media tended to cover Olympic ice skater Kristi Yamaguchi, essentializing her "Japaneseness" even though she is fourth-generation Japanese American (Kim 1999).

Model minorities are typically depicted as hardworking and high-achieving, as able to overcome obstacles and achieve success in America (Osajima 1988). However, this portrayal masks some less favorable agendas and consequences. By seeing Asian Americans as homogenized, it silences the range of voices and experiences within the group, and hides issues of discrimination and poverty (Lee 1996; Takaki 1989). The myth also helps to perpetuate controlling images and restrictive stereotypes about Asian Americans (Le Espiritu 2008). In addition, the model minority myth is a clear critique of other minority groups. The "model" in model minority inherently makes a direct comparison and critique of "not so model" minorities, and early articles about the model minority clearly made the comparison between African Americans and Asian Americans (Kim 1999; Saito 2009).

The model minority stereotype can affect Asian American men and women in different ways, but it can often be a restrictive box for both sexes. Thangaraj (2015) argues that the model minority myth has been a stifling, emasculating image for Asian American men, not to mention a source of tension for those who are not academically or economically successful. Koshy (2004) theorizes that Asian American women are held up as a "sexual model minority": not only economic successes, but also ideal sexual/gendered objects. They are particularly "model" because they are perceived to possess a combination of compliance and sex appeal that has a positive connotation for the American imagination when juxtaposed against stereotypical images of white and black women. This so-called positive imagery surrounding Asian American women contains an element of exclusion—it is her perceived foreignness, her exoticness that makes the Asian American woman desirable. What are supposedly superior feminine traits are also perceived as foreign, excluding Asian American women from a sense of normalcy. These damaging stereotypes limit Asian Americans in their potential for self-definition and influence their interactions.

Basketball as Resistance

It is important to note that the J-Leagues and their female participants are far from unexpected for most Japanese Americans. Not only are the Japanese American women discussed in this book powerful, driven, and talented, but they are also not seen as unusual in their community—they are naturalized and seen as an extension of a community project. And as the Japanese American communities of California have been crafting the contemporary story of who they are, they have made these women the protagonists.

As Asian Americans are subjected to stereotypes that portray the group as studious rather than athletic, as forever foreigners rather than undisputed Americans, and as small and feminine, rather than strong and powerful, simply playing a sport becomes a powerful site of resistance. Thangaraj (2015) theorizes that South Asian men participating in basketball might reimagine and subvert these controlling images inscribed on Asian American bodies through participation in a masculine, physical, mainstream sport. The men practice the sport in ways that help them to redefine their racialized masculine identities. They adopt tough, hypermasculine personas that help them compensate for controlling images of Asian Americans that they may feel are emasculating. Basketball, associated with African American culture and the related "cool pose" masculinity, is a useful symbol to attach to in this pursuit.

For many Japanese American players (predominantly men, but also some women), playing basketball has facilitated a similar space of masculine identification, just as Thangaraj (2014, 2015) found. It's a way to be tough, masculine, and all-American. However, for Japanese Americans, there is also a communal identity that has been negotiated and reimagined through basketball. This is where women as participants and symbols become important and complementary to the more masculine, cool, and American symbolism that men's basketball in particular evokes.

It may be, in fact, that the women's game, in its softened associations with African American masculinity, is a less problematic symbolic association for some Japanese Americans. Although participation in basketball makes sense as a community strategy in terms of emphasizing the group's Americanness and counteracting stereotypes about being small and nonathletic, the sport is increasingly associated with urban African Americans and the related hip-hop culture. For many Japanese Americans, this association might have some positive connections—a way to perform masculinity and coolness. However, for the community as a whole, the image is potentially less desirable: racist associations link hip-hop culture with poverty and illegal behavior. However, the links between basketball, African Americans, and hip-hop culture are stronger in men's basketball than in women's. The WNBA, for example, has been able to sell itself as a family-friendly activity in part because it has highlighted its marquee white players and African American players who exude a more middle-class image (Banet-Weiser 1999). Thus, women's basketball may be associated with more comfortable, middle-class symbols, while still subverting many stereotypes about Asian American athleticism.

Who Are the J-League Participants?

Participants in the J-Leagues are not necessarily representative of Asian America writ large. Japanese Americans are a unique Asian American group. They are majority US-born and have a high rate of out-marriage.[2] US census data for 2010 show that approximately one in three Japanese Americans is multiracial, the highest rate among Asian American ethnic groups (AAJC 2015, 9).

The J-League participants represent the diversity of the modern Japanese America, and even have a panethnic feel as most organizations allow other Asian Americans to join the teams in limited numbers (Chinese Americans are most visible). Nevertheless, the dominant culture of the basketball scene is made up of third- and fourth-generation Japanese Americans. They are typically the grandchildren and great-grandchildren of those who immigrated in the early part of the twentieth century and were incarcerated during World War II. Many readily identify basketball as part of their Japanese American culture, as much as if not more than attending obon festivals or eating Japanese cuisine.

Participants in the J-Leagues see themselves as part of a Japanese American "community," so I use the term often throughout this book—in part to honor how this group refers to itself, but also as a way to emphasize the importance of interactions and shared practices that occur among many Japanese Americans, particularly those in more dense concentrations along the West Coast. For many Japanese Americans, ethnicity is something that is actively "done" and not just an identifying marker. They belong to ethnic-based organizations at a rate matched in the United States only by Jewish Americans (Fugita and O'Brien 1991).

Although I spoke with J-League participants from other parts of California, the focus of this study was on the J-League participants and organizations based in the greater Los Angeles metropolis—spanning Los Angeles and Orange counties. Because of the desire among many Japanese Americans to interact as an ethnic community, place matters. "Ethnic community connotes a nested geography of populations," but the geographical boundaries can be as broad as the United States or as particular as an ethnic enclave (Kurashige 2002, xv). With Japanese Americans, the ethnic enclave no longer exists. "The internment of Japanese Americans during World War II shattered the spatial communities they had occupied in urban and rural areas" (Vo and Bonus 2002, 7). However, many Japanese Americans practice community in a way that necessitates at least some geographical proximity. The greater Los Angeles area, still home to the largest concentration of Japanese Americans on the mainland, is the place where Japanese American community most vibrantly happens. Although Los Angeles has been a hub for Japanese Americans since their early immigration, "the significance of Los Angeles grew after World War II. As farmers migrated to cities and residents in Hawaii increasingly moved to the mainland, the urban pattern of Los Angeles became the unquestioned norm of Japanese American life" (Kurashige 2002, xvi).

The Japanese Americans who represent the dominant culture of the J-Leagues are descendants of a particular wave of Japanese immigration. Therefore, the community itself identifies itself in generational terms. The issei, or "first generation," immigrated to the mainland of the United States between 1885 and 1924. The nisei, their children, were typically born between 1915 and 1935. The sansei, grandchildren of the original immigrants, are mostly baby boomers, born between 1945 and 1965 (Niiya 1993). The fourth (yonsei) and fifth generations (gosei) now represent the bulk of the youth participants in the J-Leagues. Organizers and leaders are often sansei or similarly aged Chinese Americans.

Other smaller waves of immigration from Japan have influenced the demographics of the group, but have had less effect on the culture of the J-Leagues. Later immigrants include "war brides" of the era of US occupation of Japan, as well as those who arrived post-1965, when immigration policies have favored educated and technical workers. These latter groups are not commonly involved in the J-Leagues, although there are some pockets of integration. Japanese American community centers often provide services for recently arrived immigrants and sometimes also field teams for Japanese American leagues and tournaments. One of my interviewees connected to one such community center said that the basketball component was often culture shock for Japanese-born members. Another one of my interviewees, a twentysomething nisei with post-1965 immigrant parents, commented that his athleticism had provided a bridge for inclusion in the more long-standing Japanese American community, while his sister, less athletically inclined, had ended up having trouble fitting in.

Despite the relative homogeneity of this particular group of Japanese Americans, the community is not without diversity. For example, I spoke with participants from a range of socioeconomic circumstances. Although, due to the influx of post-1965 technology workers, Asian Americans are often stereotyped as being technology and math wizards, employed in only upper-class professions, the Japanese Americans I met through my research seemed to have more diverse socioeconomic circumstances, spanning from more modest workers to high-level professionals. The most common profession among my participants was elementary or secondary schoolteacher (oftentimes combined with coach). In both Los Angeles and Orange counties, "Educational Services, Health Care, and Social Assistance" is the most prevalent occupational category for Japanese Americans.[3] In both of these counties, Japanese Americans have slightly higher household incomes than white non-Hispanics.[4] Most of my participants could be described as holding middle-class professions in areas with a high cost of living. Orange County participants seemed to have higher standards of living on average than the Los Angeles County participants.

THEORY/FRAMEWORK

In many ways this book seeks to answer the question: What circumstances have made Japanese American community investment in women's basketball possible? In answering this question, I utilize a multilevel framework, analyzing the relevant social interactions, structural and sociohistorical contexts, and representation (cultural symbols) (Glenn 2002; Messner 2002). Since both race and gender are highly salient to this analysis, I follow Glenn's (2002) suggestion that a multilevel analysis can be implemented with an intersectional approach in mind, examining the gender and race "within the same analytic plane" (6).

Glenn (2002) is helpful in providing a model for analyzing intersectionality that is true to the theoretical frame of multiracial feminism (Zinn and Dill 2003). This theory argues that gender, race, and class are primary organizing principles of stratification (82). The theory emphasizes that systems of oppression work "with and though each other" (85).

CHAPTER DESCRIPTIONS

Chapter 1, "'Everybody Plays': The Inclusiveness of J-League Basketball," examines the current place of the J-Leagues in the Japanese American community. It is the importance of the J-Leagues as a community institution that creates a foundation for a gender-inclusive sport environment. J-League basketball is a shared community endeavor that provides solutions to a number of present issues facing Japanese American communities. It has also become a source of various forms of community cultural wealth (Yosso 2005), especially in the realm of women's basketball. As Japanese Americans gain networks and relationships through J-League basketball, they feel strongly about all members of the community being involved.

Chapter 2, "'In JA Circles, Girls and Boys Are on Equal Footing': The (Re)negotiation of Gender in J-League Basketball," delves into the interactions and meaning making occurring among J-League participants that (re)construct intragroup meanings surrounding gender and sport. After a shift in perception of women athletes in the post–Title IX era, Japanese Americans today demonstrate respect for girls' and women's basketball. Unlike in the mainstream, Asian American women's bodies are assumed to be athletic bodies. In this context, coed basketball opens up spaces for challenging and playing with gender roles, archetypes of femininity such as mothers and beauty queens easily coexist with an identity of basketball players or coach, and women's leadership—even women coaching men—is respected.

Chapter 3, "'Women Who Took Sports beyond Play': How Japanese American Women's Basketball Went to College," documents the history of women's basketball in the Japanese American community, as well as the rise of numerous J-League-affiliated women in college and professional basketball. Although girls and women played in the J-Leagues as early as the 1920s, the serious and more widespread play occurred as more opportunities for women in basketball opened up in the mainstream. Several early forerunners in women's collegiate basketball not only inspired the next generation, but also became a Japanese American basketball network by coaching on women's college teams. This laid a foundation for even bigger successes.

Chapter 4, "'We're Turning Them into Stars!' The Japanese American Female Basketball Player as Icon," examines how Japanese American college-level players are understood as community celebrities. Japanese Americans follow these players as an expression of ethnic pride, but the affiliation is not only skin-deep, as the iconic players are often seen as "homegrown." Even more, those players who engage with the community are those who seem to be most well-known—the community invests in the star players who invest in them. In addition, women may make great community icons precisely because they more often do "give back" to the community and are seen as community-oriented, making them ideal role models.

Chapter 5, "'You Play Basketball?' Ruling the Court as an Unexpected Athlete," explores the experiences of Asian American women affiliated with the J-Leagues in contexts where they have announced a basketball identity outside of the leagues. Dominant discourses about which bodies belong in higher-level basketball influence the experiences of female Asian American players venturing into mainstream sport contexts. They can brush the comments off as jokes, but these women are continually reminded that their bodies aren't the expected bodies in sport.

CONCLUSION

Women are central to the story of Japanese American basketball as a community institution. Successful Japanese American female athletes are products of community investment; their achievements are not happenstance. They are seen as just one of the many positive outcomes of the community cultural wealth made possible by the J-Leagues. As icons for the community, many Japanese Americans seem to delight in how the smallest, most unlikely basketball players are the ones who are shining in mainstream sporting contests.

The community cultural wealth of Japanese American community basketball should be viewed not as a quirk of cultural practice, or as a special, model-minority resource for social mobility, but instead as part of an adaptation to social forces and power relations. As a group, Japanese Americans have been subject to a history of discrimination, exclusion, and incarceration based on a socially constructed racial/ethnic difference. They face the effects of the persistent racialization of Asian Americans as small, weak, feminine, as well as foreign and unassimilable. Within these contexts, Japanese Americans have been active agents in creating a collective identity and an enduring community. Basketball is one of the tools that Japanese Americans have used to adapt and thrive as a group.

In coming together through the sport of basketball, Japanese Americans chose a perhaps unexpected path, one where girls and boys in the community share a degree of equal footing and where women predominate as role models. However, in the greater context of the structural forces and controlling images, it can be understood as perhaps more expected than not.

1 · "EVERYBODY PLAYS"

The Inclusiveness
of J-League Basketball

It's August 18, 2007, in Long Beach, California. Dozens of children march parade-style into "The Pyramid," the basketball arena at the California State University, Long Beach, as part of the opening ceremonies for the Nikkei Games. They march in groups, with leaders holding signs atop long wooden poles that read the names of organizations sponsoring sport teams for the event: "Evergreen Church, Jets/Jetts, Norwalk Youth Sports, Orange Coast Optimist Club, Orange County Buddhist Church, Saber/Saberettes, San Fernando Athletic Association, South Bay F.O.R., SOC Youth Group, Tigers, Venice Youth Council, VFW Youth Group, Wintersburg Presbyterian Church, Nikkei." As each group marches past the stands full of family and community members, an announcer bellows out important facts about each organization represented: "Orange County Optimist Club is the largest Optimist Club in the United States. . . . Venice Youth Council is a community center that once only provided boys' teams until the 1960s when girls were included. . . . Wintersburg Presbyterian Church has been a Japanese American church since 1930."

Once the children file in and sit down on the gymnasium floor, a former Nisei Week Queen sings the National Anthem. The chairperson of the Nikkei Games tournament steps to the center of the gym and addresses the crowd: "Why Nikkei Games? For kids and families, to celebrate the traditions of our past, and to help the Nikkei Community thrive." Three speakers follow him, each attempting to motivate the children: an attorney, the founder of a major Japanese American sports organization, and a successful local high school coach. Then the youth take over, demonstrating their ball-handling and dance moves to popular music. This culminates in a ball-handling contest between four teens—boys against girls. It's a show! There are a few more short speeches, and then the current Nisei Week Royalty present tokens of appreciation to local businesses that have sponsored the event. Finally, the opening ceremonies end with a performance by *taiko* drummers.

The Nikkei Games may be the largest community sports festival of its kind. In recent years, it has typically involved ten sports and approximately 3,200 participants. Although Nikkei Games are a multi-sport event, the centrality of basketball is evident. The opening ceremonies are held at the CSU Long Beach basketball arena. In 2007, the basketball tournament alone had 89 divisions, 356 teams, and 1,400 participants.

Not only are the Nikkei Games popular, but they have a long history. The contemporary Nikkei Games began in 1994, but the festival existed in earlier eras under different names. In 1928, the "forefathers" of the Japanese American community started what was once called the Junior Olympics or Nisei Relays. Although these games have changed names and formats over the years, and there were periods when they were not held, the Nikkei Games represent a reclaiming of this sports tradition (Nikkei Games 2014).

Nikkei Games are unique within the J-Leagues in their wide variety of sports competitions and level of opening ceremony fanfare, but the basketball events represent just one of many annual Japanese American basketball tournaments held during the tournament season, which runs from late spring to early fall. These tournaments are a dominant way that basketball brings together the larger Japanese American community.

IMAGE 1.1. Nikkei Games Opening Ceremonies, 2007. Children carry signs representing their J-League-affiliated organization. (Credit: Nicole Willms.)

As the most popular and widespread sport among Japanese Americans in California, basketball has become the practice around which Japanese Americans engage in multiple layers of community building. Some of the connections made through basketball are more intimate, such as lifelong friendships among teammates. Others represent vast networks that span across Japanese American institutions, businesses, and community organizations. Japanese Americans value these connections and networks and attempt to preserve them by finding ways to ensure everyone finds their niche within the J-Leagues.

The opening ceremony of Nikkei Games illustrates the ways that the J-Leagues facilitate layers of connection. For starters, they are a shared cultural symbol, part of a cultural tradition (Hedani 2015). Within the J-Leagues, there is a collective memory of community participation, "a Durkheimian collective consciousness and collective sense of belonging" (Chin 2016, 1086). During the opening ceremony, words like "tradition," "forefathers," and "community" remind participants of this shared culture.

The tournaments also provide a very purposeful gathering of various Japanese stakeholders. They are the convergence of teams, families, and community leaders, as well as religious, business, and community organizations. Organizations that sponsor youth teams share their names and stories in the opening parade. Other organizations and businesses have booths lined up behind the bleachers.

Importantly, the opening ceremonies display the affiliations and talents of the community's youth. All of the organizations represented by the signs in the mini-parade of children sponsor youth athletic teams. These youth represent a thriving component of basketball participation among Japanese Americans and an investment in the future of this community.

The opening day of the Nikkei Games also contains messages about gender dynamics in the J-Leagues. Both girls and boys march in the parade, showing that both sexes girls and boys are important to the community investment. The battle of the sexes dribbling performance symbolizes the story of the more recent ascendency of young women in the J-Leagues. From my notes,

> Two teenage girls stand opposite two teenage boys, facing off at the half court line. They are all wearing similar basketball gear and each holds a basketball. Rap music begins playing over the loudspeakers and the four begin dribbling the ball continuously through one leg and then the other. The rap music stops, the four freeze, and "Anything You Can Do" by Irving Berlin begins to boom loudly through the gymnasium loudspeakers. The girls begin a new drill, dribbling the ball back and forth through one leg, and the boys start to do the same drill. A female voice belts out the lyrics: "Anything you can do I can do better! I can do anything better than you!" And then the male voice: "No you can't." "Yes I can!" Again, the girls switch drills and the boys follow. By the third drill, a move called the spider, one of the boys accidentally dribbles off his foot and the ball goes shooting off to a far corner of the gym. Seconds later, the second boy does the same, leaving the two girls alone at the center court, tapping away at their bouncing basketballs. Victory. Applause and cheers can be heard throughout the crowd. (Field notes, August 17, 2007)

This showdown seemed to be the perfect analogy for the gender dynamics within J-League youth basketball: many J-League girls have been excelling in mainstream basketball, and several standout players have come to occupy the center of community's attention.

The male leaders who spoke at the beginning of the ceremonies represent another side to this story. The J-League leadership is still fairly male dominated, and nowhere was this more apparent than in the suburban communities of Orange County. Still, the main distinction may be generational. Several men who are sansei, or third generation, seem to occupy a considerable amount of the leadership roles within the leagues. They are the old heads—they know everyone and everything about J-League basketball. A few sansei women are leaders in the more urban core of Los Angeles. The yonsei, or fourth generation, meanwhile represent the new cohort of basketball players, raised on female athletic role models and abundant playing opportunities for both sexes within and outside of the J-Leagues. In this generation, the basketball achievements, especially in mainstream contexts, belong primarily to female players. It remains to be seen if more dramatic shifts in J-League leadership will follow.

COMMUNITY INVESTMENT IN WOMEN'S BASKETBALL

In spite of the male-dominated leadership, women are an integral part of the success of the J-Leagues as players, role models, parents, and volunteers. The investment in girls' and women's basketball by the J-League, as an inclusive, community-run entity, seems to come naturally in support of the larger project of community solidarity. The importance of the larger project is paramount, and if it needs to rest on the shoulders of the young women who have become symbols of J-League success and potential, then that is where the community will invest.

Many Japanese Americans have come to view the J-Leagues as an important community project. In many ways the enterprise resembles a community of practice (Wenger 1998) as it is a meaningful, ongoing endeavor requiring a great deal of cooperative effort. Managing organizations, teams, leagues, and tournaments, as well as related events and fund-raisers, involves a lot of planning and logistical considerations, and it is done almost entirely by volunteers.

The J-Leagues have truly become productive of community cultural wealth (Yosso 2005), or community-specific forms of cultural capital that may not be recognized by the dominant society, but still provide rich benefits for community members. The leagues and tournaments provide venues for Japanese Americans to (re)connect with family, friends, and other co-ethnics and create networks and relationships akin an extended family. The J-League family provides meaningful engagement, social support, and opportunities in basketball and beyond—overall, it has become a bountiful source of cultural and social capital (Chin 2016). As Japanese Americans are members of an ethnic/racial group that can still experience discrimination or feel ostracized by mainstream society, especially in sport contexts, the J-Leagues provide them a wealth of resources for both practical and emotional support.

Many Japanese Americans involved in the J-Leagues express a keen awareness of the value of this community project and want to pass it along to the next generation. In the contemporary context, it is common sense that all family members are involved, regardless of sex. Since the J-Leagues are seen as a key way to be Japanese American, eschewing the J-Leagues would be akin to abandoning part of one's ethnic identity. This seems to be especially true for youth who may not be as attracted to other, more traditional cultural institutions.

The J-League organizations have kept up with this evolving community interest in basketball, leading to a large investment in girls' and women's basketball. Today, this investment is likely unparalleled by any other ethnic community. It includes extensive playing and training opportunities, numerous college-level players who act as mentors and role models, links to girls' elite club and traveling teams, and Japanese American basketball networks in mainstream women's basketball. The investment in community basketball has concurrently created a wealth of cultural, symbolic, and social capital in the world of women's basketball. This chapter focuses on the structures within the J-Leagues that have laid a foundation for this investment. Although it may seem tangential to the topic of women's basketball to speak in detail about the importance of the J-Leagues to the Japanese American community, I assert that it is the centrality of the J-Leagues and the importance of the networks and relationships they enable that has led to them being a gender-inclusive sporting space.

THE J-LEAGUES: A JAPANESE AMERICAN COMMUNITY INSTITUTION

As a community can be understood as "imagined" (Anderson 2006), it can also be elusive or fragile. Japanese Americans are linked by inscribed categories of race and ethnicity. Many Japanese Americans also share in common current and historical experiences. However, as multigenerational Americans, Japanese Americans represent a diverse range of identifications and interests and varying degrees of connectedness to ethnic identity, let alone traditional Japanese culture. They are also becoming more geographically dispersed as the ethnic enclave is no longer the center of community life. Although participation rates in Japanese American community institutions are relatively high compared to those of most other ethnic groups (Fugita and O'Brien 1991), that participation has the potential to be focused on a single community institution such as a church or community center. This isolated connection may be fragile, for example if a family moves to a new location. It may not lead to a connection with the larger Japanese American ethnic group. George, a participant involved in community development, explained,

> I think [the J-Leagues] are a lifeline—because otherwise you depend on churches, Japanese schools, other kinds of things, which are

fine institutions, but their primary loyalties are to that denomination or that church or that community center. They don't develop a sense of community. They develop a sense of institutional loyalty, but not a sense of community loyalty. And I think the leagues, because they're much broader, people come from different backgrounds, they meet other teams, it gives us much more of a feel for community, at least the community that we're trying to build. People from West Covina and people from West LA and Gardena can connect, they can meet each other, they know each other through these leagues, and they develop a sense of community, just like Facebook is doing online. It's a networking opportunity that gives them a sense of what this community is. They make those connections, and the connections they carry on in college and hopefully afterwards. They begin to get some notion of what community is.

George agreed that the J-Leagues had the size and scope necessary to create a contemporary ethnic community where lifelong connections and networks are possible. Modern life, particularly modern urban life, is not that conducive to community investment. Increasing individuality and time pressures have also meant less involvement in communal activities (Putnam 2000). Japanese Americans face these same pressures.

The flexibility and interconnectedness of basketball leagues and tournaments help to address modern community dilemmas. Many Japanese Americans seek out community engagement, sometimes due to a sense of isolation or ostracism when living far from other co-ethnics. Chin (2016) found this in her study of an Orange County Japanese American organization affiliated with the J-Leagues. Many members of the organization lived in predominantly white communities and enjoyed finding co-ethnics with whom they could share a sense of shared identity and experiences. Participants in my study from the larger Los Angeles region shared similar sentiments, but they lived in a variety of circumstances: some among co-ethnics, others mixed in with other marginalized ethnic and racial groups, and some in majority white areas. Overall, it wasn't the neighbors that mattered as much as the vehicles for community engagement.

Japanese Americans looked to co-ethnic community institutions to find connections and a sense of belonging. The J-Leagues provided a community enterprise that fulfilled these needs.

It is not a coincidence, either, that community sport has emerged as the chosen vehicle for community engagement. For Asian Americans, sport is often a particularly painful or frustrating mainstream space because of stereotypes and controlling images that often conceive of Asian bodies as dissonant bodies in mainstream sporting contexts (Brown 2015; Puwar 2004). In the mainstream, Japanese Americans are lumped in this panethnic category and often subject to racial microaggressions or feel underestimated in their playing abilities (Chin 2015). Thus, ethnic leagues provide a safe space to engage with sport without having one's sporting abilities constantly challenged.

Bridging Diversity within the Community

Basketball has become such a widespread shared engagement in some measure due to the J-Leagues relationships with a variety of important community institutions. More isolated connections to Japanese American organizations become linked into a larger network through basketball. Because the J-League basketball networks are so widespread and integral to key community organizations, basketball has become the strongest shared experience among a large portion of Japanese Americans in California.

The link between the J-Leagues and Japanese American community institutions is a central way that the sport of basketball reverberates throughout the Japanese American community. Although it is possible to participate in leagues and tournaments as an independent team, the majority of teams are connected to organizations. There are sport organizations that send teams into league play and tournaments, but more traditional community institutions such as churches, community centers, and civic organizations also engage in this practice. The Nikkei Games opening ceremonies provides a visual representation of how members from these organizations gather at tournaments not only to play basketball, but to represent their organizations and form connections with others. Image 1.2 illustrates the connections between organizations and their shared investment in basketball.

Although each of these organizations has its own role in linking Japanese Americans through common interests and cultural ties, the image hints at the large variety of ways in which Japanese Americans congregate. When a community does not share a common religion, a universal interest in learning *ikebana* (Japanese flower-arranging) at a Japanese American community center, or membership in a single business or veteran's organizations, what is the common denominator? In this case, basketball offers a link.

Basketball is not seen as the key purpose of most of the nonsport organizations, nor do all members of the organization participate in the sport, but networking and recruitment are facilitated by

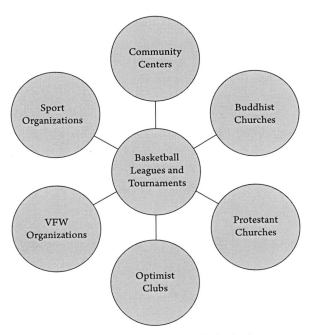

IMAGE 1.2. Japanese American community institutions are linked through their sponsorship of youth basketball teams. (Credit: Nicole Willms.)

fielding youth teams. Many members of the organization may find themselves becoming involved directly as a sponsor, coach, parent, organizer, spectator, or player. For others, the link is through association. Even if the majority of members are not directly involved with basketball, they may follow and support the teams.

During interviews, I learned of many stories about Japanese Americans joining organizations just to take advantage of playing on their teams. A few participants even seemed to be okay with switching or extending religious affiliations, for example, if it meant joining a favorite teammate or garnering a spot on a coveted team.

One of my favorite stories was from Patricia, who talked about her basketball adventures in Sacramento during the 1960s:

PATRICIA: I actually helped start up a league. See, when I was growing up in Sacramento, it was called the church league. That ran on Saturdays. I used to get involved with all the churches in the Sacramento area. Now on Sunday, the Buddhist church had their own league, the Buddhist league. They ran on Sundays, and it was more of a travel league, where they would travel and play teams from Marysville and Stockton.

NICOLE: So you were with a Christian church?

PATRICIA: Yes, I was with a Presbyterian group. We decided we'd get a little smart, so a bunch of us joined this Buddhist church in town, infiltrated their youth group, and we elected ourselves officers. So we just joined up so we got to get in the league. It was sort of like we masterminded this little—because they would not let Christian church teams into this league, because it was a Buddhist league.

NICOLE: And you wanted to play?

PATRICIA: We wanted to play, because the competition was good. We wanted to travel out of town. We couldn't get in because we weren't a Buddhist church, so we just—

NICOLE: You were going to two churches?

PATRICIA: Oh, we didn't go to the Buddhist church, so of course that caused a lot of problems from the people that really were the Buddhist parents. "These people aren't really Buddhists." But you know, they must have looked the other way, because we got away with it.

Girls' basketball was primarily offered though Buddhist churches prior to the late 1960s, so Patricia's story was not the only one I heard about girls switching or feigning religious affiliations for a chance to play. Basketball has been and continues to be both a recruitment tool for organizations and a conduit for organization members to become part of the larger community. Some church members attend because of basketball, while others are guided into basketball through the church.

Geographical Dispersion

The J-Leagues stand alone as a Japanese American institution that can be described as geographically ubiquitous, at least for a large portion of Japanese Americans in California. It spans a rather large area: centered in the greater Los Angeles, San Jose, and San Francisco metropolitan areas, but with tendrils reaching out to communities throughout the western United States.

Basketball has in some ways mediated feelings of geographical isolation, although the organizations and leagues are in the neighborhoods and suburban communities with a fairly high concentration of Japanese Americans. Two elements of basketball engagement attempt to bridge the distances between communities: (1) on a symbolic level, community members have worked toward building a recreation facility in the Little Tokyo neighborhood of Los Angeles to bring basketball to the heart of what was the ethnic enclave; (2) on a more logistical level, annual basketball tournaments, which act as regular reunions between teams from different areas, are held throughout the region by Japanese American organizations.

Budokan. Basketball has even been part of community efforts to at least symbolically recenter the community in the traditional ethnic enclave. In Los Angeles, Little Tokyo is the historical space where many Japanese American immigrants to Southern California originally came to live and work (Jenks 2008). Today, few Japanese Americans live in Little Tokyo, and the community-related businesses are gradually fading away. The Japanese American National Museum located in the neighborhood stands as perhaps the most visible Japanese American community presence. For the past two decades, there has been an active movement, spearheaded by the Little Tokyo Service Center (LTSC), to build a gymnasium in Little Tokyo.

LTSC and the San-Tai-San committee have used the fame of Hagiya, Nakase, and other prominent players and coaches to help build enthusiasm for the recreation center project (renamed "Budokan" in 2009 after the Japanese word for a martial arts hall). Since basketball is recognized as one of the stronger unifying forces in the Japanese American community of Southern California, the idea to build a gymnasium or recreation center has been circulating for quite some time (Jenks 2008). The Budokan, many believe, could bring otherwise widely dispersed Japanese American families back to the symbolic center of the community. Community leaders surmise that if teams hold their practices and games at the gym, they will be likely to have a meal at a Little Tokyo restaurant, shop at a store, or visit the Japanese American National Museum. What is difficult is that the building as currently conceived will likely house only two basketball courts. Demand for the facility may be impossible to meet, but it could still attract people to the neighborhood and stand as a symbolic shared resource that represents a more contemporary aspect of the community.

Tournaments. Japanese Americans solve some of the geographical dilemma to community participation by organizing their basketball participation around tournaments. Of course, when it comes to league play, participation occurs in discrete regions to make practices and games a feasible part of regular life. It is the numerous basketball tournaments that enable more widespread community connection. Teams not only participate in leagues, but also compete in several annual tournaments. On these occasions, participants are willing to travel for a weekend. Southern Californians, for example, frequently make the trek to Northern California for weekend tournaments, and vice versa. There are also two very popular tournaments held in Las Vegas each year.

Whereas lifelong friendships may develop between teammates and their families, the greater expansion of networks occurs when individuals and teams get together at these popular tournaments. Interactions at tournaments can occur not only through playing, but also through volunteering and socializing during tournament-related activities. Organizers of several tournaments encouraged overnight stays at hotels and an expansive array of both organized and spontaneous activities.

One of the biggest is the Tigers Tournament, organized by the Tigers Youth Club, a Japanese American athletic organization based in Los Angeles. Held over Memorial Day weekend, the Tigers Tournament is a multiday event. Games are played at local gymnasiums, while most non-basketball events are held at a large hotel where many of the participants stay. Teams from all over California and beyond attend the tournament for the opportunity to compete and socialize with other Japanese Americans. One of the co-chairs of the tournament, Ken, described an upcoming 2008 Tigers Tournament:

> This year we have 513 teams playing. It's probably the biggest one because we have men's, women's, boys', girls', as well as a master's division for the men over forty. . . . The tournament actually starts during the week for the men's master's division, and then all the other games are played on the weekend. So it's gotten pretty big. We have a golf tournament now, this is our third year. We also have the dance and bingo. So those are all good things. The dance, we've been told that the dance for the kids, they just think that's the best dance. So that's been kind of good. It's all the different functions we have together.

When I asked more about the dance, he continued, "It's big. I think last year we had a little over eight hundred kids that went in. We're trying to see if the hotel can accommodate a little bit more, because we turned people away at the door." The Tigers Tournament and its related events are hugely popular. The sports organization is able to run its entire operation almost solely based on the revenues accrued over the tournament weekend from tournament entry fees, bingo, the sale of dance tickets, raffle tickets, and tournament programs, and sponsorship/program advertising. Ken described how the funds are spent:

> Basically, it runs the club for a year. Tigers, I think we give them the best deal around. We charge eighty-five dollars for a member, and that's your dues for the whole year. And then from there, the club will pay for a league, for the girls it's JAO [run by the Japanese American Optimist Club], for the boys it's CYC [Community Youth Council]. So we pay for that league. Now, most of these leagues, they're running six hundred, seven hundred, eight hundred dollars for the season. So let's say you've got ten players, basically your membership dues is covering just that. On top of that, we pay for two tournaments. Most of these we cap it at three hundred fifty. So basically you get two more tournaments. For seven hundred dollars, you're basically getting that free, too. The only thing we ask the parents to do is work this weekend for the tournament. It seems to work.

Holding the tournament allows the organization to offer league play and entry into two tournaments for a reasonable fee, keeping basketball affordable for many families. In addition, the Tigers Youth Club is able to offer scholarships to graduating high school seniors who have played within the organization. Such tournaments are huge social events as well as fund-raising opportunities for the organizations that sponsor teams. Requiring parents to volunteer also facilitates social interactions and an investment in the group.

Basketball tournaments set the stage for numerous socializing and networking opportunities, but how does this mingling work on the ground? For the children, it is a chance to make friends. Tim recalled, "When you're young, you get to stay in a hotel and it's a great time. Everyone's going off running around going crazy. That was, like, a blast. Dude, it's like you're on a vacation with just your family and friends, but it's kind of like, you go away to camp and all the other kids are there." Nick described making new connections, as well:

The Tigers Tournament . . . there was one kid out there shooting free throws before our game, and I don't understand why I do this, but I just go over to people and I will literally sometimes go, "Hey, I'm Nick." And this is one of those cases where I just went up and started shooting around with him and we just got to meet each other. And then in Vegas we stayed at the same hotel, and ever since then, we were just close. So, every time at a tournament, I would go see their games. I actually played with them this summer, because they needed some extra players, so I played with them one game because they were short-handed. This upcoming tournament we have a pretty good chance of playing them also. It's so much fun. You see all your friends. I know I've said this probably eight times by now, but I can't explain it in words well enough to describe how strong these friendships are sometimes.

Both Tim and Nick found the environment at tournaments conducive to creating and solidifying long-lasting friendships. Players often see the same friends at multiple tournaments or at the same one each year. Tournaments provide opportunities to meet up with favorite rivals, watch friends' games, and also remix with new teammates. As Nick described, he sometimes plays at tournaments with players who are not from his league team. Although most feature typical sex-segregated, five-on-five competition, there are tournaments where three-on-three or four-on-four basketball is the standard or where there are coed divisions. These more unique forms of play invite or even require the blending of players into new team configurations, promoting the expansion of networks for players. Robert, who was a co-chair of the Nikkei Games basketball tournament when I spoke with him, felt that this integration of players from different social circles was a key part of the tournament's philosophy: "In the Nikkei Games, you don't have to play with your team. You can play with your friends who are from another organization, so we have Tiger [Youth Club] people playing with FOR [Friends of Richard] people, playing with OCO [Orange County Optimist Club] people. That's part of the extension of the friendships we talked about, that we try to embrace."

Robert viewed the tournament as a way to facilitate intergroup interactions and extend friendships across organizations.

Tournaments have the capacity to serve as a space for creating new connections, but they are also a space for reinforcing existing networks. Adults describe them as similar to reunions. This is especially true of one of the extremely popular tournaments held in Las Vegas. During this adult-only tournament held each September, at least two thousand people book hotel rooms through the tournament website. Laura described her experience:

> The tournaments, it's amazing like how many people you see and just, you know, you haven't seen them in years, since I was a kid. It's just like a huge . . . reunion. Sometimes you're like, oh, I don't want to go just because you know you're going to run into tens of millions of people and you have to stop and say hi to everybody. You can't act like you don't know them. But that's how Vegas is, because everyone stays in, they have like two hotels where pretty much everyone stays, and you know you're going to run into people. So, it's like just going from one casino from California to Main Street, there's that hallway, you're going to see probably like twenty people that you know. It's kind of like, everyone knows everyone.

Laura describes Las Vegas as almost overwhelming. Because the tournament reserves rooms in two particular casinos, attendees will very likely see other tournament participants and fans outside of the basketball games. The casinos actually offer those who book during this weekend a free weekend later in the year, providing a second, basketball-free reunion for those who wish to return. Although most participants I talked to make the Vegas tournament a yearly event, some put forth a special effort certain years to enter the tournament with members of an old team in order to create a reunion: "I'm still friends with a lot of the girls I played with back then. This last season actually—we haven't played for like seventeen years—a bunch of us, we put a team together. We played a Las Vegas tournament that was more like a reunion and more totally for fun, you know, but that was great"

(Rebecca). Rebecca had the opportunity to play with some friends who had not played together in many years by organizing a team for the Las Vegas tournament. Basketball became the conduit for seeing old friends.

Although it was mainly younger adults who spoke up in interviews about the Las Vegas tournaments, they also mentioned that many older adults attend as well. Some go to watch their or a friend's child play. Others are still playing themselves, as I will discuss later in the chapter. The tournament becomes the excuse for over two thousand Japanese Americans to converge on Downtown Las Vegas and enjoy a reunion-like atmosphere in the adult playground of Las Vegas.

"LIKE FAMILY": BUILDING RELATIONSHIPS THROUGH BASKETBALL

Why is a sport such as basketball such a useful way to link community members and community institutions? In her book *Protecting Home*, Sherri Grasmuck (2005) speaks about youth baseball as an ideal game for integrating a neighborhood community. With its long games, baseball provides opportunities for parents to meet on the bleachers and share in the experience of their children's successes and struggles. Even parents from very different racial/ethnic and social class backgrounds find themselves making friends. She explains, "On the bleachers, parents share that baseball 'suspension of time.' In contrast, parents who sit together watching basketball do not get the same opportunities. In basketball, too much happens against the pressure of the clock. The same is true for soccer. So, it mattered that it was baseball. Because it was baseball, we waited, and hoped together, and experienced moments of communion, pain and redemption in the process" (43). Grasmuck goes on to explain that since baseball leagues often require that players change teams every year, a remixing of players occurs. Grasmuck argues that after several years, parents have crossed paths with many other parents from the neighborhood through continued participation in the league, giving them the opportunity to make contacts and friendships with numerous families.

Grasmuck (2005) makes some very compelling points about the idealness of baseball for creating community connections. However, it may be that many different sports could serve in this role, especially with the help of "creative engineering" in and around the organization and practice of the sport. Perhaps because there are not as many gaps to bridge in terms of background, Japanese Americans involved in the basketball leagues practice community building not only during individual contests, but also in the activities that both sustain and augment these activities. Instead of remixing teams each year within leagues, Japanese Americans remix at tournaments. Tournaments provide a space to get together with friends and extended networks and expand the Japanese American community to those outside of the immediate geographical area.

At the team level, several practices have emerged in the J-Leagues that encourage the bonding of team members and their families. For example, participants in the J-Leagues did not often talk about socializing on the bleachers, but they frequently mentioned postgame snacks or meals. Jake said, "I think one thing you're going to hear a lot about is postgame snacks. That was always . . . you now, in the rec leagues, someone would just buy those big Costco packs of chips and sodas. That was it. [In the J-Leagues] some teams, it's almost like a picnic or a potluck, pulling on tailgates, having frys—just spreads of all kinds of food."

Additional practice of socializing occurred outside of basketball. Sandra described this as one way that the teams became "like family": "Going out to eat, celebrating birthdays or anniversaries or something together as a team or stuff like that. It becomes more like family other than just friends. . . . Once you're on the team, everybody kind of just, you know, kind of accepts everybody on the team and stuff like that . . . like [names teammate], when they were having the VFW tournament which is down in Orange County, I think nearby their own house. 'Come to my house after the game, bring the food over, just drop it off and then you can go to the game, then we'll come back, then we'll eat and go to the next game.'" Sharing food and celebrating occasions together both seem to be prominent aspects of J-League basketball teams. Having these extra opportunities to socialize provided the basis of very strong friendships and oftentimes lifelong ties to teammates and their families. Rebecca shared, "The idea is that we can come together for one thing and enjoy that. It's not necessary to have the same opinion about it, but you know, feel good about it. You know, come, play for an hour, have refreshments, go to lunch after or something. Ah, we got a couple of funny things out of that day, and laugh about those things thirty-five years from now. I think that's great." Rebecca illustrates that the practices of both playing together and socializing together provide shared memories that help to bind the team members for many years into the future. This may be community building at a different level than Grasmuck describes.

Family Connections

As discussed, many J-League teams engender feelings of family connections between players and parents who are not actually related. What also emerged in the research was that real families also use the J-Leagues to solidify bonds, especially among extended kin. Jake described his family's experiences at tournaments:

> I think it's that family bonding we have . . . a lot of our extended family that we're close with are all playing J-Leagues, for like the Tigers Tournament. So, for the big ones, my mom would just have the [tournament] book and then, just tabs all over so we know when each of the cousins' games are. We just spend the whole weekend just driving to the games. . . . So, we'd always have pretty big cheering sections. That's why it's always fun with the Nisei Week Tournament— we'll have huge cheering sections, since the whole family comes out for that one. My mom's extended family is pretty big.

So, Jake was not only finding a network with co-ethnics at tournaments, but also solidifying connections with his extended family. Keith also used basketball to maintain ties to kin. He explained how he came to play on three teams: "We have this family team kind of where it's just all comprised of cousins and, you know, friends, growing up through college. So they're like cousins and brothers. . . . I started playing with them, my cousin asked me, like, 'Hey, I've got this other team that I'm playing on, we need a player.' . . . Then they asked me to play all the time, so I was playing two games and then he asked me to play in another league." I asked Keith if he saw his family more because of playing on a team with them. He responded, "Definitely. I didn't talk to the cousin who got me into . . . playing down here . . . until I mean, like um, probably sophomore year of college, and before that, we had a family reunion probably eight years before that. So, I hadn't really talked to any of the family out here, and now I see them almost every week, which is great. I mean, it's nice knowing that I have family close around here that I'm actually close to now."

From interviews and observations, I learned that players were often pulled onto a team for league or tournament play because a cousin, sibling, or in-law invited them to play. Another draw toward family-based teams was the desire to play with one's child. Several parents I interviewed spoke about wanting to stay fit and active in basketball at least until their son or daughter was eligible to play in the adult leagues with them. For example, Sandra explained her desire to play with her daughter: "It's kind of like, one of those almost milestones, you know? It would be kind of neat to play a couple years with your daughter. . . . There's quite a few of the moms who have done that." Among my interviewees, this trend followed a single-sex pattern—fathers expressed an interest in playing with sons, while mothers wanted to play with daughters. Coed leagues and tournament divisions are becoming more popular and widespread, but tend to cater to teens and young adults, probably because for many this is a primary time for socializing with members of the opposite sex. Therefore, I heard more about playing coed with romantic partners and opposite-sex siblings than I did about father/daughter or mother/son pairs.

Not only do the J-Leagues produce a sense of family among Japanese Americans, but they bring actual families closer together. Playing with family appears to be gaining in popularity. At a planning committee meeting for the 2008 Nikkei Games, committee members proposed the addition of a family-only division within the basketball tournament. Although it was not ratified for that year, several people at the meeting expressed enthusiasm for the idea.

The Desire for It to Go On

Given the family-like atmosphere, access to networks, and positive interactions that many Japanese Americans experience within the J-Leagues and their affiliated events, it is not surprising that many participants want to pass along the experience to future generations. One way this is demonstrated is through the ethic and practice of "giving back." Giving back generally involves volunteering for a league or organization affiliated with basketball, as leagues and tournaments are organized almost entirely with volunteer labor. When asked why this ethic exists, Jake responded, "It's just something where you grew up with that and you want to make sure it continues." Sarah elaborated on this thought, explaining why she coaches at the community center where she grew up playing: "I think, just from my personal experience and playing, I've had so much fun. I met tons of people, and, you know, I've gained a lot from just playing. . . . I wanted these kids to kind of have the same experience I had, and be able to keep up this . . . like . . . tradition, or . . . I don't know, you know? I hope one day to see, like, my kids . . . involved with something like this as well."

Both Jake and Sarah had such positive experiences with the J-Leagues that they felt personally responsible for providing that experience for others. Like Sarah, many other participants expressed that it was important to have their own children involved in J-League basketball:

EMILY: I think I'll definitely want my kids to play some kind of organized team sport, preferably basketball. My daughter and my son are—hopefully they'll both play. I'll give them both the same opportunities.

NICOLE: Is it important that they play in the J-Leagues?

EMILY: Yeah, that's very important for me, for both my husband and [me], just because we pretty much both grew up—my husband grew up playing J-Leagues, too. . . . I think we both agree that—I still keep in contact with most, if not all of my friends from basketball, and it's a huge part of our lives. We're really excited for that time when we can take [our children] to their games and eat refreshments afterwards and commune with the other parents. My mom is still in touch with all the parents that I grew up with, and we're attending each other's weddings. I'm the only one, really, with kids, but I'm sure when they start having kids, I'll see those, too. It's created a real close-knit family. It's a very small-feeling community.

For Emily, getting her own children involved in the J-Leagues is an extension of the bonds she's created through her own playing experiences. She witnessed her mother's experience of making friends with the parents of her teammates, and she hopes to replicate that by reinvigorating friendships with old teammates who also have children, as well as making new friendships with the parents of her children's teammates.

Passing along J-League basketball to others was not only about sharing the joy and connections made possible throughout the sport leagues and tournaments, but also about redefining a shared Japanese American cultural heritage. Jack noted, "We're trying to build the sense that you don't have to lose this connection to your culture and your heritage. But it's not something that's frozen in the past, it's something that's contemporary and hopefully you will want to pass on to your children." Basketball became representative of a contemporary bond between Japanese Americans, attractive to youth and also a bridge between generations.

Being a part of the Japanese American community is important to many Japanese Americans, particularly those living in California. Many participants in the J-Leagues value the role that basketball plays in bringing the community together. Therefore, it becomes important to make sure the leagues continue and that their friends and family stay involved. A common belief among participants—almost invisible, as it is just understood—is that all community members should be involved. If the J-Leagues were limited to just youth, just boys, or just talented players, this would restrict how many could participate. Therefore, a community identity is forming around basketball that emphasizes making long-term commitments both to playing and volunteering as well as to providing spaces for a wide variety of participation, particularly for both sexes and also for a wide range of ages.

Community Investment: A Community of Practice

Basketball has the advantage of being a long-standing tradition within the community. The youth leagues enjoy support and encouragement from the older generations because they often played themselves. Early involvement is not seen as unusual as many families have long planned to integrate their children into the basketball community.

Therefore, it appears that Japanese Americans are moving from a more traditional ethnic community to a "community of practice" (Wenger 1998). Although this is a concept Wenger used for thinking about group-based learning, it can be usefully applied to Japanese Americans' patterns of community building around basketball. A community of practice involves (1) joint enterprise—a goal or project for group members to work toward, (2) shared repertoire—the shared meaning attached to the group goal and the tasks associated with achieving that goal, and (3) mutual engagement—the meaningful and purposeful interpersonal relations involved in completing the group enterprise. Basketball fits this model because Japanese Americans engage in the sport in a way that is both meaningful and instrumental. Most Japanese Americans already have a sense of ethnic, historical, and experiential kinship to build from, so basketball is able to borrow from these preexisting meanings since it is considered a community-exclusive activity (not purely, but symbolically at the very least). The Nikkei Games chairperson is able to speak about "forefathers" and "tradition" in his speech at the opening ceremonies, a reference to these shared meanings. Organizing basketball teams, leagues, and tournaments is an ongoing series of joint enterprises that require mutual engagement through an enormous amount of volunteer hours. Therefore, the enterprise of basketball unites many in the community to organize tournaments, year-round league play, and other basketball-related activities, and many more to participate in the fruits of the volunteers' labor. People are willing to put in the time and energy because of the meanings connected to it, but also because at a basic level they understand the social rewards they draw from it. Although the meaning is there, the activity itself and the social contacts it engenders become the focus and impetus behind community contact. Important to the relatively dispersed Japanese Americans, a community of practice does not require members to reside in the same neighborhoods. It helps that they live in general proximity to one another, especially for league play, but sometimes the practice of community on a larger scale may happen at an annual tournament or festival.

Inclusiveness

Widespread ethnic connections through basketball are not possible if only the most obvious athletes are included. Interest and skill must be cultivated, and the athletes who do not embody the dominant image of a "basketball player" still need to feel included. Overall, the sport needs to be popular, accessible, and congruent with the pace of busy urban and suburban lives. Debbie explained, "There are other sports that JAs have. There are baseball leagues. There are volleyball [leagues], of course. Bowling is another big one. But basketball—it just seems it is intergeneration[al], inter-age, inter-gender and so . . . everybody can play." Basketball was the sport that fit the community as a whole.

Basketball emerged as the link and conduit for ethnic community, but the J-Leagues also adopted certain values that they believe are responsible for the longevity of the J-Leagues as a community institutions. One key value was that of inclusiveness, voiced by J-League organizations as far back as the 1930s (Matsumoto 2014). Jack spoke about values within the contemporary J-Leagues: "I think it reflects certain community values and culture that we hope we can translate to what our community is. We want a community that is less hierarchical, that's less focused on titles and whatever. We want one that's much more group-oriented in the way we do things. We want one that's more inclusive and welcoming, one that is not sexist, classist, in terms of nature. That's what we want to build. That's not a utopia, but we're trying to build a community that reflects what we think is inclusive, positive, progressive values and build a sense about bringing people together around that." Although Jack could probably be described as one of the more visionary and progressive community leaders, these values do resonate in many of the J-League organizations.

Community Border Work

The Japanese American basketball community's commitment to internal inclusiveness also involves active border work that marks the boundaries of the ethnic community through exclusive sport activities. Teams follow rules set by leagues and tournaments, filling rosters based on criteria principally based on racial/ethnic background. Most give priority to players of Japanese descent, followed by players of Asian descent (for a discussion of the difficulties the community has in clearly defining these categories, see King 2002). Leagues are alternately described as Japanese Leagues (J-Leagues) or Asian Leagues. Some organizers have moved toward more community-defined criteria for including participants, making exceptions for those belonging to community organizations. Other peripheral leagues have opened up to all participants, but this is less common. Given these enforced parameters, what about the leagues is inclusive? They are community inclusive; once someone is clearly defined as belonging to the Japanese American community (or has attained similar status by participating through the proper channels), there is a strong ethic of inclusiveness.

Becoming defined as a member of the community can be basketball-related as well. One player, Paul, whose parents emigrated from Japan, described divergent experiences for him and his sister. Even though his family did not have many Japanese American connections because of their newcomer status, both he and his sister got involved in the J-Leagues. Paul is very athletic and fairly tall and excelled in the leagues. This translated into his gaining an acceptance into the Japanese American community. At age twenty-eight, he still plays occasionally in tournaments with his childhood J-League team. His sister, on the other hand, was not as talented of an athlete and grew tired of basketball by junior high. Between her second-generation status and lack of athletic skill and talent, she did not really fit in with Japanese Americans. Paul explains, "I think that whole experience really turned her off, because it's like, she wasn't very good and wasn't as welcomed into the basketball community." This example illustrates one of the many exceptions to inclusiveness within the basketball leagues—since most of the players are third-generation or beyond, it is more difficult for more recent Japanese immigrants to fit in (though attitudes toward newcomers and outsiders vary by location and organization). In some situations, basketball talent becomes a litmus test for belonging. However, the example also illustrates how important involvement in basketball can be for a newcomer or peripheral community member in respect to fitting in within the community. If one is not connected to the community through another source (e.g., a church), basketball can be an important way to become involved and make connections with other Japanese Americans.

Once someone is clearly defined as belonging to the Japanese American community, there is a strong ethic of inclusiveness. Community members tend to voice a commitment to keeping "everyone involved," and in providing environments where this can be possible. For example, there is a lot of discussion of making sure everyone has a place to play, and that everyone is guaranteed a certain amount of playing time. Although this is also a common goal of mainstream recreational-level play, what may make the J-Leagues relatively unique is that they have many divisions and levels, offering diverse playing opportunities.

Participants were divided on how competitive the J-Leagues are or should be (in terms of both level of play and team philosophy), probably because there is a wide spectrum levels and philosophies within the leagues, but a common response among interviewees was to tout the leagues' commitments to the values of fun and inclusiveness. For example, when asked to compare the J-Leagues to other playing experiences, Elise responded, "I think they're less competitive. I mean, they're still competitive, like, we still want to win, but it's more about everybody plays and everybody wants to have fun." Ben, a leader in both a girls' and women's league, discussed the rules regarding playing time: "I think the philosophy was to allow all the girls to play. So, that's why in the girls' program, they have to play. When we were playing quarters, they had to play each quarter. When we went to halves, they had to play a significant amount of time, so that they weren't just benchwarmers."

Some respondents, like Laura, noted that the J-Leagues' "everyone plays" ethic allows for the integration of less skilled players: "And that's the one thing that's kind of nice about the league is because, it doesn't matter, anybody can play, no matter the level. Cause they have a bunch of different divisions in the Asian League, so it's like anybody can play, even if you're horrible."

As a young man, Nick has dreams of playing in the NBA. If successful, he plans to donate a large portion of his salary to making sure more people get a chance to play in the J-Leagues: "Maybe make another team so more kids can join. I'm sure that there are always gonna be kids who want to join. There are no kids that are ever refused. If they want to play, they're gonna be accepted onto a team. But I'm sure that sometimes there's a team of ten kids out there but none of their parents know anything about basketball. They don't have a coach. Maybe I can make another team where there will be." Nick voices a commitment to the idea that all should be included, even if there may be a lack of resources.

Most tournaments and some leagues break down competition into divisions, matching up teams of similar skill and ability. This also helps teams divide themselves according to team goals. Teams that are more interested in the social aspects of J-Leagues can play other like-minded teams in a lower division, whereas teams whose focus is competition can play in a higher division. For one organizer of Nikkei Games, separate divisions as well as the three-on-three format help to facilitate an inclusive environment: "We're more into having healthy competition. We want them to have good games, so we—that's why we have, um, gold, silver, bronze, you know, copper divisions. . . . In a full-court game of five-on-five, three kids may touch the ball, two kids don't touch it a whole lot. It just is the nature of the game. . . . In a three-on-three tournament, it's for everybody, and we want you to touch the ball, we want you to play. You have to touch the ball. You have to play. But in order to make it work, you have to play against people who are your same level." Organizers paid attention to the structure of the playing opportunities, making sure that players felt included.

The care and attention paid to creating fair and inclusive playing opportunities helped resolve one important dilemma: how to keep aging community members involved in something as physical as basketball. In the adult leagues, aging teams tend to move to lower divisions over the years, allowing them to continue playing into their later years. In fact, some enjoy the leagues so much that they keep playing into their fifties and sixties. In 2008, the Las Vegas tournament had eighteen divisions of adult men's teams: from the "Gold" and "Silver" divisions down to "Lead," "Rock," and "Dirt." The AA precious metal divisions tend to be highly competitive, with other divisions progressively less competitive. The use of "Rock" and "Dirt" to name divisions shows that these players have a certain sense of humor about their level of play. Team names can also poke fun at the age or skill level of the participants. In the lowest women's division at the 2008 Las Vegas tournament, for example, one team was named "Less than Giants" and another was called "Back in Action." In the lower men's divisions, I found "Slow Break" and "Wheelchair Bound."

Although there are other ways for older adults to stay involved in the J-Leagues, such as helping to coach or organize, there were a number of participants who really valued the opportunity to play. The weekly games or annual tournaments became a comforting and consistent outlet for social engagement in their lives. One participant, Lou, in his fifties, was regularly recruited onto two or three teams each year by friends and family. A single man, Lou admitted that playing multiple times each week had even interfered with his dating life, but he still could not give it up because he enjoyed it so much. He also seemed to feel an obligation to those who invited him to play. The ties to friends and family intertwined with basketball in a way that made it difficult to disentangle.

Older players acquired a kind of notoriety. Several of my interviewees proudly told me about themselves or their parents or friends who are playing past fifty. "Some of the people I used to play with are still playing. They call it the 'open division,' which anybody past high school division, they're still running around. We always joke about it. In fact, in Northern California, they have a tournament that they call The Legend" (Danielle, fifty-eight). Although it appears to be a little less common for women to play past fifty, Danielle described a Northern California tournament aimed specifically at women in older age brackets. With men, it was a lot more difficult to get them off the court. When older players no longer felt comfortable playing in leagues and tournaments, they would still participate in semi-organized pickup games.

> I know my dad played [basketball], he played high school football too. He actually played up until ten years ago, but even now he still plays. He plays Wednesday nights, it's like a men's adult league. . . . He's like sixty-three. I mean they don't play fast, they just run the ball down and shoot, but he enjoys it. (Laura)
>
> On Wednesday night I play here at Belvedere with people that I've played with since I was in college. We all migrate to the gym every Wednesday night and some of my friends' kids, their sons come out and play with us. So, we have a lot of old and young. Our oldest is sixty-seven and our youngest is probably about in their twenties. (Andrew, fifty-eight)

Playing as an older adult may be viewed by some in the J-Leagues as humorous or remarkable, but it is also an accepted element of the J-Leagues, incorporated into many of the leagues and tournaments. Most leagues and tournaments have multiple divisions, accommodating a wide range of playing abilities. J-League networks help players find gym space and participants for more casual pickup games, favored by some older players. Altogether, the larger institution of J-League basketball provides space for older adults to continue to play.

Japanese Americans already defy stereotypes by playing basketball, a sport regarded by the mainstream as appropriate for only extremely tall and powerful bodies. Controlling images render Asian American bodies as unexpected or unimaginable against this rubric (King 2010). Whether in response to these images or in service to the larger community project—or both—it is almost as if the community has decided to throw out this rubric altogether and reimagine which bodies belong in basketball. By facilitating playing opportunities for older adults, the community subverts dominant notions of what qualifies as an athletic body. Basketball in particular seems to be associated with youthful bodies, with abilities that peak in youth: quick reflexes, vertical jumping ability, speed. The J-Leagues seem to communicate that anyone who wants to play basketball possesses the right kind of body, even if old age means an inability to run down the court. This reimagining of the athletic body and ethic of inclusiveness both easily translate into the realm of gender.

"What If a Family Was Just All Girls?"
Gender-Inclusivity in the J-Leagues

Just as Japanese Americans make room in the J-Leagues for participants of all ages, they also see a value in being gender-inclusive. This emerges in part through a recognition of the importance of basketball as a community institution. On a community level, it requires continual reinvestment by as many community members as possible. On a more individual level, many individuals and family units see a benefit to establishing a link to the institution. What has developed is a widespread ethic that all Japanese American children—daughters and sons—should have a chance to become involved.

If I still had lingering questions about why Japanese Americans choose basketball as their mode of cultural interaction, I found that at least part of the answer is that the game is perceived as appropriate for both sexes. Richard explained his view of the uniqueness of basketball:

RICHARD: It's not just the sports program. I remember when I was a kid, they even had Japanese American fishing clubs for the adults. But that was a similar type of purpose, a place to gather or get together for a common interest of the Japanese American men. A lot of 'em like to fish. And now it's the youth athletics, both for boys and girls. So it's a common denominator, a common connection.

NICOLE: Do you think that's important, that it's a sport that both genders play now, as part of community building?

RICHARD: Sure. Yeah. Because if it's just for the boys, what if a family was just all girls? They're excluded, right? But it's keeping that network and that connection so that hopefully the kids will—because it is a positive or good thing in their life that they meet people, other Japanese Americans, outside of their neighborhood, their community. LA, Orange County, Inland Empire, even up north. Make some acquaintances.

Richard recognized the value of establishing community networks and viewed basketball as uniquely positioned to meet this goal. It was an activity that attracted youth and members of both sexes. This universality seems to be the crucial element—if these were primarily leagues for boys and men, many individuals and families would not be a part of them.

Some participants spoke directly about their plans to include their children. Emily expressed some concern that her own children, a boy and a girl, would be left out if not involved in J-League basketball. She discussed the benefits: "I don't think people realize how big it is in this community, from Northern to Southern Cali all the way through. Anyone that doesn't play basketball . . . it's not that you're outcasted—you go to the games, still, you go to the tournaments, you still go to Vegas, even if you don't play. So, it's a huge chance for JAs to meet and get to know other Japanese Americans, pretty much all throughout Cali." For Emily, the worst that might occur for a non-player is that she or he might be relegated to the bleachers. She could not even imagine the idea that her children would completely be absent from the basketball scene. Emily insisted her children would have to be involved in some way, even if just as spectators, so that they did not miss out on meeting other Japanese Americans. Emily herself had taken a few years off from playing in the adult league to birth and care for her two small children. Her husband had begun encouraging her to return to playing primarily because he wanted her to be a role model to their young daughter.

The growth of the youth component of the J-Leagues over the past three or four decades has coincided—not coincidentally—with the growth of girls' and women's sports. Providing space for girls and women to be active participants in the leagues means a larger network of players and families who become involved, only increasing the breadth of the network that basketball offers. West Coast Japanese Americans have participated in women's basketball since it became popular in these communities in the 1920s; however, the growth of interest in the sport by girls and women has caused the community to react, providing more and more outlets for play. They found that a community activity that had been enjoyed for many years was only growing in popularity among the next generation.

As the center of the J-Leagues has shifted from the adult leagues to the children's programs, gender-inclusiveness has become even more important. First of all, as Richard described, families who have only daughters would, if their girls did not play basketball, be excluded from the friendships and networking available through the J-Leagues. At the youth level, being a basketball player is virtually the only way to actively participate in the leagues. Whereas adults can engage in parent- or mentor-based roles such as coaching or providing snacks for the team, children are almost exclusively players. Restricting girls' roles to ones that are traditionally feminine (i.e., not active in sport) would jeopardize the community's ability to retain families and bring youth into the fold at an early age.

As youth sports have gained popularity in the mainstream (Adler and Adler 1994, 1998; Coakley 2009; Messner 2012; Trussell and Shaw 2012), the J-Leagues have capitalized on this trend. Many interviewees involved in popular tournaments such as the Tigers Tournament spoke about the growing number of teams participating. Jimmy, who is involved with the Tigers Tournament, said, "I think the kids' part of it has really exploded within the last maybe fifteen years, because I think all the kids that are growing up now, their parents played, and from that, I guess it's like baby boomers, right, they all had kids, and they're all having their kids play. So it's really exploded in the last, I'd say, fifteen years."

The growth of the youth leagues has included opportunities for both sexes. There are multiple leagues throughout Los Angeles and Orange counties, as well as some in communities in Northern California, that offer competition for boys', girls', men's, women's, and coed teams. There are very few tournaments that cater only to one sex, although the majority of competition is sex-segregated. The Wanjettes Tournament, solely for girls, may be the only contemporary exception.

CONCLUSION

The importance of the J-Leagues lies in their strength to unite disparate elements of the community and give community members a clear goal to focus on in building and maintaining community ties. The institution of the J-Leagues—including basketball leagues, tournaments, and related events and interactions—brings Japanese Americans together in a shared activity that facilitates social ties. This shared community engagement is not fully possible without providing a wide range of playing opportunities and creating an inclusive environment. The real linchpin seems to be fostering ample and diverse playing opportunities for youth of both sexes, securing widespread loyalty to the leagues. The expansiveness of the J-Leagues translates into multifaceted engagements with sport that subvert dominant notions of which bodies belong in basketball. In the next chapter, I discuss how these diverse engagements and overall inclusive attitude that naturalizes girls' and women's involvement lead to renegotiations of the gender power dynamics often found in sport environments.

2 · "IN JA CIRCLES, GIRLS AND BOYS ARE ON EQUAL FOOTING"

The (Re)negotiation of Gender in J-League Basketball

One weekend afternoon, I stopped by a local Los Angeles Unified high school gymnasium to watch a women's J-League game. As I sat on the sidelines to watch the game, my attention became focused on a particular player who was balancing playing in the game with caring for a small child around the age of four. A man who seemed to be the child's father was tending to the boy, but could not seem to manage to keep him away from his mother. The game was occupying one half of the gym, with only one row of bleachers exposed, so there was not much space to separate the fans from the players.

The child was clearly interested in being close to mom. Just about every time the woman came out of the game, the child wound up in her lap. At halftime, she came over to the father and pointed out a few more snacks and toys that might distract the restless preschooler. During this conversation, the boy started tugging on his mom's team jersey.

"I want to wear this!" he whined.

"My jersey? I need that, Honey. Mommy's going back into the game."

"I want it!" he shouted.

The negotiations continued. After he was offered a practice jersey from his mom's bag and promised that he could wear her jersey after the game, the mother finally managed to rejoin her team for a second half. The boy still made a few trips over to the bench, but now seemed mostly pleased to be wearing his mother's practice jersey and to be munching on some of the new snacks his father was offering.

Although this story points to some of the challenges that parents, and often mothers in particular, may face in returning to adult league basketball unfettered by their families, it also illustrates another important phenomenon: the meaning making around gender and sport that occurs within the J-Leagues' female-centered and gender-inclusive spaces.

As the opening story illustrates, many J-League contexts subvert the more dominant meanings attached to sport. Here, mom is the star athlete, and dad and son her supportive fans. The cute but exasperating little boy who continued to try to invade his mother's space was a witness to his mother occupying center stage, an active position in the space. While the boy and his father watched, the mother was the focal point. The mother's embodiment of a skilled, capable, and powerful athlete—an Asian American female athlete—disrupted dominant cultural understandings of which bodies are naturalized as athletic and powerful. Moreover, the son's relentless attention to his mother and requests for his mother's jersey seem to indicate that he admired her status as basketball player and wanted to emulate it. He may have felt that something important was happening, and this led to a desire to have a jersey that would make him a part of it.

These kinds of experiences—where women are the strong athletic role models—seem to have left an impression on many J-League participants, leading them to talk about J-League basketball as "genderless" and to admire the girls and women who play as much as if not sometimes more than the boys and men. As basketball is a family-centered, intergenerational activity for many Japanese Americans in California, this renegotiation of gendered meanings is not ephemeral, but instead intentionally passed along to the next generation.

Not only do many J-League environments include women occupying nontraditional roles in the sport context, but they also appear to be conducive to the enactment of multiple femininities and masculinities. With an ethic of wanting to include everyone, the J-Leagues have created a wide spectrum of playing opportunities that easily accommodate a variety of engagements. Mothers, as described in the story, are but one example. Women playing in the J-Leagues do not necessarily feel the need to hide their attachments to children—there are teams in the J-Leagues whose members never mind if a player's little one sits on her lap during time-outs.

The J-Leagues' ability to be inclusive and accommodating produces spaces where girls and women have some ability to (re)construct the practices and meanings attached to sport and athleticism. Girls' and women's extensive involvement in the J-Leagues, accompanied by the ubiquity of basketball as a community practice, creates understandings of women's sport involvement that often subvert dominant constructions. It is this context that has helped to produce female community icons and that has also been receptive to their symbolism.

In this chapter, I examine several J-League contexts where gendered symbols, discourses, and power dynamics found in mainstream sport have been subverted or renegotiated. I also describe processes by which these alternative meanings are both (re)constructed and passed along as part of a community- and family-based cultural practice.

STRUCTURAL/SOCIOHISTORICAL CONTEXT

The reconstruction of gendered meaning within the J-Leagues is largely made possible by the structure of the J-Leagues as a gender-inclusive community institution. Although the J-Leagues are in many ways a unique social environment, larger structural forces, both historical and contemporary, have shaped the community's ideas and practices surrounding gender and sport. This includes the feminist-inspired legislation, Title IX, which led to more opportunities in women's sports, as well as the growing societal acceptance and normalization of athletic participation in organized contexts, particularly among middle-class girls. These important developments will be discussed in more detail in the next chapter.

Other structural forces are more particular to Asian American and Japanese American communities. Le Espiritu (2008) argues that the experiences of Asian Americans, including historical oppression, economic constraints, and controlling imagery, "(re)structures the rules of gender" and "relations between Asian American men and women" in Asian American communities (8–13). For example, as immigrant families facing discrimination and economic hardships, Japanese Americans arriving in the pre-1924 immigration had to pool resources as families—women and children worked to help the family subsist, and women often gained status in the family as a result (Glenn 2010; Le Espiritu 2008). Many Japanese Americans also experienced incarceration during World War II. The structure of the concentration camps had the latent effect of breaking down many of the patriarchal practices within families (Glenn 2010). Furthermore, controlling images of Asian Americans often included depictions that positioned Asian American men as less masculine than men of other races, influencing the way that many viewed Asian American men and how they viewed themselves (Chou 2012; Le Espiritu 2008).

With hardship comes adaptation—the struggles faced by communities of color can open doors for new ways of understanding gender relations and new ways of creating community cultural wealth (Yosso 2005). The social environments and interactions described in this chapter exist within this larger context and can be understood as part of the creative ways that Japanese Americans mobilize their community resources in the face of challenging circumstances.

The particular challenges facing communities of color paired with the racism specific to the sport context have meant that women of color often have different sporting experiences than white women (Smith 1992). Scholarship on women of color in sport often focuses on the experiences and representations of marginalized women, such as Asian American women, in mainstream environments (e.g., Hanson 2005; Lee 2005). However, the J-Leagues provide an intriguing case study of the experiences of marginalized women playing sports within their own racial/ethnic group. The ethnic community offers a potential site for reimagining gendered and racialized images and stereotypes that plague Asian American sporting experiences (Chin 2015).

The sociohistorical context of the J-Leagues and their current gender-inclusive structure create an environment where the connections between gender and sport are (re)negotiated in ways that scramble and reinvent traditional, mainstream norms. In this chapter I discuss several contexts, interactions, and discourses in J-League Basketball that challenge mainstream understandings of which bodies belong in sport.

THE DOMINANT CULTURE

Sports have the power to "construct differences between different femininities (and masculinities) as well as between males and females" (Hargreaves 1994, 171). Typically, this power has been leveraged for confirming male dominance.

According to Schippers (2007), women who excel at activities normally associated with men and masculinity, specifically hegemonic masculinity (Connell 2005), are often sanctioned in some way. A woman who is good at basketball, for instance, may experience some forms of backlash—the desired outcome would be to withhold the symbolic value attached to the status of "basketball player." She may become stigmatized—as too mannish, for example—due to enacting what Schippers calls "pariah femininities."

Scholars theorize that women of color in masculinized sporting environments are often treated as sporting space invaders (Adjepong and Carrington 2014; Brown 2015; Puwar 2004), as they do not possess normalized athletic bodies. Asian American female athletes in particular may seem like a paradoxical image in the American imagination (King 2006, 2010).

Especially in the post–Title IX era, girls' and women's success in the J-Leagues and beyond has complicated this formula for many Japanese Americans. From community recognition of women as basketball role models to narratives of women as possessing natural talents for coaching boys and men's teams, the discourses surrounding women's knowledge and ability in sport are transformed. From coed leagues where women are seen as strengths rather than liabilities to coed tournaments where participants play with women's basketball rules and equipment and sometimes in feminized attire, male dominance in sport is subverted.

In the J-Leagues, Asian American women's athletic participation is normalized, certainly not unexpected. As accomplished female athletes of color, in the contemporary J-League context, they are not seen as sporting space invaders (Adjepong and Carrington 2014; Brown 2015; Puwar 2004). In the J-Leagues, Asian American women who demonstrate superior basketball abilities and athletic performance are seldom interpreted by co-ethnics as exhibiting pariah femininities (Schippers 2007). As women participating competitively in a sport typically associated with masculinity, they are interpreted not as dissonant bodies (Puwar 2004), but as normalized bodies.

As such, it is fair to argue that the J-Leagues create a space in which mainstream understandings of belonging in sport are upended. With the J-League community, just as Asian American players find a place where they belong, so do girls and women. Their participation in sport is anticipated, supported, and recognized to an extent that I do not believe is reproduced in many other US contexts, helping explain the rise of Japanese American female college-level players and their status as community icons.

IMPERIALS PURPLE

Although Japanese Americans have incorporated girls and women into community sports since the 1920s, more widespread participation and high-level respect for women's play emerged in the post–Title IX era as college-level players began to make their mark on the growing J-Leagues. No team was more important to this transformation than the Imperials Purple. This is a team of women who have pushed gender boundaries and helped to redefine what women's basketball means in the J-League context.

The Imperials Purple are well-known as a women's team that took J-League women's basketball to the next level. This long-standing team has become famous, if not infamous, for their high level of play and unparalleled winning record, as well as for their intensity and aggressive play. Starting in the 1970s, these women pushed the limits of what was perceived as acceptable practice for women athletes in the J-Leagues. In the early years, they faced push-back and are still perceived by some as too aggressive for the leagues. However, the legacy of the Imperials Purple today is a recognition of their status as trailblazers and an acknowledgment of their commitment to excellence in basketball.

Imperials Purple have such a reputation in the community that they continue to be recognized and talked about even though the original players have retired or moved on to less competitive divisions. The team received coverage in the *Orange County Register* in 2016 (Fader 2016), including a photo of the most famous players (see image 2.1).

The original team members were primarily college players who earned some of the first basketball scholarships in the post–Title IX era in Southern California (see chapter 3 for more of this history). Sharing a love of basketball, they put together a team of all-stars and became known as an unbeatable team in the highest division of the women's league. Marcia Murota, one of the original players and also a former college player at California State University, Los Angeles, told the story of how several college-level players came to play on the same team:

IMAGE 2.1. The Imperials Purple are a legendary J-League women's basketball team. (Credit: Cindy Yamanaka, *Orange County Register*.)

We all kind of knew each other or it was just timing. People were finishing their collegiate careers . . . and then they were available to play and we'd ask them if they wanted to play with us. Yeah, I don't know what really got us going like that but yeah basically our whole team has played collegiately or if they would have gone out for the team, would have played collegiately. So that's cool and, yeah, I mean even from before when we first kind of started there weren't a lot of people playing collegiate ball at that time either . . . there weren't a whole lot of Japanese women playing ball. There are much more now.

In this early era of college women's basketball, the original members of the Imperials Purple found other Japanese American women who were like-minded and possessed similarly high skill levels to fill the team. Murota described the team in this way:

> The reputation of our team has been because we were always very competitive. I think and we had a coach that was pretty demanding and driven. And we were those kinds of players, too, in our younger years—definitely me in my younger years. Winning was great but then winning by a lot of points was greater! It wasn't to embarrass anybody, but that's how we played. We were aggressive and we loved the game and we wanted to play it as much as possible. That drive was, at that time I think, rare compared to the other teams. . . . It wasn't just like one person. Our whole team was driven that way. The [women's league] used to have or they still have a North/South [championship]. So, whoever would win South would play the winner of the Northern California League so we would get to play for a state championship quite a bit.

The team stood out in the women's J-Leagues for being so dominant and for their aggressive play, uncharacteristic for women's teams of that time.

Murota thought the success of the Imperials Purple played a part in raising the status of women's basketball in the Japanese American community:

> I'll tell you—before, when we were younger and playing, you know, especially from guys or men coaches that were coaching in the community, they were kind of like, "Okay, yeah, you guys play basketball. Whatever." But they'd see us play and they'd see us play over time and they were like, "Okay, you guys are like a legitimate team." So that was our reputation . . . if you talk to people who knew us because we were pretty much consistently . . . successful. That has totally changed just how kids are approached with sports now and how much younger they do actually get coaching and all the camps and stuff that they can do to develop themselves and it's a different world now.

Over the span of Murota's playing and coaching career, she had noticed a shift in the respect Japanese Americans showed toward girls' and women's basketball. When people in the community watched Purple play, they had to acknowledge the potential for female players.

In the absence of women's professional opportunities, Imperials players treated the Imperials Purple almost like a professional team, and regularly recruited from J-League college-level talent. One recruit was LeeAnne Sera, who helped win back-to-back national championships for USC with Cheryl Miller and Cynthia Cooper. Sera shared that it felt like she was joining a team of her heroes when she joined the Imperials: "Oh, sure. We looked up to all of [the Imperials], especially the Purple team. They already had a reputation as being the best, and they were. They were the team to beat. They were the best. They were all playing at a much higher level than everybody else. They were the team. They were the ones. They were the league's best women's teams for years and years." Members of Imperials Purple felt that joining the team was a way to take their game to the next level after college. It's is one of the few women's league teams that regularly holds practices. Carol Jue, another recruit who played in college for California State University, Los Angeles and at Claremont McKenna College, shared this with me when I attended a Tuesday night practice:

> We take our basketball very seriously. It's about practicing. You see this Tuesday night practice and all these women are here. This has been going over for over thirty-something years that you practice. And if you don't practice, it shows in your game and what's it's all about. It's about heart and hustle. And that's why I think we still beat people who are eighteen or nineteen years old, because of our experience. And when I first came on the team, I sat that bench sometimes. And it was disheartening for me, but I didn't—but, to tell you the truth, I wasn't good. I was good enough for high school, good enough for college, but I wasn't good enough for Imperials Purple. So, I worked my tail off to get stronger, faster, and teach myself to play post if I wanted to play.

Imperials Purple carried a level of prestige and offered post-collegiate playing opportunities for many J-League players. The intensity and work ethic pursued by the team appealed to many talented players who had a drive to take their game to the next level.

Although the Imperials Purple have been widely known as the best J-League women's team, their success and intensity have raised concern at times. Murota told this story: "There was a time in one of the tournaments locally down here where we didn't get invited to the tournament. We got invited—teams from up north wouldn't come down to play because they didn't want to. It's a big expense to come down or travel or whatever . . . but if we were playing they didn't want to come down. So, we didn't get invited so that the rest of the teams could be playing which . . . you know that was their call but that was interesting." In this early Title IX era, most Japanese Americans were not used to women in the leagues playing at this level of ability or intensity, so some teams reacted by declining to face the all-star squad.

There has also been some push-back against the aggressive play characteristic of the Purple. Some players who went head-to-head with the team regarded Imperials Purple as too intense or aggressive for what others considered recreational basketball. One of my interviewees, Janine, remembered playing against them in a fierce game. Janine's team had taken the lead, causing the Purple to become more forceful. In the intense play that followed, Janine saw many of the players on her team "going to the ground," and she became concerned about them getting injured. She explained her feelings: "I heard these women practice before you go, and we'd always just go and play. So I guess when they take it up to that level, I understand their frustration, but there's a boundary, I think. I don't know, it's just kind of—I was kind of disturbed by that [level of physical play]." Even though Janine is a very serious and passionate player herself, she distanced herself from the Imperials Purple, who she felt were too serious and aggressive for the J-League context.

Some of the reactions to the approach and style of Imperials Purple, particularly in their earliest years of success, can be understood through Schippers's (2007) concept of pariah femininities.

Schippers argues that there are practices of valorized masculinity that, when undertaken by women, are stigmatizing. Potentially, the team played with too much fervor, a little too much like elite male basketball players. They have been sanctioned—the organizers of some tournaments asked them to stay at home, and some J-League players didn't approve of their aggressive play. However, these women became trailblazers and helped change the perception of women athletes within the J-Leagues.

The Imperials Purple can be understood as a team that pushed boundaries. They were made up of some of the first women to play on scholarship at the college level. Without paid post-collegiate opportunities, these women sought excellence in the J-Leagues and tested the limits of what was acceptable practice for a women's basketball team. Some in the J-Leagues struggled with making sense of this new level of play for women's basketball. Were they too dominant? Too aggressive? Today, the team is primarily admired and revered. And for the women who played on the team, they consider just having been a member of the Imperials Purple a badge of honor.

GIRLS PLAYING—IT'S NATURAL

In contrast to the early days of the Imperials when women's high level of play in the J-Leagues and success in the mainstream were more revolutionary, in today's J-Leagues most participants regard women's participation—and even excellence—in basketball as expected. Joining a J-League youth team is now considered a natural extension of belonging to the Japanese American community. Furthermore, young Japanese American women, as well as some of their male counterparts, have been doing so well in mainstream contexts that in 2014 the Los Angeles Japanese American newspaper *Rafu Shimpo* published an article lamenting that it no longer had the staff resources to keep up with all of the Japanese Americans playing for high school varsity teams (Culross 2014) (see image 2.2).

Because basketball is such an integral part of the community, Japanese Americans tend to assume that just about everyone will

IMAGE 2.2. The *Rafu Shimpo* sports editor, Mickey Culross, is overwhelmed because he has too many athletes to cover as more and more Japanese Americans join high school and college basketball teams. (Credit: Gwen Muranaka, *Rafu Shimpo*.)

at least try the sport and that most will find something about it that they enjoy. For example, Sarah expressed some disbelief that someone would not be involved. "In Southern California?" she asked. "It's almost second nature." Attaching a stigma to girls' and women's success would interfere with basketball's role as a community-building activity. If someone is stigmatized in any way, it would be because he or she chooses not to play basketball. Many interviewees worried that those who did not play basketball would feel left out, or have to explain themselves in some way. When asked if other Japanese Americans were likely to assume that she played basketball, Laura answered, "They kind of do assume, they assume. That's why my friends feel left out—those ones that— because they'll probably always ask, 'Oh, what team did you play for?' And they feel left out of that. And you're kind of surprised if you meet somebody that hasn't played in a league and they're older. It's like, 'You never played?' They're like, 'Yeah.' It's like, 'What were you doing?' It's something that like, like everybody . . . you grew up with that and that's what you're supposed to do is play in these leagues." Basketball is such a common denominator among Japanese Americans that not being able to name a team or organizational affiliation leaves many simply out of the conversation. Laura explains that those who do not play often feel "left out." Scott goes further to say that a Japanese American who doesn't play would be "weird," although he does make an allowance for someone who lives outside of California: "I think if you're Japanese, it's kind of expected. If I meet someone new that's Japanese [American] and I found out they didn't play, I think it's weird. It's almost like the rule versus the exception. Unless they grew up out of state. . . . So, I think it's kind of—you expect them to be able to play." So, for both boys and girls, choosing basketball as a pastime is "second nature," and those who are not participating may have to explain themselves—they may be perceived as somewhat of an outsider, such as someone not from California.

This involvement was sometimes eagerly embraced by children in Japanese American families, and sometimes not. A couple of participants suggested that girls were occasionally pressured into playing basketball for at least a few years by their parents, who viewed it as a way to build or reinforce their own social ties. They also hoped to establish similar co-ethnic ties for their children. Megan described the importance many parents placed on participation, even if their children were not immediately showing athletic interest or prowess: "A lot of kids play basketball even though they—I remember some girls they didn't really like playing because they weren't very good, but their parents kind of made them play for a while and then it wasn't 'til like, I don't know, maybe a few years they let them quit. But that was because it was through church, too, because it's a very social thing. For the parents, too. Have their kids play, and they go to the games, and so they wanted them to try it."

The position of the J-Leagues as a widespread community institution meant that youth involvement was seen as nearly mandatory. Therefore, within the Japanese American community, Asian American bodies and specifically Asian American female bodies are interpreted and anticipated as athletic bodies, scrambling dominant mainstream notions of who belongs on a basketball court and providing an opening for new understandings of the meanings attached to the sport.

"EVERYONE ASSUMES YOU'RE DECENT AT BASKETBALL"

Laura described an atmosphere within the J-Leagues that takes not only women's participation but also their athletic talent for granted: "It's like, you're Japanese and a girl—everyone assumes you're decent at basketball."

When asked how women athletes were regarded in the community, Jimmy stated, "Just as much as boys, I think. There's not—I don't think—there's not that much difference. I know just outside of the JA community maybe they don't get as much respect. Maybe, I don't know. But in JA circles, girls and boys are on equal footing." Jimmy's words are important here. To assert a community attitude of "equal footing" between male and female basketball players shows a dramatically different discourse about women's sports when compared to mainstream contexts.

Girls' and women's basketball prowess also came to be naturalized through references to the female players who had achieved mainstream success. When I asked Sarah how respected women basketball players were within the Japanese American community, she answered, "I think if anything, it's actually more respected for females because more of them are playing at the collegiate level, whereas the males don't tend to either try out or make it at the collegiate level." Because women had achieved a greater level of mainstream success, several participants argued, women's basketball received a lot of respect. Women were able to leverage this symbolic resource to assert themselves as strong players, and some women became comfortable playing side by side with men.

Female participants noted that male sporting spaces were often easier to transgress within the J-Leagues than in mainstream contexts. One could imagine that even if girls and women in the J-Leagues are recognized as players, this may not necessarily translate directly into a respect for their playing knowledge, skill, or ability or give them a free pass to transgress into male-dominated spaces. However, there was evidence that this is exactly what was happening in many of the J-League contexts. Women, particularly women of color who excel at sport in spaces symbolically reserved for men, often experience feeling like a "sporting space invader" (Adjepong and Carrington 2014; Brown 2015; Puwar 2004), However, in Japanese American contexts, women did not commonly report feeling this way. Several women shared that they felt much more comfortable talking about or playing basketball with Japanese American men than with men from outside of the community, and that these men were generally respectful and receptive to sharing sport spaces with them on equal footing. Meredith played in a coed league and said, "[Japanese American men] are not afraid to say that word: 'good.' Like I know some guys are afraid to say 'hey, she's pretty good.' You know, like, 'We're playing against a girl that's really good.' They're not. I guess you could say they're not embarrassed to get scored on by us, you know, where some guys are like embarrassed if a girl scores on them, but I don't think the guys are that embarrassed because they know that we can probably hold our own." For Meredith, the general respect for women's play in the J-Leagues removed any stigma from playing with women. In the J-Leagues, to be scored on by a female player was not synonymous with being scored on by a weaker player.

Grace felt this appreciation of women's talent extended to any men who "know about the Japanese Leagues." She explained, "It's easier to play with other guys that know about the Japanese leagues . . . like, they know you can play, they've seen you play, versus someone that doesn't know anything about leagues and thinks it's just girls playing basketball." In this statement, Grace voices exceptionalism not only for those who are affiliated with the J-Leagues, of whom she assumes a certain degree of awareness and respect, but also for the female participants in the J-Leagues. She seems to imply that even she might not expect girls and women who were not in the J-Leagues to be strong basketball players.

Lena echoed the sentiment that Japanese American men are aware of the women's athletic abilities, but admitted that certain aspects of their participation could still take some men by surprise:

> I mean, I think in general Japanese guys know that it's a big part—most girls now growing up play in the leagues. So, I think they know that we can play. But even when I met my husband, I remember him being really surprised when I used to play in the men's leagues at college. And I remember saying to him, "What do you expect? We grew up playing this." I remember being surprised that he was surprised that I would want to play in the men's leagues. But I think there's generally more understanding amongst the Japanese guys because they go to a lot of games. They see us play. They know that we're playing in the same tournaments. They are in the same leagues.

Although women's participation was anticipated and their abilities were often acknowledged due to mainstream successes, some spaces such as men's leagues were still seen as somewhat transgressive for Japanese American women.

"'BASKETBALL MOM' HAS A DIFFERENT MEANING ALTOGETHER"

In the story at the start of this chapter, I shared the account of a player whose son both interfered with and idolized his mother's role as basketball player. Some readers could have been wondering—why bring a four-year-old to a basketball game? It may very well have been quite intentional. A few of my interviewees suggested that exposing children to their parents' play is part of the process of folding their children into the tradition of the J-Leagues. Some parents spoke explicitly about girls' exposure to female basketball role models, starting with their own mothers. Emily nonchalantly shared with me that her husband, Logan, had been encouraging her to rejoin the adult J-League with the intention of bringing their two small children, Jenny and Erik (about ages four and two, respectively), to watch her play: "Even Logan said to me the other day, 'You've got to get Jenny [involved].' Because I'm going to start playing in a league this Sunday. 'I really want to get Jenny out there so she gets accustomed to seeing you play.' So he's very encouraging of—he thinks that Jenny has to play just as much as Erik." Emily had been on hiatus from playing since having her two kids, but was planning to return to her adult league that week. Her husband was already planning to have their daughter watch Emily play so as to spark her interest in the game. This shows the importance placed on investment in girls' basketball. Women, and especially mothers, are active as role models in this process. Emily's daughter Jenny, only four, will have the chance to see her mother play basketball in an organized league with referees and scorekeepers, and the air of importance that comes with both. This role modeling was important not only to Emily, but also to her husband, who was actually the one to suggest her return to the team.

The stereotypical role of mothers in sport is usually characterized by the labor involved in providing sport experiences for their children: washing uniforms, driving their children to practice and games, and helping out with team snacks. In one election season, the "soccer mom" became an archetype of American middle-class suburban culture, symbolized by the stay-at-home mom with a minivan full of children seemingly perpetually in route to the next soccer practice (Swanson 2009; Vavrus 2000).

Women's roles in the J-Leagues are complex. There are certainly many mothers who perform the stereotypical "basketball mom" labor for their children. For example, after-game snacks are a big deal in many J-League organizations, and preparing snacks is often a duty left to mothers. Some mothers did not appreciate the extra effort required to provide "snacks" for the team. Debbie shared, "Because I am the mom. . . . It doesn't necessarily fall on the dad . . . there is still that division, that sexist division. I mean, it was grueling to have to come up with what creative fabulous thing are you going to provide and so I was very glad when our team said yeah, just bring your own drinks. What was even greater was that this team always went out to eat afterwards. Let's just go have dinner together." Feeling burdened by the expectation of elaborate postgame snacks, Debbie and other parents spoke up on one of her son's teams and suggested that they skip them. However, she suggested another activity, going out to eat together as a team, to compensate for any lost social opportunity surrounding snacks.

Even though women take on many of the roles traditionally assigned to mothers, since many women participants grew up playing basketball, they engage in a wider range of roles within the leagues than might be anticipated in mainstream sports leagues. They occupy leadership roles in some organizations and often sit on committees. At the actual games, women can be seen acting as scorekeepers, referees, coaches, and players. In their families, they may be driving their children to practices, but they are likely a coach, whether officially or informally, training their children on the side or giving them advice on their play.

In this context, as one participant explained, "'Basketball Mom' has a different meaning altogether." Rachel, a sansei (third-generation Japanese American), had a father who took an interest in her playing career, and this led her, as a mother of three, to replicate his parenting practices with her son.

> My father would take me to all my games. This made him more involved in my life. He knew all of my teammates and my teammates came to know him, even opposing teams. He would always sit quietly in the stands, keeping score, cheering the team on. After the games, I would be able to look at his score sheet (a folded up piece of scrap paper) and see how I did, and how my teammates did. We'd talk about the game in general and he was always supportive, win or lose, if I played good or bad. Watching my son play over the years, I would keep score (on a piece of scrap paper) at games for him. I have come to know all his teammates, we discuss the games and we have a great relationship.

Rachel also added this thought: "Kids see their mothers out on the court playing and see them in a different light, not just a typical old frumpy housewife. Basketball mom has a different meaning alto-gether." So, not only did Rachel play the role of sideline coach with her son, filling a role her father had once occupied in her own life, but she viewed herself as presenting a different image of mother-hood through her own adult participation in the J-Leagues.

WOMEN LEADING—"WHOEVER IS CAPABLE"

As Japanese American women's participation in basketball repre-sented a normal, expected engagement with the community, most participants regarded women's leadership within the J-Leagues in a similar manner. Leadership roles included serving as a commis-sioner, organizer, or board member overseeing a sport organiza-tion, league, or tournament and acting as a coach of an individual team. Although men outnumbered women in most of these roles, women were a consistent presence. Moreover, the discourse on women in leadership, particularly in regard to coaching, was gener-ally very affirmative, praising women's capabilities.

Since there are so many J-League sport organizations, leagues, and tournaments, it was difficult to determine the exact percent-age of coaches who identified as female. In order to acquire an estimate, I analyzed the 2006 Tournament Program for the Tigers Youth Club Tournament, purportedly the largest J-League tourna-ment. I located the name of all head coaches listed with each youth team, coding the names as male, female, or ambiguous. Taking all teams into account, 85 percent of coaches had male names, 10 per-cent had female names, and 5 percent had names that were ambig-uous. Counting only unambiguous names, women coaches mainly coached girls' teams—about 20 percent of the girls' team coaches were women, whereas only 3.5 percent of the boys' team coaches were women. Although these percentages are comparable to or slightly better than those found in other studies of youth sports (e.g., Messner 2009), they are far from equal or representative. In mainstream recreational leagues, women tend to coach primarily in the younger age groups, where coaching is believed to be less intensive, and less knowledge-dependent (Messner 2009; Messner and Bozada-Deas 2009). In contrast to these findings, J-League women were not necessarily relegated to coaching at the lowest age divisions. The largest percentage of women coaching boys' teams (17 percent) occurred in the seventh grade division.

Unaware of my estimates, a few participants believed that women coaches were abundant in the J-Leagues. Nick, age fifteen, was on a team coached by a young woman named Marissa. He informed me, "There are actually a lot of women coaches around the league, a lot of people's moms. I see a lot of moms as coach. So having Marissa as coach is really no different than some of those other teams. I'd probably say fifty–fifty women to men coaches." Evidently, Nick saw enough women coaching, mostly mothers he believed, to lead him to estimate that women made up half of all coaches. This provides evidence that at least in some leagues, women are quite visible and accepted as coaches.

Only one interviewee, Kevin, who lived in Orange County, discussed the dearth of women coaching youth teams. He was involved in planning the Nikkei Games event, so I asked him why I had mainly seen men gathering during the youth basketball tournament coaches' meeting. It didn't seem congruent with the abundance of female talent and did not match what I had observed in Los Angeles County. His answer was that women were too busy raising children to participate. Evidently, there may be obstacles to a greater number of women coaching that have to do with expectations of middle- and upper-middle-class motherhood, as has been found in other contexts (Messner 2009).

WOMEN COACHING BOYS' AND MEN'S TEAMS

In the J-Leagues, women regularly coach boys' and men's teams. Male coaches far outnumber women coaches, but the discourse about the women who did coach is worth exploring as another example of the renegotiation of gendered roles in sport occurring within the J-Leagues. Participant narratives about women coaching typically showed respect for women's coaching abilities and basketball knowledge. Women coaching boys and men was seen as a normalized, even idealized practice.

In mainstream sports, it is rare to see women coaching boys' or men's teams (Acosta and Carpenter 2014; Knoppers 1992; Walker 2016). There are a few very recent examples of women cracking through that barrier, including Becky Hammon and Japanese American Natalie Nakase occupying positions on NBA coaching staffs. In intercollegiate sports, the percentage of men's teams coached by women has remained remarkably consistent since 1972, at around 2 to 3 percent (Acosta and Carpenter 2014; Kamphoff and LaVoi 2013). Women also rarely coach boys' teams in high school and youth recreational sports (LaVoi 2009; Messner 2009; Messner and Bozada-Deas 2009; Walker 2016).

One discourse among J-League participants about women coaching men was that these women were able to be "one of the guys." Nick explained that his coach Marissa is "just as much one of the guys as any one of us." Even though she's a woman, she acts like one of the guys sometimes. . . . After every practice, we go out and put our hands in and after every practice we have a tradition of, whoever did the best in practice, we pull him in the middle. It's usually more like a congratulations and we all do it to him, but the kids turn it into, "Hey, let's push him around and be funny." Marissa sees that no one's seriously trying to hurt anyone, so she'll be the first one to pull you in. She's one of the instigators of the whole thing. She's like, "Get in here, you're the one getting beat up today." So, I don't think anyone thinks of her as a woman more than just a coach. I think that's what everyone really sees her as. For Nick, the highest praise he could give his coach was that she fit in perfectly with a group of young adolescent men, understanding even their rougher team rituals. Women may be on equal footing in the J-Leagues, but Nick's interpretation suggests that some of this esteem may still rest on a masculine embodiment of basketball player.

Another discourse centered on a meritocratic argument, asserting that coaches were chosen based on their skills and not their gender. Barbara had a son in sixth grade whose team was coached by a college-age woman. I asked Barbara about female coaches in general, and she responded, "[The J-Leagues] recognize the talent. When a woman is good at something, it's respected." She had no doubt that there were many women who were good at coaching and that they got the respect and placement that they deserved. When I asked about her son's coach, she thought that there may have been a little bit of disrespect for her because she was so young, but in general refused to incorporate gender into her appraisal: "I don't really categorize between male and female. A good game is a good game." Barbara felt strongly that there were no gender biases in the J-Leagues. She shared with me that one of the players on her son's team had an older sister who had played in college, and that the sister would occasionally come out to practices to play with the boys. Barbara had been coached by women growing up. She summed it up: "Whoever is capable." Barbara voiced a gender-blind meritocracy argument—if they're good enough, they'll be chosen to coach.

A third discourse was voiced primarily in relation to the men's league. At the Los Angeles–based Nisei Athletic Union, for example, male board members talked about women coaching adult men's teams as if it was the best thing going on in the J-Leagues. In this discourse, women were seen ideal coaches for men's teams due to their penchant for being more responsible and organized than men. Women who coached men tended to assert that men respected their basketball expertise. Both perspectives seemed to resonate with many participants' experiences.

At the adult level, coaches were primarily organizers. They made sure the dues were paid and disseminated game schedules. At games, they would run the substitutions and occasionally give suggestions to players, but they rarely held practices or implemented complex game plans. In this context, men and women described women coaches as capable if not superior coaches to men, utilizing discourses that both contested and reproduced traditional gender ideology.

Most women who talked about coaching men had coached for teams where they knew one or more of the players, usually a boyfriend, husband, or male family member. Tammy's experience seemed to be fairly typical: "I was twenty-one or twenty-two. [The guys] were probably mid-twenties. It was my boyfriend's team. . . . It was cool because—I don't know, I just told them what to do. At that level, you just substitute them and give them pointers here and there. Because I know basketball, how to match up. 'You should do this: go to the zone, press them.' Just those things, because when you play in an adult league, you either know how to play or you don't. You don't really practice any more. They just need someone to tell them what to do sometimes. So, that was all I did." Tammy mentioned her role as coach as somewhat limited, but also described herself as guiding the players. One could imagine that in a mainstream men's league, it might be met with skepticism if a player brought on his younger girlfriend as coach. Nevertheless, Tammy spoke about it as if her role was unremarkable and did not mention any player push-back.

To some extent, coaching close family members may help smooth over any objections to behaviors perceived by some to be outside of feminine norms. Cheryl, a Chinese American, has coached numerous family members, including her father.

> I coach my husband's team still today. It's funny. It's a lot of my nephews, my brother, my husband, and friends and everything. I get well respected from them because they know I know what I'm doing. And we've won many championships. And it's funny one of the friends of my nephew's—older guy, lawyer. I said something—it would be okay for a man to say it to a man, but not a woman to a man. And he kind of made the comment, "I could never get coached by you." And I go, "Why?" And he goes, "Because, you coach like a man, and you don't hold back." And I forgot what I had said and it was funny. Like, it was just something like, "What the heck are you doing?" I guess it's funny coming from a woman. And when a woman says it to a man, especially a very macho man, ah, the guy in the stands couldn't take it. And so he told me. But my players who are men—my husband and everyone—it's okay, because they know that I'm just doing my best to make them win. And I coach my dad's team and they're okay with that. There's a mutual respect.

Although an onlooker felt Cheryl had overstepped her boundaries as a woman coaching men, Cheryl felt that the men on her team accepted her and her coaching style. They knew her and that she was a great coach. Evidently she did not alienate her players—she shared with me that she met her husband when she started coaching his team. Cheryl had coached in the Chinese and Japanese Leagues and always felt her players thought of her as capable and appreciated her strong coaching.

Whereas women coaches talked about how their knowledge was respected, men often described the women coaches in more feminine terms. When I was chatting with some of the leaders from the NAU, they proudly volunteered that there had been several women's coaches who coached highly ranked men's teams, a nod to the quality of coaching by these women. However, in their narratives about the subject, they described women coaches not only as capable, but also as "having it together." They thought that men's teams often sought out good female coaches because they needed a woman's help to get the team organized. According to them, most of the men would rather just play and appreciated someone to step in and keep the team on track, picking up tasks such as getting players enrolled or organizing substitutions during games. They viewed the women as knowledgeable of the game, but also felt women were better than men at responsibilities that could be described as caretaking tasks. The women coaches, at least through some of the men's eyes, seemed to be part "Team Mom" (Messner 2009; Messner and Bozada-Deas 2009) and part coach. In many ways, this could be seen as capitalizing on feminized labor. However, the men were also submitting to the direction and expertise of a woman in an athletic context, scrambling some of the gendered meaning attached to the role.

One woman, Cassidy, not only coached men's teams, but decided to start a men's league. She was probably the true definition of "one of the guys." While I was interviewing her, there were several games going on at the gyms on the property (a public school). As the boys and young men walked by, they all seemed to know Cassidy. A respected coach and leader, she also in many ways took care of these young men. She even started the leagues as a favor to some of her friends who could not find enough playing opportunities in that part of town.

J-LEAGUE BASKETBALL IS "GENDERLESS"

How did the J-League participants make sense of the gender-inclusiveness of the leagues and the general respect for female athletes and coaches? Like Nick, quoted earlier, many participants noticed the high level of play and coaching expertise by women and began to overestimate the actual proportion of players and coaches who were women. This gave an impression of equality and led some to describe the J-Leagues as "genderless."

Some believed that within the community, basketball had shed its label as a "men's sport." Sandra viewed the J-League opportunities for play and coaching as egalitarian. She had grown up in Northern California playing basketball in the J-Leagues. Now a parent of two children, a boy and a girl, playing in the Southern California J-Leagues, she thought that basketball was becoming "genderless." Even growing up, she said that she definitely perceived basketball at the professional level as a male sport, but on a local community level, she didn't really think of it that way. It was "everybody's sport."

Musto (2014) suggests that, in attempting to understanding the social construction of gender, it may be important to explore the way that groups might understand gender relations across contexts. In a few of my interviews, J-League participants seemed to be constructing different meanings about women's athleticism within the J-Leagues in contrast to more elite mainstream environments. When asked about the status of women's basketball in the J-Leagues, Jake made a similar distinction to Sandy's: "I think within the JA, it's mostly like a rec league. We don't really—I don't think it's like the . . . how people feel about the WNBA . . . like it's inferior or. . . . It's just, you know, we all know it's just something we're doing for fun . . . at this level. I don't think it's really much of a difference. I mean, it's not like you can really tease them for playing something that's inferior, when we're out playing rec leagues as well." Jake implies that there may be a common sentiment that the WNBA is inferior to the NBA, but within the J-Leagues, everyone sees each other as being at the same level. He does not see a reason to tease the girls and women in the leagues, since he sees himself as at an equal level to them.

By rebranding basketball within the community as a Japanese American thing rather than a men's thing, participants seemed to renegotiate some of the gendered meaning in sport. Gender difference is still reproduced through mainstream symbols in basketball, but to some extent subverted within the community league context. At the professional level, women's sport is still viewed by some participants as less important or less serious than men's basketball, whereas in the J-Leagues neither men's nor women's participation is typically perceived as serious, discouraging gender comparisons and creating more gender egalitarian discourses.

Sometimes the "genderless" belief system led participants to be somewhat blind to any lingering disparities between men's and women's opportunities. Sandra, Nick, and others who had contact with women coaches seemed convinced that women coached just about as often as men. I could not find evidence of this in any of the contexts I observed.

COED SPACES: "GOOFING OFF" AND SERIOUS RESPECT

Coed leagues and tournaments were another example of the J-League's ability to incorporate and accommodate a wide spectrum of abilities and interests, leading to spaces where meanings attached to gender and sport are reimagined in the context. Coed leagues seemed very popular among young men and women and several participants reported that the coed leagues have been expanding.

On the day that I interviewed Meredith, a Japanese American Division III basketball player, I also watched her compete in a coed J-League with her brother. She described the division in which she and her brother played: "I know they have different coed divisions, and so I know in the lower ones they don't really care too much. The lower ones are more goofing off. This one, they tend to play more serious." During the game, Meredith's brother scored a beautiful three-point shot. A few minutes later, Meredith hit her stride, sinking back-to-back three-pointers for the team. Some male teammates chided the brother, "Who's the better shot?" The brother answered, "No contest," and cast his eyes toward Meredith. In this league, several of the women, including Meredith, play or have played on college and university teams. The men understand this, and their play demonstrates respect for the women's athleticism. Keith, twenty-two, who plays in the same league, elaborated,

> [Girls are] pretty much the keys to winning the game, I think, because if you have two solid girls, they can—they're groomed to shoot, that's what they're made to do, that's what they've trained and worked on. I mean that's what they do. So, I mean, if you get two girls that are shooters and they just hit a bunch of shots outside, I mean. . . . They could take over a game basically. There is a mutual—there are times there's three girls in, and um, two guys in so a guy has to guard a girl, which is always an interesting kind of feel, because the girls are not afraid of those guys. I think they almost welcome them. Like, if I make him look bad, then, people are—it's going to look great. So, but I mean, I've definitely—I mean, I've blocked girls. I just view them as . . . as another guy because I think that's how they want to be viewed. They don't want to be viewed as dainty, like they can't play or they should be treated differently. If a girl's going to drive in for a layup and I have a chance to block her, then I will block her.

Playing in the higher division coed league, Keith views his women teammates "as another guy." He is clearly impressed by the skill and abilities of the women he plays with in this league, perceiving them as a challenge. In order to win, he can't afford to treat the women differently. In this coed league, there is a rule that two women must be on the court at all times. Nevertheless, as Keith alludes to in the interview, it is not uncommon for teams to field three. There are many women in the J-Leagues who are skilled players, and the teams benefit from having them on the court.

On July 24, 2009, I observed at the Jets/Jetts Tournament coed competition and discovered a bit of what Meredith meant by "goofing off." There were two divisions playing that night: high school and adult. As the high school teams warmed up, I noticed one straggler enter the gym, a young man of about sixteen. A fellow teammate, a young woman, met him at the side of the court. "Yes," I heard her say in a raised voice, "you *have* to wear the socks!" I glanced at some of these players' teammates and realized that all of the players on this particular team had polka-dot socks and had a different colored background on each foot: one black and one white. The young woman stood over the young man until she was satisfied that he was going to comply. As this process unfolded, a man with a camera, likely a parent, came over smiling and snapped a couple of pictures of the young man putting on his socks.

As more and more teams cycled through the three courts, I realized that quite a few had uniforms or accessories that could be described as costumes. On one team, it was just one young man who had decided to wear a pink sweat band on his head, as well as rainbow socks pulled over tights. Later, another boy entered the gym with sparkly pink and purple face makeup, as if he had had his face painted at a carnival. This time, several people gathered around with cameras to take photos of him or to pat him on the back. As for the girls, one was wrapped in plastic over her clothes and dragged out onto the court for photos. Other teams showed their creative energies in less ostentatious ways, such as with homemade T-shirts reflecting the individual personalities of players. A few teams had more conventional uniforms.

Just when I thought this was only the silliness of high school students, the adult teams arrived. Several players wore crazy accessories. Again, a lot of the symbols were feminine. For example, two of the coed teams wore uniforms of pink T-shirts—one team wore hot pink and the other light, pastel pink.

"Goofing off" in this context seemed to refer to the tendency for players to engage in a bit of play with feminine symbols. The

IMAGE 2.3. Coed leagues and tournaments have become popular among young adults in the J-Leagues. In this photo, Nikkei Games 2008 basketball tournament participants play four-on-four coed basketball. (Credit: Nicole Willms.)

level and intensity of play were fairly high, and not much joking occurred on the court. However, the use of costumes, accessories, and nontraditional colors made this event into more than just a basketball game. They gave a jovial feel to the coed tournament. Many of the players' accoutrements were gendered—the theme seemed to be for both male and female players to dress in exaggerated feminine symbols. It seemed to be a space where "doing gender" (West and Zimmerman 1987) in basketball took on a whole new meaning. In some ways, the gender performances of the young men in the tournament call to mind "rituals of reversals" as described by Foley (1990) in the context of powder-puff football. In powder-puff, high school boys, usually from the football team, dress up as cheerleaders and cheer on high school girls, typically the real cheerleaders, as they play a game of football dressed in football attire. Foley notes that the boys tend to exaggerate femininity to the point of caricature—this way, it is clearly a joke and the stigma of dressing and acting

like a girl is diminished. The girls more often take it seriously, trying to prove that they can be tough athletes.

The young men at the coed tournament may have been participating in a ritual of reversal by putting on polka-dot socks, wearing tights, painting their face, or wearing pink shirts. The reactions
of others indicated that these practices were intended to be funny,
as the participants got their pictures taken or pats on the back
from peers as well as parents. However, other than the perhaps
inherent caricature associated with the aforementioned apparel
and accessories, the young men did not appear to be overtly making fun of their female counterparts. As the sock incident implies,
it may have been that the young women team members were the
ones who organized the costumes and that some young men were
sometimes reluctant to participate. Also, the goofing off did not
really show itself in the play of the game. Play was fairly serious,
and the male athletes appeared to respect their female counterparts. The only aspect of play that was somewhat lopsided was
that the young men tended to be the ball-handlers in most games,
although this was not true of all of the games, and the position
sometimes rotated.

The playful atmosphere and feminized forms of dress I
observed at this tournament represented an engagement with
a range of gender performances that are not usually found in
basketball. They seemed to be yet another example of how the
gender-inclusive environment had provided room for renegotiated engagements with sport and also encouraged a playfulness
surrounding gender norms.

Participants often spoke fondly about coed leagues and tournaments, showing a level of mutual respect between the young men
and women. Recall that many female participants found J-League
men more respectful and aware of their basketball talent. They felt
more comfortable entering men's playing spaces. Correspondingly,
many of the male participants saw J-League men and women on
equal footing. I was able to observe one league where men and
women competed as equals in a competitive atmosphere and
at a tournament where they did so in a fun, playful atmosphere.

As I discussed in chapter 1, the wide range of options make the J-Leagues accessible and enable participants to negotiate the content and meaning associated with basketball participation.

THINKING ABOUT COED SPORTS

Wachs (2002) argues that "coed sports are an anomaly in the recent history of modern sports" (301). The recent model of equality in modern sports, she explains, is based on a concept of separate but equal (single-sex competition). This creates a paradox because "equality is predicated on definitions of difference" (302). Coed sporting environments, however, may be spaces where participants can challenge assumed categorical differences between the sexes, and where both sexes have the opportunity to recognize and respect each other's abilities. Wachs found that in coed softball, gendered rules tend to undermine this challenge to gender dichotomy, instead reifying and drawing focus toward gender differences.

In the highly competitive league where Meredith and Keith play coed basketball, Meredith's brother's recognition of her shooting abilities and Keith's comments about the competencies of female players show signs of mutual respect among players and even challenges to gender norms. One reason for this is probably the skill level of the female players—since many Japanese Americans have access to solid coaching, clinics, and numerous playing opportunities, most players, both male and female, are highly skilled. Thus, there is less reason to doubt female abilities. This also means that there do not have to be as many rules that serve to "protect" or provide opportunities for female players. The absence of complex gendered rules may, in turn, aid in making gender less salient on the court.

Rules for coed competition in the J-Leagues can vary widely, but are generally fairly simple, in contrast to the elaborate rules that Wachs (2002) encountered in her study of coed softball. The most common rules center around what Wachs describes as "affirmative action": rules that mandate a certain number of girls/women on the court at all times. Although these types of rules provide access to playing time and preserve the notion of "coed," they also insinuate that a team would choose to have fewer women if possible. Keith's descriptions of his experiences in the coed league imply that it is somewhat common to play the minimum number of girls (two), but that "there are times there's three girls in." So, at least in this league, this gendered rule does not prevent more women from playing than the rule implies would be desirable. The most egalitarian rule that I encountered was at the Nikkei Games three-on-three basketball tournament. Instead of singling out women as a protected category, they simply decided that the coed competitions would be four-on-four and that two players must be male and two must be female. This rule does reify gender categories because it forces teams to categorize players and make lineups and substitutions based on gender, but does less to imply that there is anything lacking in the abilities of either sex. It could simply be interpreted as an enforcement of the idea of "coed."

Another very common rule in coed competition within the J-Leagues is that teams play with a women's ball. In high school and college basketball, for instance, women play with a ball that is slightly lighter and smaller in circumference than that which men play with. Thus, when playing in coed competition within the J-Leagues, men must make an accommodation to play with the women. Although it is not unheard of for a coed league in the mainstream to institute this rule, this could be interpreted as one of many ways that the male players are asked to make accommodations. When teams wore pink shirts, for example, this seemed to be another symbolic gesture of men playing with the women on the women's terms. At least in one case, the young woman on the team was insisting that her male teammate wear polka-dot socks. In many ways this is radically different from what is asked of women in many sports contexts where they enter environments that are already established by and for men and have to prove themselves worthy to compete, often on men's terms. In the J-Leagues, some of the rules and practices seem to infer that the men are the ones entering a feminized space.

BASKETBALL WITHOUT
THE HYPERMASCULINITY

Since the Japanese American collective identity is formed, in part, through the J-Leagues and the forums and interactions they make possible, this identity formation works in concert with and helps to create patterns of inclusiveness. It also seems to discourage hypermasculine approaches to sport. J-League participants view the leagues as highly organized activities providing a family atmosphere. They view themselves as community-oriented and as kind to one another. Thus, the J-Leagues are structured with the intent that everyone should have the best experience possible. This is interpreted as competitive play against appropriate opponents in a kind environment that is not overly physical or aggressive. Rules establish boundaries of the community, who belongs and who does not, and promote inclusion of all community members. Rules also prohibit unkind behavior, and there are strict sanctions for those who do not comply. The inclusiveness creates a structure of opportunity, particularly important for girls and women in the league, but also for men who possess a range of engagements with masculinities. The kindness prevents hypermasculinity from dominating play and discourages behaviors that put down or alienate other players (male or female).

DIVERSITY OF ROLES, IDENTITIES, HYBRIDITY

While I was perusing an article about the Nisei Week beauty pageant contestants one year, I noticed that half of them had listed J-League playing experience in their bios. I remember thinking, "Playing basketball is seen as a qualification for a beauty pageant?" It turned out that a few of my interviewees had also been Nisei Week Royalty, including LeeAnne Sera, who was crowned Nisei Week Queen in 1987, and Jamie Hagiya, who was Miss Tomodachi in 2010.

This fluidity in roles between basketball player and beauty pageant contestant points to the flexibility of gender performance among female J-League participants. Rebecca noticed this trend,

"I'm saying that consistently along the way it's been . . . [it's] not like just because you play ball, you're not feminine enough to be in the beauty pageant either. You know? So, I think that's really nice because they're really well-rounded people. . . . When it's time to play ball they could be out there with the best, and when it's time to be in the beauty pageant it's—they could be there, so it's nice." One interpretation of her words is that she is making a claim that J-Leagues do not inherently masculinize its participants: Certainly, a few other, usually older, participants hinted at this. When women participate in sports that are viewed as masculine or male-dominated, they can sometimes be labeled in potentially stigmatizing ways—as too masculine and/or lesbian (Hargreaves 2002). These are labels that Schippers (2007) included in her description of pariah femininities—she argues that women were often sanctioned with these labels when they trespass into spaces reserved for valorizing hegemonic masculinity.

However, rather than being defensive in asserting the women are still regarded as feminine, Rebecca and others may instead be indicating that the J-League women remain unsanctioned. The J-Leagues are open to a range of women's engagements with practices of femininity and masculinity. The majority of women playing basketball in the J-Leagues are not aspiring beauty queens, but as Rebecca indicates, one role does not preclude the other. In addition, because Nisei Week Queens are chosen to be representatives of the community, basketball participation helps their candidacy—for their participation they are seen not as unfeminine, but as involved community members.

In the women's league, participants reported a growing acceptance of women who identified as lesbian or bisexual, although there is room for more exploration of this subject. Maggie and Laura, two women who had played at the top level in the women's league, related that some teams, including theirs, had become known for having several lesbian players:

LAURA: Well it was weird, even like growing up, we used to, since we started in adult league out of high school, there was this one team that everyone thought that everyone from there—thought they were gay. And it was like, the kind of thing where everyone just assumed. And now it's funny. It's because nobody else on any other team was open about it . . . and it wasn't until the last few years. We were at this Vegas festival . . . and they were really open about it, making out, walking out of the casino holding hands. Which is great, you know, but it wasn't until more recently that I guess they felt, I don't know.

MAGGIE: Now everyone—seems like everyone is open about, and everybody's gay. Haha.

In earlier years, some women's teams were subject to a degree of speculation and gossip, but in the contemporary era of the J-Leagues, more women felt comfortable being out about their sexuality, and the J-League participants seemed to be more accepting. Later, when asked "who best fit in" in the J-Leagues, one of these players, Laura, said, "I think anybody does. I mean there's so many, there's a variety of different people who play and I never feel like, you know, well somebody at our age right now, just somebody who knows how to play basketball. That's all. I mean there's not a personality thing, it's not what they're into, or what their sexual orientation is, or anything. It's just anybody. Like you know how to play." Laura illustrates the gender-inclusivity of the J-Leagues: it's not perfect, but in many ways open to a wide range of participants.

CONCLUSION

Many interactions in the mainstream sporting world are structured by masculinized institutions and are reproductive of gender inequalities (Messner 2002). Although certainly not yet gender egalitarian, the contemporary J-Leagues provide illustrations of some of the interactions and discourses made possible by men and women playing together in the same community network on relatively equal footing. The interactions tended to be respectful of girls' and women's play and coaching abilities, and discourses often reaffirmed their equal standing within the J-Leagues. This led to some flexibility and variety in how the athletes engaged with femininities, masculinities, and sexualities on and off the court.

As Musto (2014) has argued, when male and female athletes compete in contexts where their abilities are perceived as similar, it can lead to interactions where gender is less salient and understandings of gender are nonhierarchical. Because so many of the young women in the J-Leagues advance their skills on high school and club teams, not to mention the considerable number who go on to college-level play, these women step into contexts such as coed play with a lot of skills and confidence. The J-League men are aware of the women's competence and tend to treat them as equals. In some leagues, this occurs in a competitive, more serious atmosphere. In others, perhaps to diffuse any gender tension or to demonstrate men's willingness to step into feminized territory, feminine symbols become part of the playful interactions between men and women during coed competitions.

The J-Leagues are part of a very specific community made up of members from a shared racial/ethnic group. Therefore, the contexts produced by the J-Leagues within the Japanese American community are far from generalizable, nor are they easily reproduced in other situations. Still, examining the patterns that have emerged in this group's community of practice surrounding basketball reveals several important issues for further reflection.

First, the J-Leagues show it is possible for a group, community, or institution to view girls' and women's participation in sport as important and valued. Japanese Americans seem to appreciate this active participation as instrumental to the group's goals such as cohesion and the maintenance of group ties. It is probable that the more central the sport enterprise is to the community, the more important it may become to facilitate gender-inclusivity.

Second, the interactions in the J-Leagues suggest that when sport opportunities are expansive and flexible enough to accommodate a wide range of participants, this may facilitate more openness toward a wider range of individuals. The upshot is that many types of men and women are able to play and experience an identity as a basketball player. In the J-Leagues, gender-inclusivity appears to extend to an array of gendered practices and, to a certain extent, sexual identities, such as lesbian-identified players.

Third, the goals of community building, particularly for a group facing past or present discrimination and controlling images, appear to be strong enough to disrupt some of the dominant gender patterns in sport. Despite Asian Americans facing racialization in US culture as feminine, weak, and small, the J-Leagues cannot be viewed as simply a project to shore up masculine identity among its male participants. It may be most notable that the many male community leaders who run the J-Leagues do so in a way that is inclusive of not only girls and women, but also men of different ages and abilities. Organizers do not appear to be creating basketball experiences for the sake of giving male participants access to hegemonic masculinity. Instead, they eschew aspects of hypermasculinity by strictly monitoring behavior in the J-Leagues.

An expansive, basketball-centered "community of practice" has provided a fertile ground for a gender-inclusive sport environment. Not only do the J-Leagues provide ample opportunities for both sexes, they also provide a spectrum of opportunities that appeal to a wide variety of women and men who are free to engage in a range of gender performances and roles in relation to basketball. In particular, the greater diversity of options open to the JA women in these leagues allows for girls and women to be active participants, thus increasing their involvement and devotion to the leagues. Gender-inclusivity seems to be a key component of the growing prosperity of the leagues, especially at the youth level, and by extension to the continuing construction of an ethnic community.

The impact of the patterns seen in the J-Leagues is that most Japanese Americans view other Japanese Americans as potential (even assumed) basketball players, no matter their sex, height, or disposition. Particularly among younger generations, J-League participants view themselves on equal footing and acknowledge the basketball knowledge and skills of both men and women. The resulting attitudes toward women as basketball players and coaches are to some extent egalitarian.

3 · "WOMEN WHO TOOK SPORTS BEYOND PLAY"

How Japanese American Women's Basketball Went to College

The Japanese American National Museum, located in the Little Tokyo neighborhood of Los Angeles, holds a fund-raiser each year that includes a Gala Dinner. In 2014, the theme of that dinner was Evolving Pastimes: Connecting Communities and Generations through Sport. Among the honored speakers that night were three basketball phenomenons: Wat Misaka, Natalie Nakase, and Jamie Hagiya (see image 3.1). Misaka is a historical figure, a Japanese American who played at the University of Utah and then went on to be the first person to break the color barrier in the National Basketball Association when he played for the Knicks briefly in 1947. Sharing the stage with Misaka were two women who are probably the most well-known Japanese American basketball players in recent history. The program read, "The 2014 Gala Dinner theme *Evolving Pastimes: Connecting Communities & Generations through Sports* will be an evening of enlightening stories of history making men and women who took sports beyond play to inspire, unite, elevate, and shape who we are as Japanese Americans." Placing an NBA player of historical significance on a stage beside two young women who

IMAGE 3.1. Jamie Hagiya speaks at the Japanese American National Museum Annual Gala, 2014. Natalie Nakase and Wat Misaka stand beside her on the stage. (Credit: Mario G. Reyes, *Rafu Shimpo*.)

are contemporary community icons demonstrates the significance of these women for the Japanese American community. It is also emblematic of a shift from a time when male Japanese American basketball players tended to be the focus of the community to today when it often seems like all eyes are on the women.

In this chapter I address how Japanese Americans women have become community icons for many Japanese Americans, principally examining the sociohistorical and structural factors that have enabled their success. Today, Japanese Americans can point to several women who have "made it big" in basketball. Success is difficult to define, but the two most well-known and beloved icons of the 2000s have been Jamie Hagiya and Natalie Nakase. There is a reason that they stand beside Wat Misaka as honorees at the JANM Gala Dinner.

The story of these women's success begins with the generations of Japanese Americans who have laid a foundation for girls' and women's basketball within the community in response to widespread exclusion and racism in mainstream contexts. It continues with the women of the 1960s to 1980s who began to make progress in mainstream high school and collegiate basketball as players and coaches, capitalizing on increasing opportunities for women. Their story evolves today as a one of the power of community networks and investment in women's basketball.

Inspired by the early forerunners, in the 1960s and 1970s the J-Leagues began building even more structure for girls to receive early training, support, and extended playing opportunities in basketball. About this same time, a burgeoning women's movement and the transformational legislation that came with it, Title IX, acted as a match that lit ablaze Japanese American girls' and women's basketball. Although Japanese Americans were ahead of the curve in offering basketball for girls, the new opportunities in secondary schools and institutions of higher education added mainstream societal acceptance for women in sport. Japanese American women were now receiving accolades and opportunities for what previously had been a community-based activity.

When the community devotion to basketball intersected with growing opportunities for women's sport in the mainstream, the community responded by investing in girls' and women's sport. Contemporary mainstream women's basketball provided channels for success that have proved to be more constricted in men's basketball, so in many ways attention shifted toward the women's game. Successful female players became role models and inspired new generations of players.

Recognition of these local sports icons appears to have reinforced the popularity and investment in J-League basketball, and increased interest in developing college-level talent. The star players, along with other J-League affiliates, built networks in club, high school, and college sports and offered opportunities to the next generation of J-League players. According to the sports editor at *Rafu Shimpo*, there have never been more Japanese American high school and college players—so many, they are having trouble covering them all in the newspaper (Culross 2014). Successful girls and women have captured the support and admiration of community members of all ages and both genders, contributing to an overall respect for women's basketball and shared belief in the value of investing in young women's playing careers.

EARLY FOUNDATIONS

The early inclusion of women in Japanese American basketball is important to understanding women's contemporary status as sports icons. The Japanese Americans who settled along the West Coast, and their descendants, have made a remarkable commitment to providing sporting opportunities for *all* members of the community, regardless of sex. This commitment has been in many ways unique to this community, as they have often offered more opportunities for girls and women than in mainstream or other ethnic league contexts. However, the community has also been responsive to social forces in the larger society, adapting to the changing opportunity structures and cultural trends present in the United States and on the West Coast over the past century.

Foundations of Women's Basketball in Meiji Japan

Japanese American openness to women's participation in athletics may have roots in nineteenth-century Japanese culture. Japanese immigration to the United States began in the late nineteenth century, known as the Meiji period in Japan. Before this time, women's access to sport in Japan was limited, although women may have been recognized practitioners in certain types of martial arts, particularly judo. The Meiji era marked a period when Japan sought to "modernize" in the image of the Western world. Japanese educators traveled abroad and brought back knowledge of sports and physical education, including notions about the appropriate inclusion of girls and women (Kietlinski 2008). The opportunities for women to participate in Japanese athletics continued to be rare and limited to higher socioeconomic classes. Still, one American writer observed sufficient evidence of it to write a book on the topic, proclaiming that the Japanese participated in "the kind of athletic work that has resulted, undoubtedly, in making the little Japanese women the strongest and most cheerful members of their sex to be found anywhere on earth" (Hancock 1904, as cited in Kietlinski 2008).

One Japanese woman had a noteworthy exchange with the mother of women's basketball, Senda Berenson. Inokuchi Akuri traveled from Japan in 1899 to study with Berenson at Smith College. Berenson was a physical education professor who first introduced women to the sport of basketball around this same time. Despite this intriguing, perhaps foreshadowing, connection, Inokuchi appears to have focused her studies on gymnastics and physical education in general. When she returned to Japan, she was highly influential, teaching at the Tokyo Women's Normal School and establishing a physical education department there (Kietlinski 2008).

There is no evidence that the issei, or first-generation, immigrants had any knowledge of basketball before arriving in the United States, but Japan's adoption of physical training for girls and women in the late 1800s may have influenced Japanese migrants to the United States in that era to be more open to the idea of athletics for women. Although a common refrain among nisei is that their parents were often "too busy working" to concern themselves much with sports, the experiences the issei had in Japan may have contributed to the openness many appeared to demonstrate toward their sons and daughters engaging in sport in the United States, not to mention their own enthusiasm toward sports and recreation (Regalado 2000). Likewise, there is little to no record of issei women engaging in organized sports, but they did participate in organizations that would later provide a foundation for their sons and daughters to become involved (Regalado 2000).

Women's Basketball in the Pre–World War II Era

As Japanese immigrants became more established in California, they and their children began to embrace sport in an era when organized sport and physical education were gaining in popularity in the United States (Matsumoto 2014). In the late 1910s and early 1920s, YMCAs, YWCAs, and other organizations in California began offering sporting opportunities, many specifically targeting the children of immigrants as part of the "playground movement" (Cahn [1994] 2015; Cavallo 1981; Niiya 2000). This time period was significant for the development of Japanese American sports, particularly in Southern California, because it reflected a growing nisei population, the children of the biggest wave of Japanese immigrants (Waugh 1978).

Japanese American nisei women became caught up in the sport movement, right alongside their nisei brothers. The 1920s and 1930s have been described as a golden age of sports for women in the United States (Hult 1991). Women's basketball was immensely popular in California during this era (Emery and Toohey-Costa 1991). In Southern California, Japanese Americans created a Women's Athletic Association (WAA) and a Women's Athletic Union (WAU) (Matsumoto 2014). The WAU emerged from nisei women playing at the Japanese "Y." The women originally called their league the Southern California Women's Basketball League, which then became the WAU. In its early years, it fielded eighteen teams in two divisions (Costa, Adair, and Jackson 1991). In addition to the YMCA, Japanese American Buddhist temples also responded to the enthusiasm for sports and began forming teams and leagues. Japanese American girls and women seemed to find a particular niche in the leagues provided through the Young Women's Buddhist Association (YWBA). For example, YWBA teams existed in Alameda and Stockton, California. The Stockton team, the Busy Bees, was particularly successful, playing from 1928 to 1940 with purportedly only four losses (Franks 2016).

Beth, a longtime Southern California Women's Athletic Union (SCWAU) board member, described her experiences playing for her Buddhist temple as a teenager in the late 1930s in San Jose:

> It was an activity of the Buddhist temple. We had teams up there. We had a league, so we traveled from city to city and had competition, games . . . it was all among friends. . . . We all went to the same temple. The team was composed of members of the temple. We all went to school together. It was a rather close group. . . . In those early years, the temple was the main social place. We did have a gymnasium, so

it was a place where we all got together. My brother was actively—my brother was a good athlete. I wasn't. I tried, but I was just one of those that tagged along and played. We used to compete with teams around the area . . . they were mostly Buddhist temple teams.

Beth describes the Buddhist temple as the center of community social life. Sports became embedded in this existing institution by building gymnasiums in or near temples and coordinating with friends who belonged to the temple. Beth also described how women's basketball was played in a different format in these times: "Yeah, [laughs] like, a long time ago, the girls used to play three courts, it was divided into three. You had your forward and your center and your guards . . . I remember playing—was I playing three courts? We used to play half-half, forwards on one side, guards on one side. I remember playing that way. I think—was I playing when we had three divided? I might have been. But I know it was that way at one time." Beth's participation through her Buddhist temple appears to be very typical of the time, as was the format of the women's game: split court.[1]

By the 1930s there was a golden age of sport for Japanese Americans in California (Regalado 2000). Chris Komai, nephew to one of the men who played a big role in the men's league in Los Angeles before and after World War II, saw the development of sport for Japanese Americans in this way:

Our issei grandparents thought that they had a problem with their nisei parents, which is hilarious to us sansei, because the nisei are our parents. They called it the "nisei problem." Really, it was a matter of, they were worried that their children were not growing up the right way. Now, the thing was that what the issei really need to have in perspective was that this is America, and your children are going to grow up Americans, not Japanese. They're gonna act like Americans, they're gonna talk like Americans, they're gonna do everything that Americans do, and that may or may not be something that they wanted. But that was the reality. So what they wanted was to be able to control some of their free time. So that's why they organized so many sports leagues. That's probably why they also had something for the girls, as well, because they wanted activities in which their Japanese kids would: one, be playing in organized sports so they wouldn't be doing something bad, but two, they would be interacting with other Japanese, which is still true in our sports leagues.

Komai thought, in line with an essay he later referenced by Niiya (2000), that the issei were motivated to embrace the concept of sport clubs due to concerns about negative mainstream cultural influences, as well as a desire for community cohesiveness. This led some issei to build, and others to encourage, sport teams and leagues for their children. As he notes, having boys and girls participating together helped achieve the goal of cultural continuity and co-ethnic affiliation.

World War II

The incarceration of approximately 120,000 West Coast Japanese Americans during World War II was devastating for the Japanese Americans communities of California. It also disrupted the growth of the popular sport leagues along the coast. However, in an effort to maintain a sense of normalcy, many Japanese Americans continued to play sports within the detention centers and concentration camps.

Sports became an important part of life at the camps. Japanese American teams played among themselves within the camps—the camps were separated into "blocks" and teams formed within each block—and also against local high schools and Native American teams (Franks 2016). Camps favored different sports depending on the residents and the facilities (Niiya 2000). At the temporary detention center in Merced, California, in 1942 there were leagues for boys' baseball, girls' volleyball, girls' softball, men's and women's basketball, and sumo (Franks 2010). At Manzanar, photographers including Ansel Adams and Francis Stewart captured Japanese Americans playing basketball (see image 3.2), as well as football, baseball, and volleyball.

On the whole, basketball appeared to match baseball/softball in popularity among the youth. At the Topaz Relocation Center in

IMAGE 3.2. Young women playing basketball at the Manzanar Relocation Center during World War II. (Credit: Francis Stewart.)

1943, the newspaper reported that a block council had requested twelve baseball fields and a basketball gymnasium to be built at the site (Regalado 2000). Although softball was probably the most popular sport for women, "had there been better facilities to accommodate indoor sport, female basketball clubs, based on its prewar popularity, would have rivaled softball for attention" (Regalado 2000, 439).

The men of the camp tended to be the organizers of the sport leagues, but readily included girls and women. Relocation camp newsletters and newspapers covered the women's progress. Women played basketball at Heart Mountain, a common destination for Japanese Americans in Northern California, and were covered by the camp newspaper, the *Sentinel* (Franks 2016). At the assembly center in Stockton, the center's newspaper, *El Joaquin*, regularly covered the popular women's team, the Busy Bees (Regalado 2000). Journalists were also impressed by women's basketball at the Rohwer Camp (Franks 2016). The Manzanar newspaper, the *Free Press*, encouraged male readers to attend women's softball games to check out potential mates. Occasionally, older men's teams played against top women's teams (Regalado 2000).

Post–World War II to 1965

After the war, Japanese American communities began to rebuild on the West Coast and gradually brought basketball back to its earlier glory and beyond. Niiya (2000) points to the growing urbanization of Japanese Americans in the postwar era as a key reason why basketball thrived in the major cities where Japanese Americans resettled after the camps.

Girls' and women's basketball remained a popular community activity for many Japanese Americans, even as interest tapered off in the mainstream. From 1947 to 1967, girls' basketball was a quite popular social activity for Japanese Americans in San Francisco (Kawahara 2000). The Japantown Buchanan Street YWCA sponsored the Arbees—they held practices in the YWCA gym, but played their games at the San Francisco Buddhist Church gym, Hamilton Center, and Booker T. Washington Community Center. In 1948, the Arbees became part of a nine-team league, "probably the first [postwar] non-church/non–Japanese Association basketball league for Nisei girls" (Kawahara 2000, 176–77). In 1948, some nisei women organized an unofficial, intercollegiate basketball game: Fresno State versus East Los Angeles Junior College (Franks 2016). A newly formed Young Buddhist Association in Stockton revived the Busy Bees (Franks 2010).

In Southern California in 1946, Akira "Aki" Komai reestablished one of the principal Los Angeles Japanese American newspapers, *Rafu Shimpo*. Soon after, looking for some positive news to print, he and friends would also revive the Los Angeles area men's basketball league. When the league returned in 1946, they renamed it the Nisei Athletic Union (NAU) (Komai 2000; interview with NAU board).

For girls and women of Southern California, the churches were again a primary source of competition. Ed Takahashi, one of the men responsible for expanding teams and leagues for girls and women in Los Angeles in the late 1960s, spoke about the earlier postwar period of Japanese American women's basketball: "Before the girls' sports program or SCWAU got formed, there was a program called Buddhist Churches of America. BCA was in various temples that belonged to a certain religious sect that had basketball tournaments. So, they would have these basketball tournaments in Northern California, Southern California, and Central California . . . I think in the late '50s, until SCWAU got started in the late '60s, there was a gap in terms of playing independent of any Christian or Buddhist league, but there was always the Buddhist Churches of America program." At least in Takahashi's recollection, there was not a lot of play available outside of the Buddhist church leagues. However, interest would begin to swell again in the 1960s and 1970s, leading to a new epoch in Japanese American women's basketball.

1965–1975: The Birth of a New Era for Women's Basketball

Japanese American girls' and women's opportunities to participate in basketball expanded dramatically in Southern California starting in 1968 when the girls' league, the Junior Athletic Union (JAU), was expanded and a larger, women's league was established. The SCWAU fielded around seventy teams (Komai 2000). Takahashi took over the JAU girls league that at the time went up only to age fifteen and determined that there was more interest for teams in higher age brackets: "So I reset the age bracket in the girls' sports program to midgets, fourth, fifth, and sixth grade, juniors, seventh, eighth, and ninth, seniors, tenth, eleventh, and twelfth. So, they can play until they're seniors regardless of what age they are. And then they could move into the SCWAU program or they can actually play simultaneously, but I recommended they did not. When I had the program, we had I think six teams in the junior and six teams in the senior in '69. At the time that I left the program, we had I think sixty teams." In addition to his efforts to expand the girls' and women's leagues, Takahashi also decided to do away with separate women's rules: "What I did was, I changed the rules. Instead of the setup where you had three girls on defense and three girls on offense and they could never cross the line—you had two dribbles and you had to pass—I changed it to boys' rules, with the thirty-second clock, if you asked for it. And once you ask for it, it's on for the rest of the game." Around this same time, in 1969, one of the more powerful mainstream rule-making bodies called the five-player, full-court rules for women's basketball "experimental," delaying the widespread adaptation of this official rule until 1971 (Hult 1991). Takahashi was instrumental in changing Japanese American women's basketball in the Southern California region as he greatly expanded opportunities and adjusted the rules, even a couple years ahead of most mainstream basketball.

Today, Southern California is home to many Japanese American sport organizations that grew out of this postwar era and incorporated women during the 1960s. The two biggest organizations are Friends of Richard (FOR) and Tigers Youth Club. FOR most likely held the first official tournament in Southern California in 1960, said to have been a replacement for a prior tournament in Salt Lake City (Franks 2000). Another prominent athletic organization in the Los Angeles area is the Tigers Youth Club. A group of nisei athletes who had played in the pre–World War II era as the Has Beens started this youth sports club in 1953. It began with just one boy's baseball team, but quickly grew to sponsor several baseball and basketball teams. In 1962, the club added a girl's program. Later, the Tigers grew to incorporate men's and women's teams, as well. The Tigers started their own basketball tournament in 1976, and today it is one of the more popular tournaments, accommodating over five hundred teams (Tigers Youth Club n.d.).

Mainstream Opportunities: Women's Basketball Post–Title IX

As the second wave feminist movement began to develop in the late 1960s, alongside a reinvigorated US interest in sport and fitness, in part inspired by the Cold War (Montez de Oca 2013), interest and opportunities in women's basketball began to grow. The mainstream had taken a rather long midcentury hiatus in its enthusiasm for women's sports, and women's basketball had never really been

institutionalized in high schools and colleges prior to this time outside of niche arenas such as women's colleges and in high schools
in regions such as Iowa (Cahn [1994] 2015; Cain 2000). Iowa has
had a unique long-standing enthusiasm for girls' high school basketball (Beran 1991, 2008). Japanese American women, as well as
some women from other marginalized racial/ethnic communities (Abney 1999; Liberti 1999), also kept the game alive. During
this early rebirth of women's basketball, several Japanese American women, with extensive experience basketball experience, were
uniquely positioned to excel on mainstream teams.

Excelling is perhaps an understatement. These women could
not find mainstream opportunities that matched their level of skill
and ability. Japanese American women who were in high school
and college during the late 1960s and early 1970s shared experiences of disappointment at the level of play and coaching available
on high school and college teams. Colleen Matsuhara shared her
experiences as an adolescent in the J-Leagues as compared to her
experiences playing in high school during the late 1960s in Northern California:

> [In the Japanese American community] it was just the thing to
> do. There wasn't any stigma attached to it, because it was boys and
> girls. . . . Whenever we had tournaments, it was always boys' and
> girls' teams, not just an all-girls' tournament and all-boys.' The
> [boys'] team in Sacramento that we traveled with, we'd go watch
> their games and they'd root for our games. It was a very close-knit
> group. In the outside, meaning high school . . . I started playing on
> my high school teams, but the level of play I thought was really not
> very good. In fact, I stopped going out for my high school team when
> one day the high school coach asked me, did I want to help coach the
> team? I thought to myself, what's wrong with this picture? If I have
> to help him.

Matsuhara's experience in the J-Leagues reflected a level of support
and respect for girls' basketball that was not mirrored in her high
school team, whose assigned coach was in her view unqualified.

She eventually left high school basketball, but she did end up playing for Sacramento State University, though there were no scholarships available for women at the time. Matsuhara eventually became a college basketball coach herself and continues to coach women's basketball to this day.

Another prominent player and coach, Marcia Murota, also did not bother playing for her high school team during the early 1970s, but in college she decided to try out for the team at California State University, Los Angeles (CSULA), where she had firsthand experience with the early college opportunities and scholarships offered in response to the Title IX legislation. She described her playing experience (1976–1980):

> Well, at that time . . . basketball for women wasn't a big deal yet, so a friend of mine was playing on the team here and when I came to the campus she was just like, "You should come out for the team." . . . So, the first year I was here I came out for a practice and they weren't very good and they were doing basic things at practice, so I said, "Ehhh, I'm not going to play this year." Then the following year my teammate . . . came out of high school, so I convinced her to play. I said, "Come here and we'll play." And our other friend here was on the team so . . . that's how it got started . . . then it was cool because . . . we ended up being on a scholarship so it was like . . . you're going to pay me to play basketball? Okay! That's cool!

Though initially discouraged by the basic level of play at the college level, Murota and her friends gathered together some J-League players to help build the team. With a roster of six Asian Americans and six African Americans, Murota and her teammates enjoyed many successes. They went to the playoffs during her last two years of play, with Murota playing starting point guard. Suzie Iwami played alongside Murota for CSULA from 1977 to 1980, setting the school record for most career points, broken only by another Japanese American player from Hawaii, Monica Tokoro, in 2004. Iwami was named to the school's Hall of Fame in 1986. Murota and Iwami received some of the first athletic scholarships offered to women athletes. Murota went on to become the head coach of women's basketball at CSULA from 2001 to 2007.

JAPANESE AMERICAN NETWORKS

Since the early forerunners—Matsuhara, Murota, Iwami, and others—Japanese American women have continued to join college and university teams, solidifying a pattern of achievement in women's basketball. In the 2000s, several J-League women made it onto Pac-10, Division I teams: some examples include Natalie Nakase and Allison Taka at UCLA, Jamie Hagiya and Daniela Roark at USC, Corrie Mizusawa at the University of Oregon, and Kristen Iwakawa at UC Berkeley. However, most Japanese American players find spots at smaller California colleges and universities. At certain schools, there is almost a legacy of Japanese American participation.

While interviewing several of the college athletes of the past few decades, I began to see a common practice of J-League-affiliated women helping each other—whether by offering advice and training, putting in a good word with established contacts, or purposefully recruiting fellow J-League women for basketball opportunities. It became evident that many Japanese American women benefited from a form of women's basketball social capital available in part through J-League affiliation.

This social capital was built on the shoulders of the initial waves of successful Japanese American women. The J-Leagues helped develop a critical mass of talented basketball players, many of whom have continued playing, coaching, and mentoring in women's basketball, producing a powerful social network. There are now established pathways and social connections that pave the way for the most driven and talented players to pursue basketball outside of the community. With the help of this network, more and more young women are able to go on to college-level play and beyond.

Investment in mainstream women's basketball social capital can be considered an extension of the existing ties fostered within J-League-affiliated community institutions. As discussed, the J-Leagues are already a fertile ground for social and cultural capital. Through community institutions such as the J-Leagues, Japanese Americans are able to create social capital through "weak ties," which can be described as loose bonds that may be based on shared membership in groups rather than by close relationships (Fugita and O'Brien 1991; Granovetter 1973, 1982). Chin (2016) found that relationships formed within a suburban veteran's organization linked to the J-Leagues led to a "co-ethnic social network" providing support and resources. She theorized that this created an opportunity to "share cultural capital" that sometimes extended outside of the sport context (1083). Other scholars have connected sport with cultural and social capital, originating in the work of Pierre Bourdieu (1978, 1984).

What does mainstream women's basketball social capital entail? Broadly, it is a women's basketball network primarily centered in California. The network includes former college players who act as mentors who pass along skills, knowledge, and insider information: these are women who coach J-League and AAU/club teams, as well as offer camps, clinics, and training sessions all aimed at J-League youth (and often girls in particular). These links not only are a foundation for training and preparation for higher levels of basketball, but also provide valuable information and opportunities that may help young women succeed in women's basketball.

Perhaps more importantly, the network also includes Japanese Americans who have gained positions of influence in mainstream institutions. In California, there are a number of high school, college, university, and even professional women's basketball coaches and administrators who emerged from the J-Leagues. Many of these individuals give back in small and large ways to J-League participants.

Although some J-League-affiliated women have held positions of influence in women's basketball, this influence has been hard-won and exists only in limited contexts. Many of these women still feel as if they are swimming upstream. They often face push-back or feel overlooked, and much of it seems to be attributable to perceptions of them as Asian American women. Therefore, my interpretation of their efforts to help other J-League women is not that they are creating an unfair or undeserved advantage. Instead, their efforts are compensatory—they hope to give players a chance to be seen, provide an opportunity when most doors have remained closed.

On the Shoulders of Those Who Came Before: Networks of Opportunity

The story of Japanese American social capital in women's basketball is a story of women helping women. As mentioned, a few Japanese American women stood particularly poised to capitalize on the growing mainstream opportunities in women's basketball during the 1960s and 1970s. Several of these early achievements, for example those of Colleen Matsuhara and Marcia Murota, paid dividends for the community in the form of social capital. Both women went into coaching as a profession and leveraged their positions in ways that helped other Japanese American women succeed. Some of their protégés have continued these practices, following in their mentors' footsteps.

Marcia Murota's mentorship of Carol Jue helps illustrate how one of these chains of mentorship began. Remember that Murota was one of the first scholarship recipients at Cal State LA in the early 1970s and later became a coach for the team. When Jue began her collegiate basketball playing career there, Murota was the assistant coach. Although Jue transferred and finished her degree and playing career at Claremont McKenna, she stayed in touch with Murota because they played together for the Imperials. Murota became the head coach at Cal State LA and Jue became her assistant coach for six years. After an interim coaching job at Claremont McKenna, Jue went on to become the head coach at Chapman College, where she remains today.

Jue regularly has J-League players on her roster at Chapman, an NCAA Division III program. I asked if she recruited directly from the J-Leagues. Her answer, "A lot of it is word of mouth." As she still plays on a J-League team in both the SCWAU league and at several tournaments, she keeps abreast of who has talent and who might be interested. This is how she came to have community favorite Lauren Kamiyama on her team. Right before Kamiyama's senior year, Jue shared with me, "I knew about Lauren, but I thought Lauren had wanted to go higher, because a lot of times the really good kids go to higher schools. If I got her, I thought that was a plus. . . . But here she is with me—she's going to be in her senior year this coming year. It's been a blessing. You know? She's just absolutely— somebody like me except she's a lot better. We have the same passion and the same kind of values when it comes to basketball. I feel lucky that I get to coach her." Jue knew about Kamiyama from her connections with the J-Leagues and was able to recruit her even though she felt Kamiyama was likely good enough for higher-level, scholarship basketball.

The mentorship of Kamiyama represents another link in the chain. Lauren Kamiyama now coaches varsity girls' high school basketball for North High School in Torrance, California. This area is home to a relatively large Japanese American population, and her high school varsity roster contains a number of Japanese American surnames. Several of her players are likely affiliated with the J-Leagues.

Colleen Matsuhara is another early pioneer who has often helped other Japanese Americans. She has coached in many collegiate and professional basketball contexts, including her position as head coach at UC Irvine from 1991 to 1997. When I asked her if J-Leagues connections had ever come in handy in her coaching career, she said, "At Irvine it probable was, because I knew the guy that does [a J-League] organization. He would call me up and say, 'There's a good kid' here or there."

Matsuhara would later link up with Jamie Hagiya and Natalie Nakase. Hagiya and Nakase both developed their love for basketball in the J-Leagues, but did not capitalize directly on a J-League connection to help them secure a spot on their USC and UCLA college teams, respectively. Prior role models mattered—Hagiya mentioned that both LeeAnne Sera, former USC player, and

IMAGE 3.3. Coach Carol Jue gives player Lauren Kamiyama encouragement during a Chapman College basketball game. (Credit: Kevin Jue.)

Nakase, who played a few years before her at UCLA, had provided inspiration and proof that big time college play was possible. Nevertheless, both Nakase and Hagiya made their collegiate rosters in part through development in AAU/Club teams and also by good fortune. They were both chosen for scholarship positions late in the recruitment period, last minute additions to the roster.

It was after their college careers when Matsuhara attempted to capitalize on her own networks in women's basketball to help Hagiya and Nakase. In her later career, Matsuhara settled in as head coach at West LA College. She took Nakase under her wing as an assistant coach, and they also ran clinics for Japanese American youth together, sometimes including Jamie Hagiya.

Hagiya eventually started her own name-brand basketball camps and she also continued to privately train up and coming athletes. In a conversation that took place not long after she returned from playing professionally in Greece, she said that often community members wouldn't believe her that she would come to team practices or work with players one-on-one, but that is what she really enjoyed:

Just because I've been around [basketball] so long, I feel like I know the game. And I want to help out other girls or guys who are trying to get there. And it's really neat because I've been like training a couple girls. Like I'm going to [a local high school] tonight to help out. And, ah, I work with a team for an hour and then with girls individually for the next hour. And it's really neat because you can tell that they just love the game, you know? And they're like so passionate already and just listen so well. They want to learn, you know what I mean? So, like helping correct just even like simple things like dribbling moves and stuff like that or shooting and stuff like that. So, yeah, it's really fun and really rewarding for me.

Many of the former college- and professional-level players are able to use their skills and community connections to make a little money working with young athletes. At the camps, clinics, and training sessions, the star players pass along skills and fundamentals to the young athletes, but also act as role models and guides for the larger world of mainstream women's basketball.

Reaching for the Dream

When Hagiya and Nakase each independently decided to fight for their dream of playing in the WNBA, Japanese American networks attempted to intervene on their behalf. This was a big test of the reach of Japanese American social capital within women's basketball.

Natalie Nakase in this case was poised to benefit from her connections to Matsuhara, as Matsuhara had built her own professional network in mainstream women's sports. Not only was Matsuhara a college coach at several different institutions, but she also held the position of assistant coach on the Los Angeles WNBA team, the Sparks, from 1998 to 1999. Over time, she had met a lot of people and established a fair amount of connections. Matsuhara shared this story of when she had put in a good word for Nakase:

When I went to the [Women's NCAA Division I] Final Four, I ran into the new assistant coach for the Seattle Storm, the WNBA. I said, "What are you looking for?" She said, "I needed a backup point guard for Sue [Bird]." "Look, I know you guys probably are flooded with people that think they could come there, but my assistant coach, Natalie, when you see her you're gonna think that I have led you astray, but I'm just gonna tell you about her. She plays on Pro Am [semipro], too. She's five foot two, but she is just a little hellion out there. She's over in Germany right now." It turns out the new head coach had already lined up some people. But I was saying, "She'll fly there on her own just to get looked at." She actually went to the Phoenix Mercury last year and was invited to training camp.

Matsuhara tried to use her own networks to speak up on Nakase's behalf and help her get seen by decision makers. She wanted to make Nakase's WNBA dream come true. Nakase was also proactive on her own and ended up trying out for Connecticut, Los Angeles, and Phoenix before giving up on her WNBA prospects and concentrating on coaching. She did play in the National Women's Basketball League (NWBL), a semiprofessional league for two years before it folded in 2008, and then abroad in Germany for one year.

Hagiya had a comparable story about two community members who tried to help her join a WNBA team. Hagiya also played professionally in Europe (Greece) after completing her college career at USC. However, she also had dreams of playing for the WNBA. After years of tryouts and false starts, Hagiya and two prominent community members embarked on a campaign to advertise Hagiya's talents to the Los Angeles Sparks. Hagiya gathered a collection of letters attesting to her popularity in the greater Los Angeles area among Japanese Americans. She asked me to write a letter describing what I had learned in my research, which I gladly did. There was eventually a meeting with the Sparks business office that resulted in an "Asian American Night" with a clinic before the game run by Hagiya. Hagiya thought that they sold a thousand tickets to the game that night through J-League connections, but no offers for playing opportunities followed.

The stories of both Hagiya and Nakase illustrate the loyalty and advocacy enacted by several Japanese Americans in support of the two women's sport careers. There is a real sense that the community is rooting for them and advocating for them in any way possible. In these cases, the networks did not end up leading to WNBA playing opportunities, but did result in more exposure and encouragement for both women. It is somewhat exceptional, particularly in the case of Matsuhara and Nakase, that these networks exist at all.

"Club" and AAU Basketball, J-League Networks, and the Development of Female Talent

Club or Amateur Athletic Union (AAU) traveling teams provide a key channel through which high school players achieve visibility and vie for college scholarships. This is especially true in women's basketball, where college recruiting budgets are typically lower than those for men's teams. University teams can send scouts out to the national AAU championship in lieu of scouring the entire country looking for recruits. Club teams are often like all-star teams; players are exposed to high-level competition, building toward a future in college sports.

Today's J-Leagues have links to club teams—some teams' rosters are primarily made up of J-League players; others are coached by J-Leagues participants who often recruit at least a couple players from the J-Leagues. These are mainstream teams with no official ethnicity rules. They compete regionally and nationally against other teams who have no J-League affiliation.

Club teams are often expensive, due to not only league and tournament fees, but also the travel expenses associated with competing at the regional or national level. There are scholarships available, but one critique of the growing reliance of women's basketball on club tournaments is that it has made women's basketball, as well as other women's sports, more elite. For the most part, unless you are a standout star, these teams are accessible only to those with the financial means.

Though AAU club teams were not always a part of the J-League network, these networks do exist and seem to be growing. This represents another area of Japanese American social capital within the field of girls' and women's basketball. Now that several

Japanese American women have gotten college athletic scholarships in women's basketball, more and more Japanese American families are willing to invest in this prospect, often using J-League connections to club teams as well as the personal training, clinics, and camps offered by several of the former college-level players.

Having club team experience seemed to have played a role in the success of both Nakase and Hagiya. Both grew up in Orange County and played with club teams. Hagiya's first club coach was Japanese American, but as she got older and more successful, she moved on to other teams without connections to the J-Leagues. Nakase mainly played with unaffiliated teams, but later coached two teams with many J-League players. Nakase talked about coaching club: "I started my own club program, so it's like high school girls who want to play on the off season and they want to pursue college and continue their career. I started out with a club program here, but then I just wanted to do my own, just wanted to do it in my own way." I asked her if there was a Japanese American connection to her club team. She explained, "My following is mainly Japanese girls. When I announce, if I have trials or whatever, I do get a lot of Japanese Americans. I've noticed that. So people, the girls around here, the ones that want to go on to college, I do have a couple Japanese, five or six of them. Last year it was more, but then this year it's a lot less because they either graduated or they switched programs. But yeah, I noticed I do have Japanese—actually, I just coached last year a seventh and eighth grade club program in Orange County, because that's where I grew up, and my whole team is Japanese American." As a Japanese American, J-League-affiliated coach—and a well-known one at that—Nakase mainly had Japanese Americans try out for her club team. The J-League networks influenced but did not fully dictate the rosters of her teams, as her high school club team was only about half Japanese American.

Nakase helped to pass the torch to at least one other Japanese American, in part through her role as a club coach. After admiring Nakase as a player, Allison Taka began playing on Nakase's teams, including her club traveling team. When it came time to make a decision about college-level play, Nakase mentored Taka in her decision. Taka shared, "Yeah, I was looked at by [two California State University coaches]. I wanted to stay close to home, so I turned down anything that was out of Southern California. . . . I really, really liked the coach [at a California State University], and Natalie just kept telling me, 'Don't sign yet, wait, wait.' . . . She goes, 'Just wait, you never know what's gonna happen.' I was like, 'OK.'" Nakase not only was a mentor and coach, but also was able to use her networks in college women's basketball to help Taka. Later on that year, Nakase was able to get the UCLA coach to take a look at Taka. Taka shared, "We went to a tournament in North Carolina in March, and the UCLA coach came to see me because they had a point guard transfer that spring. . . . So, she [Natalie] called her and told her to come. She [the UCLA coach] saw me play and then they offered me a scholarship." Nakase had played under this same coach and was able to contact her and let her know about Taka.

Taka was not a starter at UCLA during her playing years there, 2006 to 2010, so did not get quite as much attention as Nakase or Hagiya. However, she did have a solid career as a scholarship player. Japanese Americans came out to support her, and she became a role model herself. She had a few public appearances at San-Tai-San and at a Japanese American church that sponsored youth basketball.

Nakase's mentorship of Taka is an excellent example of how Japanese Americans in California create college-level women's basketball players through the institutions and networks made possible by the J-Leagues. Taka started playing at a young age in the J-Leagues—her dad was involved in the J-Leagues and was well connected to the Japanese American community in Venice, California. He knew where to find opportunities. When she got older, she took advantage of the higher level training and competition in J-League-affiliated club teams and worked with former college player, Nakase. Taka then took Nakase's advice and benefited from Nakase's connections to land a scholarship playing opportunity at a basketball powerhouse: UCLA.

Taka was also able to pay Nakase back in a small way. Nakase became a professional basketball coach, at first in Germany coaching women and then in Japan coaching a men's team. In Japan, she made some NBA connections and began to solidify what had always been a dream of hers—to coach in the NBA. She returned to Los Angeles to try to make it happen. When Nakase's own connections did not pan out immediately, she did not know how to proceed. Then, one day, Taka invited her to a youth clinic offered by the Clippers. At the camp, the two women were able to demonstrate their talent and knowledge of basketball in front of some of the Clipper staff. Nakase translated that encounter into an invitation to a practice, where she took meticulous notes. Soon, Nakase had an internship as a video coordinator. The internship developed into a paying gig, and now Nakase does video analysis and trains players. She remarked, however, that she may not have caught the coaching staff's attention if Taka had not invited her to be part of the youth clinic. Also of interest, it was Darin Maki, a J-League participant who played in college and then professionally in Japan, who helped Nakase find a job coaching a men's professional team in Japan. In the world of basketball, you never know when a J-league connection will be helpful!

Whose Capital?

Is this women's basketball network an example of social capital as Bourdieu imagined it or more of a niche network, an example of community cultural wealth (Murjani 2014; Yosso 2005)? Bourdieu defined social capital as "the sum of the resources, actual or virtual, that accrue to an individual or a group by virtue of possessing a durable network of more or less institutionalized relationships of mutual acquaintance and recognition" (Bourdieu and Wacquant 1992, 119). At face value, this is what Japanese Americans have developed, albeit in niche areas. They are able to mobilize their access to mainstream networks within women's basketball to create opportunities for many of the best J-League players.

Simultaneously, some J-League-affiliated networks are fairly closed networks and less reliant on mainstream connections and channels. Most of the basketball social capital is developed in the J-Leagues and mainly by co-ethnics. Although this capital has been useful in navigating mainstream institutions, it is primarily leveraged among group members only in marginalized contexts (women's basketball versus men's). It may be more accurately conceived as an adaptive resource for the community, as "cultural wealth" (Yosso 2005). The value of the network and even the related achievements are not necessarily recognized in the mainstream to the extent that they are among Japanese Americans.

Women's basketball social capital could be compared in some ways to how other communities of color have used community-based social capital to help them navigate institutions. Yosso (2005, 79–80) explained, "Historically, People of Color have utilized their social capital to attain education, legal justice, employment and health care. In turn, these Communities of Color gave the information and resources they gained through these institutions back to their social networks." Many top-level players shared stories about being overlooked by coaches and other decision makers due their race or size (see chapter 5). The J-League-affiliated networks in women's basketball facilitate opportunities for J-League participants that may lead to college and even professional playing opportunities—which might not be easily available without the extra help. J-League participants mobilize both mainstream and community-based networks to find playing opportunities, some of which pay off, for example, in college scholarships or admittances. This needs to be contextualized, however, by a sporting environment that often marginalizes or trivializes Asian American participation in basketball (Chin 2015; King 2006; and see chapter 5).

It must also be contextualized that this social capital exists in a field that is also, relatively speaking, marginalized in mainstream sports: women's basketball. Although some of these networks extend to boys' and men's basketball, they are not as numerous nor can they be leveraged in the same way that the women's basketball network can. This investment by Japanese Americans has paid off more in the field of women's basketball, providing incentive for concentrating their efforts in this direction.

GREATER SUCCESS THAN THE MEN

In earlier eras, it was mainly Japanese American men who would occasionally make it onto mainstream high school and college teams. In the late 1940s, Wataru "Wat" Misaka played for the University of Utah and later the New York Knicks (Franks 2010). He is said to be the first nonwhite player in the NBA. Kaz Shinzato played for USC from 1955 to 1960. Former *Rafu Shimpo* sports editor Chris Komai could name several male players from the 1970s who had gained spots on California State University teams. During most of this early period, mainstream opportunities were just not available for women.

In the 1970s—right around the same time that Japanese American women began making their mark on the California college women's basketball scene—men's basketball started to become increasingly competitive and more and more associated with African American athletes and African American urban culture (Campbell 2015; Hoberman 1997). Unlike from the 1920s to the 1970s when a few prominent Japanese American men were able to play on mainstream high school, college, and even professional teams, from the 1980s onward, Japanese American men were largely absent from big-time collegiate and professional teams and rarely made their high school varsity squads. In a time when women's mainstream opportunities were increasing, men's seemed to be constricting, creating a new context for community icons.

In the contemporary era, mainstream women's basketball is far more competitive than it was in the 1970s and 1980s. However, Japanese American women may continue to have some advantages over men in securing college playing opportunities. For starters, it is still not a widespread trend to start girls in basketball at age four and provide them with year-round playing opportunities throughout their youth—the J-Leagues have an advantage here. Second, the style of women's basketball may be more accessible to Japanese Americans. Although less universal than stereotype or community identity would suggest, Japanese Americans do seem to be, on average, shorter than the typical basketball player. Women's basketball is often described as more about finesse and fundamentals than is the men's game, and it is commonly played "closer to the ground," with far less dunking and aerial displays. Therefore, at least when selecting guards, height is seldom used as a disqualifying factor. The theory that height matters more for the men was voiced by many of my participants, as well as by participants in other research on J-League basketball (Chin 2012).

J-League participants widely believed that Japanese American girls and women had a better chance of making it to higher levels of basketball. Maggie gave her impression:

> Even though guys and girls play basketball, for Japanese, a lot of guys, they don't play high school. Well, number one, they're not good enough to play and it's only like the elite players that actually make the team. I mean varsity. They'll play like freshman, JV ball maybe, but very few of them actually make varsity. It is kind of different, do you see that? . . . Or some of them don't even play, won't even try out for high school, because they know they probably won't make the team. It's just girls, Japanese American girls, you know, everyone plays varsity. It's rare that you find someone that didn't play varsity.

Mas articulated the different style and athleticism argument: "I think boys, they're always trying to play above the rim. Less fundamentals. They're more athletic. The girls, they're usually stronger fundamentally. I think they're better shooters, in general. They just try to play the game with more smarts than boys. I think boys try to play with too much athleticism nowadays." Many of my participants, like Mas, attributed the male star deficit to a height issue—the perceived height difference between Japanese Americans and other ethnicities seemed to matter less in women's basketball.

A third factor that may be influencing opportunities for Japanese American men is gendered racism. As I will describe in more detail in chapter 5, Asian American players seem to be viewed as universally small, or as "playing small" (King 2006, 2014), in spite of their actual size, causing coaches and recruiters to be less likely to invest in Asian American athletes. Although both men and women in my study reported being underestimated and overlooked in many basketball contexts, it is possible that differences in how Asian American women and men are racialized create greater barriers for men. Japanese American women may carry associations with smallness and femininity, but these images may not hurt them as much in a women's basketball environment. Japanese American men who potentially carry similar associations would have more to overcome in proving their merit. Two male players mentioned "dunking" as being a kind of litmus test for Asian Americans in men's basketball. Not all male players can dunk, but Mike had a high school coach require that he prove his ability to dunk if he wanted to play on the varsity team. For some Asian American men, the dunk emerged as a unique, racially charged requirement. In women's basketball, even players who are highly skilled at dunking seldom do so in games because it is not as much a part of the style of the women's game. Accordingly, no Japanese American women mentioned feeling the pressure to dunk or perform a similar test of their vertical reach.

Whatever the exact reasons, over the past fifteen years, Asian/Pacific Islander women have tended to have double the proportion of players in NCAA Division I basketball as men (NCAA 2010). In the most recent report, for the 2009–2010 season, women of Asian descent made up 1.2 percent of all Division I women's basketball participants (fifty-five athletes), while their male counterparts composed 0.5 percent of participants (twenty-six athletes) (NCAA 2010). As Asian Americans are about 5 percent of the total US population, Asian Americans of both sexes are underrepresented in the highest levels of collegiate basketball.[2]

Of note, in the time since I was "in the field" during my research, a small handful of Japanese American men have played at small Division III programs in California, following an established path of many of their female counterparts. I hypothesize that the achievements made by Japanese American women have influenced a few of the young men to reach a little higher and perhaps led men's college basketball coaches in the area to be more open-minded about their recruitment.

CONCLUSION

Over its long history, organized basketball in the Japanese American community has provided opportunities for Japanese Americans to become skilled basketball players. These skills have at times translated well in mainstream contexts, allowing some of the players trained in the J-Leagues to excel in school sports at the high school level and beyond. Women have long been involved in the community project of the J-Leagues.

In a transitional period for women's sports in the 1970s, Japanese American women playing in the J-Leagues found that their skills and passion were now rewarded in the mainstream context. Several women capitalized on college scholarships and coaching opportunities. As this first generation became established in women's college basketball, many used their skills or positions to mentor or provide opportunities for the next generation of talented J-League players.

The modern context, influenced by the growth of organized youth sport (Adler and Adler 1994) and the growth of women's sport, has continued to create opportunity structures for Japanese American women to succeed in the mainstream. The J-Leagues offer Japanese American girls training not typical for young girls in the mainstream—they start early and provide playing opportunities throughout the year. This paired with J-League-affiliated "club" traveling teams make numerous Japanese American women competitive for college scholarships. In the early years following the passage of Title IX, many Japanese American women dominated in mainstream basketball environments. Now, women consistently play for local colleges and universities, and some have had great success that in most cases surpasses the achievements of their male counterparts.

In addition to the early and consistent training offered by the J-Leagues, Japanese Americans have also built an extensive women's basketball network with connections in many mainstream contexts including club, high school, college, and even professional women's basketball. This social capital has aided the most talented of the J-League participants to pursue college basketball scholarships and make attempts at professional opportunities.

The J-Leagues in general have provided a source of community cultural wealth, but the community investment in women's basketball in particular has become a font of riches. The social capital created by a network of mentors, supporters, and connections has provided channels of success for the most talented J-League-affiliated women. This is a story of women supporting women and of co-ethnics supporting co-ethnics. In a context where Asian American women are symbolically excluded from an identity as a college-level basketball player or coach, it is a story of women using community resources to fight back and give themselves—and others like them—at least a chance at playing ball in the big leagues.

4 · "WE'RE TURNING THEM INTO STARS!"

The Japanese American Female Basketball Player as Icon

On a Saturday morning in May 2008, I was trying to find some shade from the sun with some other volunteers during the San-Tai-San ("Three-on-Three") tournament in Little Tokyo. Suddenly, Jamie Hagiya, one of the "special guests" recruited for the event, walked by us. It was almost as if a hush passed over the nearby crowds. One of the volunteers said to me and anyone in earshot, "That's Jaime Hagiya. She plays for USC and she's really amazing." As Hagiya made her way through the crowd, those who knew her were saying hello and others were murmuring to each other, looking her way. This was someone really important walking by.

Events such as San-Tai-San both (re)create and capitalize on the fame of the J-League players who have achieved success in collegiate basketball and beyond. This tournament in particular, where basketball is played on the streets of the Little Tokyo district of Los Angeles, visibly links the current generation's version of Japanese American culture—basketball—with a historical site of ethnic community. Moreover, it is an event that raises money and awareness about a proposed recreation center, "Budokan," that community leaders hope will soon be built in Little Tokyo. This would create an even more permanent link between the historical and contemporary Japanese American community in Los Angeles. The college-level female basketball players become a vibrant part of this ritual, and others like it. They become symbols of community unity and continuity, of the hopes and desires of the youth, and of Japanese American identity.

Several women have been taken up as Japanese American community icons. They are, above all, accessible heroines and role models to many youth in the community. At San-Tai-San, Hagiya—and other "special guests" over the years—are often given roles that place them on a pedestal: sharing an encouraging speech at the beginning of the tournament or giving out raffle prizes and awards at the close of the event. The star players have also engaged in more hands-on activities: leading stretches, playing basketball-related games with the children, or just mingling with the crowd (see image 4.1). Little girls in particular tend to follow the special guests around at events, wanting a chance to talk to their favorite player or obtain her autograph.

As established in prior chapters, the majority of Japanese American women who have played at the college level and beyond owe a great deal of their success to Japanese American community resources, such as the structures of opportunity offered by the J-League-affiliated organizations and the existing women's basketball networks. Now that there are many women succeeding at this level, there is another layer of community support that helps accentuate their fame and visibility. The community cultivates a degree of celebrity-level attention for J-League participants who have played or coached at the higher levels of mainstream basketball. These community stars, primarily women, are highly recognized and celebrated. They are regularly featured in community-based media outlets and at community events. Self-promotion also occurs when athletes host their own name-brand basketball camps and clinics, as well as when they post information about their athletic careers via social media.

IMAGE 4.1. Jamie Hagiya leads a basketball drill at the San-Tai-San tournament, 2012. (Credit: Gwen Muranaka, *Rafu Shimpo*.)

The symbol of the successful female college basketball player has become a community resource in itself. An important source of community cultural wealth (Yosso 2005), the women engender ethnic/racial pride, serving as a source of inspiration and aspiration. They also often become symbolic of an idealized Japanese American identity. On a more practical level, these women are sought after as "special guests" in part because they can draw a crowd and in doing so help to replenish community interest in and financial support of Japanese American organizations and community projects.

A community chooses its icons for what they represent. What does it mean that many Japanese Americans in California have embraced a group of talented young *female* athletes to hold up as role models? How is their celebrity (re)created, understood, and consumed by community members? In this chapter I examine the meaning making that occurs surrounding the most prominent contemporary basketball stars. The level of visibility and success achieved by some of the women in particular is a product of not only larger social forces and the structures, networks, and interactions made possible by the J-Leagues, but also the processes by which the women have been taken up as cultural symbols. The meanings inscribed on these icons have been responsive to community debates surrounding Japanese American identity, and embedded in larger gender and racial projects.

FEMALE ATHLETIC ICONS

It is often assumed that male athletic heroes have more importance and bring more pride to the groups whom they represent—they have infiltrated a more esteemed side of mainstream sports. There are exceptions, however, that disrupt the ubiquity of male athletic icons.

It may be fruitful to compare athletic icons representing ethnic groups to those representing nation-states in international competitions. Why have certain female athletes emerged as national icons? One way this question has been approached is the "medal hypothesis," which proposes that when women have more success than men, they will get a boost in popularity, measured in levels of media attention. For example, if it is women who are bringing home the gold medals for the United States, Americans will turn their national pride toward the women. Research of media coverage during the Olympics suggests that greater women's success does typically result in more media coverage for women, but it is a nuanced picture and differs nation to nation (Bruce, Hovden, and Markula 2010).

A related thesis explains sport heroines through their symbolic value to the nation. This is particularly common in Olympic competitions where stories about successful women athletes can inspire a sense of national pride. Although masculinity and whiteness are more commonly part of these nationalistic projects, women, including women from marginalized racial and socioeconomic positions, have had moments of national glory. For example, Gardiner (2003) found that during the Sydney Olympics in 2000, the Australian press embraced indigenous athletes Nova

Peris-Kneebone and Cathy Freeman as symbols of national identity and unity. Depictions were not free of racialized and gendered imagery, but such images became co-opted, helping to build a sense of Australian national identity. In the case of these athletes, the nonwhite female body became a symbol through which some degree of racial reconciliation could take place, at least in the eyes of the predominately white mainstream press.

One could argue that part of the reason that women have more rarely served as athletic icons is that they have had far fewer opportunities in "big-time" sporting environments. This is likely why the Olympics have stood out as a unique circumstance where women receive higher amounts of media coverage (Bruce, Hovden, and Markula 2010; Messner, Duncan, and Willms 2006). It follows then that Japanese American women were able to transform their status as co-ethnic recreational players to community icons in the post–Title IX era when higher level play in women's basketball became more legitimized.

Although Japanese Americans are not embarking on a project of nationalism, they are working on a similar project to sustain and define their ethnic identity. The difference is that they do so in a space of marginalization, particularly in the world of sports. Could the context of marginalization influence the potential for women athletes to be taken up as athletic icons?

Symbols of Cultural Belonging

The Japanese Americans who have had successful playing careers in mainstream contexts may be lionized in part due to their symbolic claims to American cultural citizenship (Lim 2006; Rosaldo 1997), or a sense of belonging to the larger society. The symbolic power of a Japanese American who is successful in a popular mainstream sport such as basketball may be in its ability to produce "counternarratives to the mainstream construction of racial minorities as unassimilable peoples occupying a liminal space outside the imagined nation-state" (Lim 2006, 12). Thus, the Japanese American who can successfully play an American sport in the mainstream can be a confirmation that Japanese Americans do in fact belong.

During the first half of the twentieth century, both community sports and successful Jewish American athletes became important elements of Jewish American life. There is some scholarly debate as to whether Jewish athletes who became successful in the mainstream were celebrated by Jewish American individuals and communities because these athletes represented acceptance by mainstream society (indicating the possibility and desirability of assimilation), or rather because they engendered a sense of ethnic pride, heightening feelings of ethnic solidarity (Kugelmass 2007). The simple answer is both—the ability of these icons to simultaneously symbolize a sense of belonging to the larger society and to the ethnic group was probably what solidified their appeal as icons. It created a middle ground—a supportive ethnic safe space, but also a feeling of belonging to the larger culture (Levine 1992).

Japanese Americans likely find similar rewards in their own practice of basketball and have much of the same feelings toward those athletes who succeed in mainstream contexts. Sports can often provide at least symbolic access to the larger society, a sense of citizenship for populations feeling excluded in some way from mainstream life (Kugelmass 2007; Levine 1992). It is, however, important to remember that the way that these symbols get taken up influence the feelings that they evoke and the potential that they have to change the image of the group (Lowe 2016).

Pride

Many J-League participants described feeling a sense of pride whenever Japanese Americans made it to higher levels of mainstream basketball. One player, Danielle, noted, "[Japanese Americans] can vicariously experience the level of competition, the thrills. I think it's a source of pride, really, just for the community or the group as a whole." Especially when the success was perceived as momentous, the sense of connection to a successful player could be simply a shared racial or ethnic background. However, many of the homegrown college players inspired a more complex, and more intimate sense of pride, built on intersecting symbolic identifications with race/ethnicity, school/college, hometown, and league/organization. Connections to the icons at times were "real" when the successful players were teammates, friends, or family. Participants based their pride and identification on concentric circles of belonging, each athlete possessing unique signifiers of group affiliation.

Ethnic/Racial Identification

For many marginalized groups, seeing a group member excel in a mainstream context can be empowering. Particularly in the history of US professional sports, ethnic-community icons have been a source of pride and identification, especially when these stars were among the first to break into a particular sport (Levine 1992; Gems 2013). Today, scholars have begun to write about what contemporary Asian/American male athletic icons, such as Jeremy Lin and Manny Pacquiao, mean to Asian Americans (e.g., Arnaldo 2016; Combs and Wasserstrom 2013; Park 2015).

Asian Americans have not had very many standout players in US collegiate and professional basketball, so there is still a lot of excitement about any co-ethnic or co-panethnic Asian American basketball stars. The best recent instance of this is the emergence of NBA player Jeremy Lin. There is evidence of Japanese American community excitement. During a 2016 archival search of articles from *Rafu Shimpo*, Jeremy Lin's name appeared in fifty-four sport stories. In addition, an article in the magazine *Colorlines* connected some of Lin's fandom with the popularity of Asian basketball leagues (King 2012). However, Lin is not Japanese American and did not play in the J-Leagues, and therefore has only limited, panethnic connections with Japanese Americans. I would also imagine he is not perceived as accessible or as known personally by J-League participants. In other words, Lin's concentric circles of belonging do not run very deep. However, his level of success bridged some of these gaps, as he was taken up as an Asian American icon.

When speaking with J-League participants, some of the identification and pride they felt toward successful athletes seemed to be primarily ethnic affiliation, influenced by a sense of marginalization within the world of sport. For example, Brandon said, "I think it's great when I see JAs in professional sports or in higher-level sports. I feel proud that they're in it. I know they've overcome a lot to get there, just like any athlete. But I think it's great . . . but you just don't see that many JAs in higher-level sports, so when they do make it, it's nice to celebrate it and acknowledge it, highlight it." Brandon is proud to see Japanese Americans succeed. He was not necessarily concerned if he knew the players or if they were involved with the J-Leagues. He could identify with the players because they shared the same ethnicity. For Debbie, the ethnic connection was also about the satisfaction of seeing Japanese American players challenging stereotypes: "It's just pride. You know? People assume that Japanese Americans can't play basketball."

Long before Jeremy Lin, Japanese Americans had two earlier co-ethnic, mixed-race professional basketball players emerge in the late 1990s: Lindsey Yamasaki and Rex Walters. Yamasaki is a mixed-race Japanese American woman from Oregon who had a very successful career at Stanford University (1998–2002) followed by a few solid years of play in the WNBA (2002–2006). The Southern California community embraced Yamasaki by covering her in *Rafu Shimpo*, inviting her to community events, and attending her college and professional games. Debbie described the local enthusiasm: "She was very good . . . there was a couple times we all went to watch her play a couple of her WNBA games so we'd all go to see her . . . just me with San-Tai-San people . . . but the audience, the spectators were all JA [Japanese American], just filled with JA little girls." Debbie describes enormous excitement for a co-ethnic making it to the WNBA. Yamasaki was embraced as a role model, particularly by girls and women involved in J-Leagues and related events (San-Tai-San is the tournament described at the beginning of this chapter).

Yamasaki acknowledged the Japanese American community support by granting interviews and participating in some California-based Japanese American events. At the time, the community seemed to view her as the most successful Japanese American woman so far in basketball, as she had played at a major university with a strong women's basketball program and later became the first Japanese American woman to play in the WNBA. However, she did not fully fit the bill as a local, Southern California Japanese American heroine. For one thing, she is not fully of Japanese descent, but more importantly, she did not play in the California J-Leagues. Like Lin, Yamasaki's level of success overcame some of these barriers.

Rex Walters is an interesting example on the men's side. Also a mixed-race Japanese American, Walters grew up in Northern California and played in the J-Leagues with the Zebras organization. Walters played first for Northwestern University and then transferred to the University of Kansas, where he went to the Final Four in 1993. He played in the NBA from 1993–2000. He coached college basketball for several years, most recently at the University of San Francisco. In 2016, he left USF to coach an NBA D-League team, the Grand Rapids Drive, an affiliate of the Detroit Pistons. Several participants brought up Walters as a source of pride, but he was not mentioned as often as the current female stars. There are a few probable explanations for this. At the time of my interviews, his success as a player was already far in the past, and whereas my participants had connections to Southern California, Walters is affiliated with a Northern California J-League organization. When participants did speak about Walters, they often mentioned that he had played in J-League tournaments, suggesting that perceived accessibility and community contact were meaningful to establishing community attachments to sport icons.

Darin Maki is another Japanese American example on the men's side. He played at East Los Angeles College (1998–2000) and at California State University, Dominguez Hills (2000–2002). Because his mother was born in Japan, he was able to create a career playing professionally in Japan for several years. Although his name came up in many conversations as one of the few men from the J-Leagues who had made it to college-level play, he did not have the local exposure and fame of Nakase or Hagiya. Maki did participate in a few camps and fund-raisers—often alongside one or both of these women—but he lives abroad and has not been able to continually stay in contact with Southern California fans.

Community Connection

Other interviewees felt pride in the college-level players primarily because they emerged from the J-Leagues or share a particular league or organizational affiliation. Beth talked about the college-level players: "They're doing very well, I think because they grew up playing in the Japanese American leagues. They're doing quite well, and I'm very proud of them. It really makes you say, 'Oh, wow, all this playing in the league has really helped them.'" Beth has been on the board of one of the girls' leagues for many years and therefore has a lot of pride in the women whose skills first developed within these leagues. For her, it extends beyond racial/ethnic and community connections to a sense of ownership over the leagues and, by extension, the players' successes.

As I interviewed J-League participants from all over Los Angeles and Orange counties and spanning several organizations, it was remarkable to me how many of them knew or had met many of the "mini-stars" who were playing at the college level—or at the very least, they knew someone who knew the player. These were clearly not distant icons. For example, one interviewee said that Jamie Hagiya's mother had worked for him and he had also attended a funeral where he discovered that the minister was Hagiya's father. Several interviewees whom I recruited from diverse sources said that Hagiya was their cousin.

Many of the players who played on all-star teams or in the top divisions at tournaments follow their contemporaries, as several of them continued playing in college. Allison, twenty-two, plays Division III basketball, but also follows players her age, particularly in her conference, "just because I know so much about them. I mean, if I read a clipping about someone, it's like, good for her! Or teammates playing in different places, it's like, good for them! A really powerful thing."

Men who were over forty tended to be very knowledgeable of Japanese American women playing basketball in college and unself-conscious about expressing their enthusiasm and support of these women. Not only do these (mostly sansei) men appear to be the contemporary keepers of the J-League culture as organizers and promoters of J-League basketball, but they also often know the parents and former J-League coaches of the successful women. For example, Andrew is a Chinese American man who is very active in the leagues. He could, like many men in his cohort, rattle off the names of the prominent J-League players: "So there's a few people . . . Natalie [Nakase] and Jamie [Hagiya]. For women, they look up to them. You may not notice it until—when Jamie played at SC, they have a home game, the majority [in] attendance were Japanese Americans. I don't know if you noticed that. . . . She brought in a lot of people. Natalie brought in a lot of people, at least the Japanese Americans that were interested in basketball came out to watch Jamie or Natalie play. I noticed that. And even at Chapman College, we have Lauren [Kamiyama] that plays out there. Every time I watch her game, everybody goes out to watch her play. So, you have a lot of the spectators who are Japanese American at Chapman."

Even though Andrew indicates that it is mainly women who look up to Nakase, Hagiya, and Kamiyama, he shows his own interest by indicating that he has attended several games and currently attends Chapman College games. The men's knowledge and support of the women athletes are demonstrative of the leadership and community loyalty in which many of the sansei engage.

"WE'RE TURNING THEM INTO STARS!" LOCAL COMPETITION AND COMMUNITY EVENTS CREATE STARS

The San-Tai-San tournament had an established tradition of bringing high-profile Japanese American basketball players as "special guests" at the event. Although the committee often brainstormed possible guests, it seemed to be protocol to go through two women who were members of the LTSC board. The committee often solicited these women's help in both suggesting and communicating with proposed special guests. They were connected with the J-Leagues and seen as the ideal sources for information on which players were currently popular and which might be available to attend the event. J-League networks, thus, were influential even in the process of deciding which Japanese American athletes and coaches qualified as community icons.

However, in an effort to include men and some new women, one year the committee decided to cast their net wider, seeking out potential guests from the rosters of all local colleges and universities, not just the bigger programs. They had all of the volunteers on the planning committee scour team rosters and check with any networks they had. They also suggested including some prominent Japanese American high school and college coaches. The committee felt that since some of these players and coaches might be less well-known in the J-League community, the tournament would be an opportunity to introduce new role models to the children involved in the tournament. Charles, a committee member and employee of the Little Tokyo Service Center, commented, "We're turning them into stars" (Field notes, March 21, 2007). That year, the committee was able to secure three guests, all women who had played at the collegiate level.

Other tournaments did not utilize guests or speakers, but the organizers did sometimes encourage star players to play in the tournament or spread the word if such players signed up to play on their own. For example, at the popular adult tournament in Las Vegas, there did not seem to be as much desire to feature community icons as speakers as is done at many of the youth tournaments. However, when I asked Rebecca, a Las Vegas tournament organizer, if she ever invited any of the star players, her focus was more on the "celebs" who attended the tournament. She responded, "No, we don't make a point to do it, but, a couple of years we've had like uh, Rex Walters, 'cause he's half Japanese . . . he played actually, when he wasn't playing pro ball. But other than that, only like the celebs that come are self-made celebs . . . we have one girl who just finished playing at UCLA. . . . Those kind of people are pretty much known to a lot of the community or a lot of the people who played. But other than that, we don't necessarily force the issue to have somebody there. If they're there, they're there." As mentioned, other participants remembered watching Rex Walters at J-League tournaments or checking out the Imperials Purple, a team filled with former college players. The presence of these star players increased the tournament's status, while at the same time players gained visibility.

Many members of the community have enjoyed watching the more prominent Japanese American basketball players in action at local college and professional games. Some of these games have become events in themselves. For example, when Jamie Hagiya's team (USC) played Corrie Mizusawa's team (University of Oregon) on January 4, 2005, *Rafu Shimpo* and the Little Tokyo Service joined with USC to promote the event, advertising the competition as the "Downtown Showdown" (see image 4.2). Even though Mizusawa graduated later that year, the same parties held a similar themed event a year later on February 11, 2006. The USC athletics website described the event as a way "to celebrate the rich tradition of women's basketball as well as raise funds and awareness for the Little Tokyo Recreation Center building project" (January 31, 2006). The Downtown Showdown events formalized what was already a strong following of Jamie Hagiya's career at USC. The university was able to grow their audience and *Rafu Shimpo* to grow their readership, and the LTSC raised funds and awareness for their project, a recreation center in Little Tokyo. *Rafu Shimpo* also distributed a feature article on Kai Felton, who was then an assistant coach for the USC women's basketball team. She is half Japanese and grew up playing in the J-Leagues in Southern California.

Not all Japanese American basketball enthusiasts had the time or interest to attend games in person when Japanese American athletes were playing. However, they could still follow the success of the players through other sources such as through word of mouth or newspaper coverage in local and Japanese American publications.

Start the New Year off on the Right Foot at the

DOWNTOWN SHOWDOWN!

presented by

🈴 ⚘ **RAFU SHIMPO** 🈴

USC vs. University of Oregon Women's Basketball

Sunday, January 2, 2005, 2:00 PM
Los Angeles Memorial Sports Arena

Women of Troy
SC
Basketball

Jamie Hagiya
USC Sophomore Point Guard
Torrance, California

Support the Women of Troy on New Year's Weekend
and help the Little Tokyo Recreation Center realize a dream!

For each $5.00 LTRC-USC Ticket sold, USC will donate $2.00 to the Little
Tokyo Service Center for the Little Tokyo Recreation Center building fund!

TICKETS AND INFORMATION
(213) 821-0782

IMAGE 4.2. The Little Tokyo Service Center paired with the
University of Southern California athletic department to host
a fund-raiser for the proposed Little Tokyo Recreation Center. (Credit: Mike Murase.)

CREATING AN ICON: MEDIA COVERAGE

When Japanese Americans do well in sport, community publications often follow their success and share about the athletes
through articles and photographs. Historically, there were several
California daily publications aimed at Japanese American audiences, but *Rafu Shimpo* in Los Angeles is the only one still in print.
There are a few publications with web presences and some limited

publication: *NikkeiWest* in San Jose (1994–present), *Nichi Bei Times*, once a daily in San Francisco, and the Japanese American Citizens League national publication, the *Pacific Citizen*.

Through editorial choices, these publications help to (re)create and define which players qualify as worthy of community attention. The content then frames the athletes' stories in ways that guide readers in how to interpret the success of these athletes. When I interviewed the sports editor and sport reporter at *Rafu Shimpo*, I learned that the editorial decisions were driven not just by the newspaper staff; community members are also involved. Readers often send in recommendations for stories. They may contribute photographs or scores from a recent event. And they send in feedback about the sports page. Thus, the sports page is not only a reflection of the sports editor's view of the Japanese American sport landscape, but also an outgrowth of requests from the more vocal community members.

There is evidence that media run by marginalized ethnic and racial groups have been more attentive to women's sports than is generally found the mainstream (Paraschak 1990; Williams 1987; Willms 2014; Yep 2009). The coverage has also been transgressive in terms of content. Jamieson's study (2001) of media portrayals of golfer Nancy Lopez in a mainstream magazine (*Sports Illustrated*) versus two magazines aimed at a Latino/a audience (*Nuestro* and *Hispanic*) showed qualitative differences in how the two media sources constructed meaning around the subject of Lopez. One strong departure between the two types of magazines was in how they interpreted family and cultural influences on Lopez. Similar to Yosso's (2005) theory of community cultural wealth, magazines aimed at Latino audiences saw Lopez's family and background as assets, while mainstream publications seemed to imply they were obstacles. Yep (2009) found comparable media divergences in her qualitative archival research on mainstream and ethnic community news coverage of Chinese American athletes during the 1930s and 1940s. The mainstream press during this period tended to treat women athletes in a stereotypical fashion and depicted Chinese American athletes in stereotypically racialized and gendered ways. Conversely, ethnic community presses such as the *Chinese Digest* tended to treat Chinese American women athletes with respect. Paraschak (1990) found that from 1968 to 1980, a newspaper based on the Six Nations Reserve in Ontario, Canada, featured local women athletes in 78 percent of their publications. The coverage indicated that girls and women athletes from the reserve were excelling both within the "All-Indian" leagues and in mainstream athletic competition.

The findings in these three articles indicate a departure from mainstream trends, first by covering women athletes and second by covering them in ways that diverge from stereotypical portrayals. These niche publications all appear to be resisting mainstream interpretations of sports, finding alternative ways to cover their own communities.

Rafu Shimpo

In Southern California, the Japanese American newspaper *Rafu Shimpo* plays a large role in defining player success. My participants often became aware of standout players by reading about them in the paper or talking to people who had read the coverage.

The content of the sports coverage in such a paper can provide clues as to how the community understands itself and how they prefer to present themselves through narratives and images. It can also represent a negotiation within an ethnic community (Bacon 1999) about how the communal ethnic identity should be understood, since readers have the ability to respond to coverage and submit ideas for stories. When I interviewed the sports editor, he explained, "We really rely heavily on word of mouth from readers. That really is the bedrock of our local coverage. . . . We hear about people from staff members, parents, coaches. . . . We get a lot of emails." Because Japanese Americans are active in the production and consumption of what appears in *Rafu Shimpo*, they influence the content and express ideas about sport that are meaningful to them. As girls and women have become markers of mainstream success in the community's favorite sport of basketball, coverage of these women in the community newspaper has become a key site for negotiating their visibility and image.

It is in this context that I found that *Rafu Shimpo* dedicates more of its basketball coverage to girls and women (54 percent) than to boys and men (20 percent) or to coed/neutral coverage. This asymmetrical coverage of women's basketball stands out as different from the paper's general treatment of sports coverage: men's sports represented 60 percent of all articles, whereas coverage of women represented 18 percent (Willms 2014). For both sports in general and basketball in particular, these percentages are dramatically different from what is found in most mainstream media outlets. Women now receive very little sports coverage on mainstream television, as little as 2 percent of coverage on ESPN's nationally broadcast *SportsCenter* (Cooky, Messner, and Musto 2015). The print media also exhibit tendencies toward the "symbolic annihilation of sportswomen" (Pedersen 2002, 306). At best, when narrowed down to only the sport of basketball and only in print outlets, women's coverage is 25 percent or less of total basketball reporting (e.g., Dozier 1999; Kian, Vincent, and Mondello 2008; Silverstein 1996).

The content of the coverage in *Rafu Shimpo* is also very respectful. Photographs of female athletes, for instance, are just as likely as photographs of male athletes to be action shots (Willms 2014). Yep (2009) also found in pre–World War II Chinese American publications that photographs depicted female athletes "in positions of strength or authority" (106) and did not focus on feminine qualities. Thus, even though some more recent scholarship suggests that the mainstream media may be more respectful of female athletes (Cooky, Messner, and Musto 2015) and standardizing its photographic depictions of men and women in sport (Pedersen 2002), Chinese American publications of the 1940s appear to be far ahead of their time.

As has been documented in early twentieth-century Jewish communities (Kugelmass 2007; Levine 1992), sports stars (typically male) have been a source of pride for many ethnic communities. In addition to Yep's (2009) findings about Chinese American newspapers, studies of the black press, Latino magazines, and a newspaper from the Six Nations Reserve in Ontario (Jamieson 2001; Paraschak 1990; Williams 1987) demonstrate that racial- and ethnic-based communities can find a similar pride and appreciation in their successful female athletes as well. It appears that when it comes to sports, depictions in race- or ethnic-based media tend to emphasize pride in the community member's accomplishments and not on reinforcing a gender hierarchy.

Word of Mouth—Reading the Newspaper and Beyond

Newspaper coverage is only as important as its readership, so I asked the majority of my interviewees about their exposure to *Rafu Shimpo* and other sources of information about standout Japanese American basketball players. Although the newspaper was a dominant source of information, it was the word of mouth surrounding the paper, the passing of information from the paper on to friends and relatives, that appeared to be most effectual in creating buzz about basketball stars.

The newspaper played a role in creating an iconic status for the local college players. One of my interviewees, Keith, was dating a local college player, and indicated that the newspaper was behind a lot of the attention that she received from Japanese Americans: "Katie I think is a perfect example of that because I hear people all the time, I mean just people who meet her like, 'Oh you're Katie! Oh yeah, I follow you in the *Rafu*. I see you all the time.' I mean, that's, yeah, it's something that's—they're little mini-stars because the paper tells them, everybody reads that— not everybody, but I know a lot of . . . um . . . Japanese Americans that read that paper, they follow people all the time. So yeah, I mean they're mini-stars." Keith implies that the paper plays a large part in publicizing the standout athletes and, in effect, creating "mini-stars." When they are out together, Japanese Americans recognize Katie from the articles that consistently follow her career and stop to talk to her about it.

Many younger interviewees admitted that they did not read or subscribe regularly to the paper, but mentioned that older relatives commonly passed along articles or shared the paper with their younger relatives. For example, Beth, eighty-three, read the paper regularly and remarked, "I read the newspapers. They're

doing very well. . . . There's quite a big [number] playing in college now. . . . I read the sports page, read up on all those girls doing
well." Beth regularly follows the college-level players in *Rafu
Shimpo* and therefore knows a lot about who is currently successful. Younger participants were more infrequent readers and
often relied on older relatives to clip articles and share them or to
tell them the news in person. Jake, age twenty-five, said, "We get
[*Rafu Shimpo*]. I don't have the chance to read it too often anymore, but I guess within the community, if something big is happening, I have enough people around where someone is going to
send me an email on it or mention it . . . if one of our pictures is
in it, someone will usually—my mom will get it first and show us,
but other than that, we don't really look too much," Jake's comments reflect a trend I commonly heard from younger players—if
they themselves were written about in the paper, a relative would
quickly clip out the article and send it to them or their parents.
As Jake also described, when "something big is happening," such
as the success of a local player, someone will get the word out by
email or other means.

As a reflection of this word-of-mouth phenomenon, most
J-Leagues participants were able to name at least one player who
they knew had played or currently played in college. For example,
Grace said, "Their names are out there if they play, like at USC or
big-time schools. They're so proud of someone that's Japanese
American that plays at that level. Or Natalie [Nakase], she played at
UCLA for a while. So everyone kind of knows them, even though
they may not know them personally. Everyone knows who they
are, how they're doing. Especially in the higher divisions, everybody knows the really good players, the ones that play in college."
Newspaper coverage becomes a reflection of—and an inspiration
for—conversations happening in the Japanese American community. The coverage of the young women who have had mainstream
success in basketball clearly demonstrates a community interest
and pride in these individuals and what they mean for the community. As Grace expressed, there is a sense of knowing the players, even if one does not really know them. This is, of course, what

often gives icons their mass appeal. People tend to feel a sense of pride when someone to whom they feel connected does well. Whether through a sense of ethnic/racial pride, community pride, or league/organization pride (or all three), people had their eyes on the successful players.

Expanding Existing Networks: Social Media and Subcultural Celebrity

In an era of social media, Japanese American players can also more easily manage their own image and visibility. As far as I can tell, just three Japanese American players could be described as subcultural social media stars: Jamie Hagiya, Natalie Nakase, and Darin Maki all have a substantial social media presence. All three played some form of professional basketball and have careers related to their athletic pursuits that have gained them fame outside of the Japanese American community.

Jamie Hagiya has a Facebook page with 4,961 friends and 1,421 followers. She also has a celebrity page for her career as a CrossFit athlete with 3,143 likes. She has professionalized her athletic status as she offers name-brand basketball camps and training, owns a CrossFit gym, and is also a sponsored competitor in CrossFit competitions. Hagiya has a Twitter account with 400 followers. Her profile reads, "USC & Overseas pro hooper, Hagiya Basketball camps & clinics, Baller turned CrossFitter. Co-owner &coach @ Torrance CrossFit. Newest member of NPFL Phoenix Rise" (statistics as of March 2016).

Natalie Nakase has a Twitter account with 1,389 followers. Her profile simply reads "Basketball Coach." She is currently on the coaching staff for the Los Angeles Clippers. She has a Facebook fan page with 301 likes (statistics as of March 2016).

On the men's side, Darin Maki has a Twitter account with 2,285 followers. His profile reads "Ret. pro basketball player • Partner at @kabotip." His Instagram has 5,264 followers (statistics as of March 2016).

Media scholars have written about subcultural stardom and how it can be built by connecting with audiences and fans in multiple

ways, including "transmedia," which is across different media plat-
forms: "Performances, promotional appearances, interviews, posed
and candid photographs, and gossip publications all contribute to
the discursive construction of the star. Thus, the transmedia story
of the star is formed through repeated connections between these
discursive sites. Its production involves entertainment industry professionals, corporate interests, and promotional labor by the stars
themselves" (Ellcessor 2012). As Hagiya, Nakase, and Maki have
overlapped their basketball playing careers as Japanese Americans
with their corporate connections, their media visibility has grown.
Furthermore, each has taken at least some initiative in constructing
an online presence that helps to further their careers and put forth
an image of themselves as athletes and coaches.

The path of these three athletes is, of course, extraordinary.
Most of the players followed by the local Japanese American communities of California never play professionally and enjoy visibility
only in community publications, by word of mouth, and in direct
interactions within the J-Leagues.

"It's a Small World": Visibility and Weak Social Ties

Japanese Americans create sport icons in part by simply being a
highly networked, tight-knit community. Emily explained how she
and others knew about college-level players: "When someone gets
onto a Division I team . . . I feel like the JA community is really
small and everyone kind of knows who the best players are and
who ends up going off to college." It was sometimes hard to pin-
point exactly how community members became aware of college-
level players—it was just common knowledge. Jimmy felt that the
J-League community was even more of a "small world" than the
larger Japanese American community: "In these basketball circles,
everything is a small world. All of the many thousands of people
that play, it's still very small. You run into people; you have some
kind of connection with most of these people somehow."

The extent to which college-level players' parents were embedded in the Japanese American or J-League community also contributed to how well-known the players became. During the time

of my research, this phenomenon led to the popularity of a Division III player, Lauren Kamiyama, who played at Chapman College for Coach Carol Jue. Despite Chapman being a smaller school in a non-scholarship division, *Rafu Shimpo* regularly covered and a number of community members frequently attended Kamiyama's games. As it turned out, Kamiyama's parents were widely known in the J-League community. Her father co-ran an organization that trained and scheduled referees for the J-Leagues, and her mom was a powerhouse player in the Southern California Women's Athletic Union (SCWAU). Kamiyama's mother was famous for loving the game so much that she once played in the league for several months while pregnant. This led to Ed Takahashi instituting a new rule that prohibited playing while pregnant, although the league leader seemed more proud of her stubbornness than the new rule implies. Sadly, Kamiyama's mom passed away during her first year at Chapman, and she tore her anterior cruciate ligament twice during her college career. The community was really eager to see her succeed given these tough turns. Even so, these circumstances do not entirely explain her following—the enthusiasm was clearly also due to her talent. I was able to see her play once at Chapman and another few times in a coed community league game, and at two tournaments—she did not disappoint. Despite her injuries, Kamiyama was quick and excelled as a ball-handler. Her shooting from behind the three-point line was also impressive. While at Chapman she broke the school record for career three-pointers and assists.

For Kamiyama, her J-League social capital not only led her to a spot on the women's basketball team at Chapman, but also helped her to acquire status as a community icon. Her parents' connections helped to build a buzz about her, and many J-League participants took note and began to attend her games and read about her in *Rafu Shimpo*. She was able to translate this experience and her degree into a high school coaching position.

In another flexing of the muscle of symbolic capital, Japanese American organizations help to publicize successful players who are current or former members. For Mas, who is involved with one of the big Japanese American sport organizations, this connection is his primary source of pride: "Occasionally in our newsletter, they'll mention a player who's doing well at a certain college. That just—I think that's like any organization, to be proud of having a member do well." LeeAnne Sera (USC, 1983–1984) described her feelings about the support and acknowledgment from both the "community" and a particular Japanese American organization, the Zebras:

> As far as the community, I'm still . . . especially when I moved home, where I grew up. . . . I always just in general felt a lot of support from the people here. I guess it's just helped the kids to know it can be done. And I talk to-I was asked to speak to teams and to tell my experience, talk to them as a guest speaker. . . . The organization I played for up here is called the San José Zebras. They have a tournament every year . . . and they talk about the history of the Zebras. I'm the first mentioned in the history of the Zebras. They talk about how many of the players have gone on to play at higher levels, where I went to USC and won the national championships. . . . I would realize later that a lot of the younger kids coming up after me who played for the Zebra organization . . . they felt that I was someone to follow, that I was a role model. If I did it, it can be done. So, it gives them incentive to try; it's something to reach for.

Sera enjoyed recognition as part of the history of the Zebras organization. The organization utilized its successful members as symbolic resources to encourage youth coming up in the organization.

MEANINGS SURROUNDING FEMALE ICONS

Public appearances and newspaper articles help to feed the Japanese American community's appetite for appealing images of Japanese American success and help to co-create the iconic status of many of the Japanese American women who play college and professional basketball. These are stars whom people can reach out and touch, as many in the community feel that they know them through family, playing, or other community connections. Little girls want to hug them and get their autograph. The more that the women give interviews and volunteer their time at events, the more celebrity and esteem they gain for giving back to the community.

Given the clear sense of pride and ownership many in the community have for the players who have been successful in the mainstream, what can we make of the fact that most of these players are female? In the following section, I discuss some of the gendered meanings behind the players' iconic status and also share some of the ways that J-League participants make sense of the greater successes and attention given to female athletes.

During my interviews, I asked several questions to try to understand how the participants in J-League basketball viewed the success of Japanese Americans in college basketball. With the same intent, I also analyzed articles about the star players in *Rafu Shimpo*. Prominent themes that emerged in interviews and content analysis included Japanese American pride (racial/ethnic, community, or organization/league), overcoming obstacles, role models/good girls, and discussions of women being more successful than men.

"Little Dynamos"—Overcoming Obstacles

One way that community members and journalists articulated the pride and esteem felt for the female basketball icons was through a narrative of overcoming obstacles (Willms 2014). Debbie noted, "People assume that Japanese Americans can't play basketball and especially when you see these girls, they are so little. Some of them are barely five feet one, five feet two and yet they are little dynamos." In this depiction, the women's successes in mainstream basketball were all the more remarkable because they represent accomplishments in the face of adversity. Although being female is in some ways thought by many in the J-Leagues to be an advantage in terms of one's chances of competing in the mainstream, it is also seen as the ultimate marker of an underdog status in mainstream basketball. If Japanese Americans saw themselves as small, Japanese American women represent the smallest members of the community. In a game where height is considered a major advantage, Japanese American female success is interpreted as a great accomplishment.

To what extent is the women's status as underdogs key to their popularity as community figures? Wang (2016) argues that the painting of Taiwanese American Jeremy Lin as an "underdog" was part of his appeal: "We champion underdogs not just to see them beat the odds but to see them overcome some kind of injustice that explains those odds. The underdog is an implicitly aggrieved actor, someone who has been treated unfairly and, therefore, their struggle to succeed is inherently redemptive, rather than just statistically unlikely" (79). Wang concludes, however, that "these stories merely reify a familiar, conservative worldview of American meritocracy and exceptionalism" (80).

Small size became a prominent symbol of disadvantage in the *Rafu Shimpo* features, particularly for the female players (Willms 2014). Many feature stories about Japanese American female athletes engaged with a narrative of overcoming obstacles, where against all odds, the small heroine proved herself in the face of adversity—against the "giants" present in the world of mainstream basketball. This theme was more common in features about female players. While female players' heights were almost always included in feature stories, male players' heights were seldom included (Willms 2014).

Role Models/Good Girls

Many members of the Japanese American communities select college- and professional-level players to include in public forums in large part to provide visible role models for the youth of the community. As role models, they are lauded not only for their basketball talent, but also for possessing good character and for giving back to the community. Along these same lines, the Japanese American press often highlights the players' academic abilities and community service (Willms 2014). It is the players who meet these standards who appear to be the most adored as "ideal citizens" of the community.

It may be that this image of "ideal citizen" is a vital ingredient to the female icon's appeal. Like other women who have become symbols of Japanese American communities, such as community pageant contestants, they are seen as "nice girls" (Willms 2014; Yano 2006). A few of my interviewees spoke about the women college-level players in ways that acknowledged not only their athletic abilities, but also other attributes as students, family members, and community members. For example, when I asked Bob about J-League athletes who went on to play in college, he spoke about two female players whom he and his family were keeping an eye on: "Both of them were in clinics through this organization that we play with and I've seen them both play, and you can just see the fiery edge and where they are. And they're good students, too. They're really good students, and just good kids—always come home, take care of mom, and see what the mom's doing. You know, really family-orientated. So, I know they're well grounded, which probably helps in their studies and in their sports life quite a bit." As he hints, many of the players who have local fame run basketball camps and clinics targeted at Japanese American youth. So, right away they earn esteem by giving back to the community. Moreover, Bob emphasizes the players' status as "good kids" who are family-oriented and do well in school. Bob could feel good about exposing his daughters to these women and encouraging them to learn from their example. One of the organizers of the Nikkei Games spoke about the opening ceremonies where he invites prominent Japanese Americans (athletes and coaches, but also other professionals) to give short talks to the kids and families in attendance:

> I've gotten a lot of emails from parents giving me feedback about our guest speakers and how they really enjoyed them because some of the things they talk about . . . because audience for those opening ceremonies are the kids and they tend to be, oh, eleven years old and younger. . . . Those parents, you know, really enjoy the speakers, because they're tremendous role models. Yeah, we have coaches come . . . successful players . . . that come and speak, but they're more role models talking about the importance of giving it their all,

you know, working hard, developing strong work ethic, and talking about the importance of school.

Although not speaking directly to just female players, he echoes some of the values and traits that are important to the community when considering whom to invite to speak at events such as the Nikkei Games. Often, the female players embody these values and traits and are therefore selected for appearances at tournaments and other community events.

Leaders and parents spoke most often about the off-court attributes of the female athletes, but some younger interviewees did point to their peers as both top-level athletes and quality people. For instance, Grace, thirty, talked about an SCWAU teammate who had played college basketball: "She's great, because one . . . she's one of the top players in our league. She's just a great person. She teaches PE right around here now. She coaches at [names school]; she's been coaching there for years. She's really involved in the whole community."

It feels good to have role models who also possess good character and who are down-to-earth and accessible. The community produced an image of the Japanese American female basketball players that matched these expectations and rewarded those who most fit the description with newspaper coverage, guest appearances, and a loyal following.

Resistant Capital

Even if to some extent the symbol of the successful female basketball player was taken up as a gendered community symbol, as a good girl, there was also a concurrent discourse of empowerment. In this discourse, the female basketball icons were breaking down barriers and dismantling stereotypes. The symbolic capital of the female athletic icon emerged in part as resistant capital (Yosso 2005), from her power to resistant dominant narratives about Japanese Americans.

Other communities of color have invested in women as resistors (Robinson and Ward 1991; Villenas and Moreno 2001; Ward 1996, as cited in Yosso 2005). Young women learned "to be oppositional with their bodies, minds and spirits in the face of race, gender, and class inequality" (Yosso 2005, 81). For most Japanese Americans, race and gender inequalities may be more common problems than economic struggles in their lives. Japanese Americans, on average, are less likely to be facing poverty than many other ethnic communities of color—8.2 percent reside below the poverty line (2007–2011 American Community Survey as cited in Macartney, Bishaw, and Fontenot 2013). However, in their struggles for both acceptance and upward social mobility, many Japanese Americans have felt the sting of racism resulting in a desire to push forward prominent figures whose successes contradict the falsehoods present in controlling images about Asians in general and Japanese Americans in particular.

One of the more prominent symbols of basketball success, Natalie Nakase, talked about why she thought Japanese Americans loved basketball so much. She saw resistance behind their passion: "I think part of it is because it's starting to be, again, like a sport where it's very popular and to where you can kind of just be crazy, you're not—like, say, golf or something or tennis, it's kind of more a quiet sport and very respectful and very appropriate. Basketball is just like, you let loose and you can be whoever you want to be and no one will really judge you. You just kind of play. I think that's where the Japanese community is turning a little bit. I think it's really trying to get away from the stereotypes." For Nakase, playing basketball was a way that she symbolically broke through stereotypes.

What Is a Heroine?

When a Japanese American succeeds, pride still reverberates through the modern ethnic community. Tears filled one participant's eyes when he related a story about a Japanese American being appointed as a federal judge. Another remembered getting excited when a local fishing prize went to a Japanese American sport fisherman. In this vein, it is perhaps not unexpected that those Japanese Americans who have excelled in mainstream basketball have enjoyed a devoted following. Even so, during the time of my research, I was astonished by the level of visibility and reverence many of the Japanese American college-level players received. Heroines may be particularly difficult to define:

> A culture is remembered for its heroes and heroines, and sport constructs them and influences our perceptions of them continuously. In popular consciousness, heroes and heroines are men and women who are "larger than life," "inspirational icons," special people with extraordinary qualities that are constructed and represented in particular ways to encourage us to admire and idealize them. In other words, heroes and heroines are socially constructed through discourses and meanings and values that change over time. But heroes are more easily defined than heroines and there is greater social importance attributed to the production and celebration of male heroism. (Hargreaves 2002, 1)

Overwhelmingly, though, the shining stars for contemporary Japanese Americans are women athletes. These athletes, as role models and symbols of what is possible, have helped provide ideological support for the gender-inclusive structure of the J-Leagues. They have also become symbolic of the aspirations of the community as a whole, solidifying the connections between Japanese American ethnic identity, basketball, and the female basketball player as icon.

Heroes versus Heroines

Does it matter that this mainstream athletic success is achieved by women more often than by men? It is likely that a male basketball star would be a dream come true for many Japanese Americans, and that the right player in the right situation might enjoy more esteem and renown than the current female icons. For one thing, men's college and professional basketball occupies a space at the center of American sports (Messner 2002). Access to this space carries more mainstream social and symbolic currency, and therefore might mean more in terms of cultural citizenship and access to more forms of dominant cultural capital. The popularity of Jeremy Lin, the Asian American NBA player of Taiwanese descent, among

Asian American groups, and certainly many Japanese Americans, lends credence to this idea. In addition, a male figure might do more to recuperate the masculine status lost to racist controlling images of Asian American men (Thangaraj 2015).

Nevertheless, with some exceptions, most J-League participants spend very little time dwelling on what is not currently occurring (i.e., the dream of a top men's college or NBA player of Japanese ancestry trained in the J-Leagues), and more time on embracing the J-League women making exciting inroads to top-level college programs and knocking on the doors of professional play. They have found a niche in women's basketball and made many community investments to build ever more successes in this field, in part eschewing the mainstream focus on men's basketball.

It may be that the masculine cultural space represented by high-level basketball competition can be permeated by female actors with similar meanings attached. For example, Konagaya (2005) found that taiko, a very physical and powerful form of Japanese drum performance, became popular among Japanese Americans in the United States beginning in the late 1960s. He viewed this resurgence of the cultural form as "responding to both the need to build Japanese identity . . . and a perception that popular culture portrayed Japanese men as silent subdued, and studious . . . taiko performances became locations to negotiate between the ethnic and popular cultures an evolving conveyable sense of masculinity among Japanese American men" (134–35). Konagaya viewed participation in taiko as a performance of masculinity. However, complicating the issue, he found that after taiko's initial resurgence in the 1960s, the drumming became increasingly popular among women who now outnumber men as participants. He described this transformation: "Women's participation in leading and supporting taiko groups has been essential to the making of a Japanese American taiko tradition and to the maintenance of community ties. . . . There is a sense among leaders of the taiko movement that the revival of taiko in America required the participation of women if it was to be successful in rallying the whole community around a cultural tradition" (147–148). Just as I have argued about the J-Leagues, Konagaya observed that participation by women was a key strength of the activity in its potential for community building.

A final, overarching claim by Konagaya may be the most relevant; he argued that the masculinity embedded in the performance of taiko was more important than the gender of the performers. "The manliness in the performances could be interpreted as emboldening Japaneseness and not just the egos of men" (148). For Japanese Americans, then, it may be powerful to see one of their own participate and succeed in a masculinized space of cultural citizenship. Success in this area by any member of the community—man or woman—confirms a sense of belonging and a counternarrative to dominant constructions of Asian Americans.

THE SYMBOLIC CAPITAL
OF WOMEN'S BASKETBALL

The women who have become basketball icons for Japanese Americans are able to enjoy a certain status and reap certain rewards for themselves, as individuals, as well as for Japanese Americans as a group, due to the relative visibility of their achievements. In other words, they possess symbolic capital (Bourdieu 1989). Yet, how can we understand the nature of this form of capital?

Using critical race theory, Yosso (2005) suggests that marginalized communities have their own unique forms of capital that may be transgressive or unrecognized by mainstream society, but still yield positive outcomes for group members. In a discussion of forms of capital that may be unique or uniquely understood by a marginalized racial or ethnic group, Yosso does not address symbolic capital, perhaps because Bourdieu defines it as an outgrowth of other forms of capital. It is "the form that the various species of capital assume when they are perceived and recognized as legitimate" (Bourdieu 1989, 17). Once a person has made some achievement or gain in a form of capital, she or he is rewarded with prestige, or "symbolic capital."

Using Yosso's theory (2005), one could argue that symbolic capital built on community cultural wealth would not necessarily yield benefits in a conventional way. It might not be exchanged readily for other forms of mainstream capital or directly rewarded by the dominant culture. However, it might be experienced as rewarding and empowering by the marginalized community, even in the absence of mainstream legitimacy, or indirectly lead to positive outcomes.

Symbolic capital in women's basketball may straddle these two theories of capital. On the one hand, achievement in women's basketball has some degree of mainstream legitimacy and can translate into symbolic capital recognized outside of the community. On the other hand, this mainstream recognition may be limited due to the marginalization of women's basketball. It is more difficult—as I will discuss in more detail in the next chapter—to leverage athletic symbolic capital as a female basketball player and particularly so when you possess a racialized, gendered body that is not recognized as the ideal sporting body.

Despite the challenges in the mainstream, achievement in women's basketball can lead to status and accolades within the Japanese American community. Furthermore, it helps produce the unique community cultural wealth (Yosso 2005) made possible by the J-Leagues: a gender-inclusive sporting environment, ethnic pride, and community engagement. Successful female athletes are more easily able to capitalize on their symbolic capital within the community, and the community mobilizes this fame toward its community projects.

Becoming a college-level player can translate into many positive outcomes in mainstream environments. It can provide access to higher education and can lead to job opportunities for those players who have pursued coaching or professional sports, even in hard-to-access spaces such as the NBA. Inside of the community, however, this status creates a wealth of community resources. College-level players can use their status within the community to gain economic capital: several of the women have earned money through coaching, training, and hosting clinics and camps. Their status also brings them a lot of subcultural symbolic capital: glory and adoration, coverage in community publications, and requests for public appearances. To many of the youth especially, these women are heroines. The community in turn consumes the symbolism of their success.

CONCLUSION

How does a female sports figure become a valued icon? First, as with the gender-inclusive structure of the J-Leagues, the production and consumption of successful women basketball players seem to fulfill the goals of the community. For many Japanese Americans, community building and community (ethnic/racial) pride are viewed as paramount. If these goals can be fulfilled by looking to women as sports heroines, then these women's images will be the ones that community members create and consume.

This may be a parallel situation to female icons in the Olympics. At times, female athletes representing their country have received more media attention than is customary for women's athletics. In these cases, the goals of the nation (i.e., nationalism) provide the incentive to follow and cheer for female athletes. However, images and narratives surrounding the female athletic icon are often manipulated to support existing rhetoric, making them less subversive and reifying race, class, and gender stereotypes.

For women who represent a racial or ethnic community, most come to represent this "community" in some way, and media coverage specific to this community tends to embrace them. The few studies that have analyzed gendered sports media coverage by niche or racial- or ethnic-based media (Paraschak 1990; Williams 1987; Willms 2014; Yep 2009) all found similar trends of relatively respectful and ample coverage of female athletes. This trend spanned Native American, Latino, African American, and Asian American news sources. This does not mean that these niche presses did not also manipulate the images and narratives surrounding female athletes for the purpose of asserting a collective identity. What is different about the niche representations is that they subverted not only many ethnic/racial stereotypes, but also gender stereotypes. These niche media outlets portrayed a positive, respectful image that treated women very similarly to men, and avoided trivializing or marginalizing women athletes' accomplishments. We may be able to interpret this as a degree of solidarity between men and women within these groups producing a context where images of successful women bring pride to co-ethnics to a similar degree as those of successful men.

Second, the female icons from the J-Leagues are often viewed as having close connections to the community. These women are not untouchable stars, but seen as friends of friends, daughters of friends, extended family, and so on. In this way, J-League participants feel as if these successful athletes belong to the community. Speaking about the successful women can be a way to establish community connections, as many of my interviewees tried to establish a direct or indirect connection to one or more of the successful players. Enjoying their successes becomes a community and family activity. Family members enjoy clipping out articles in *Rafu Shimpo* and other newspapers and mailing them to the featured players. Other community members enjoy talking about the players and attending their games in groups. This closeness of icons may not be a crucial component in producing greater media attention for female athletes, since similar trends have been found in other niche or ethnic- or racial-based media.

Finally, the female icons seem to embody something that feels good to the community members and that may symbolize idealized aspects of J-League or Japanese American identity. The coverage of female basketball players in *Rafu Shimpo* is often respectful, but the successful players are honored not only for their athletic accomplishments, but also for their academic and civic achievements. In the Hawaiian Japanese American community, beauty pageant contestants portrayed the image of the "nice girl" that Yano (2006) argues is also an idealized image that the entire community has of itself. Similarly, the Japanese Americans depicted in *Rafu Shimpo* and spoken about by interviewees were often praised for their approachability and commitment to service in the community. The college and professional players were beloved not only because of their accomplishments, but because they remained active participants in the community and gave back through their appearances and other volunteer work.

5 · "YOU PLAY BASKETBALL?"

Ruling the Court as an Unexpected Athlete

During Jamie Hagiya's time at USC, she would sometimes work on her game by joining pickup games with mostly male players at the university gym. She shared with me that as a five-foot-four Japanese American woman she often got picked last for teams. One night she arrived at the game just as the last spot on the court had been secured. The tenth man, feeling generous, took a look at Hagiya and said, "I'll shoot you for it." Her eyes twinkled as she told me this portion of the story, her expression communicating what she would not say: with no defenders, she does not miss. "So, I got into that game," she said, smiling.

Hagiya's "gotcha" moment is probably familiar to many strong female athletes who venture into male-dominated sport spaces. However, listening to many Chinese and Japanese American women from the J-Leagues talk about playing in mainstream environments, they described ways that stereotypes associated with their Asian ancestry intersected with gender to influence their interactions in mainstream sport contexts. Asian American women's bodies, in particular, were taken up in the discourse as unnaturally small and unsuitable for engagements with basketball.

Sport gives salience to bodies and plays a part in symbolically "naturalizing" beliefs about racial and gender differences (Birrell and Cole 1990; Carrington and McDonald 2001). Scholars have suggested that, due to prevailing racialized imagery surrounding Asian Americans, their presence in sport is often perceived as anything from humorous novelty to paradoxical (King 2006, 2010; Yep 2012). It seems evident that part of Lin's climb to celebrity status in 2012 was due to how novel it was to see an Asian American basketball player on equal footing with white and African American stars (Wang 2016; Yep 2012). Deloria (2004) has suggested that we can interrogate moments when people or events emerge as surprising to better understand our cultural expectations and what they reveal about what is normalized and what is constructed as different or other.

Interviews with Lin indicate that he experiences real consequences to his unexpected identity as a competitive basketball player (Chu 2008; Leitch 2012). In his earlier career, he was continuously overlooked for collegiate and professional playing opportunities. He described hearing racial slurs from the opposing team players and fans and experiencing what could easily be labeled as racial microaggressions, or verbal slights and behaviors that communicate that a person, due to her or his perceived ethnic/racial identity, is different or unwelcome (Sue et al. 2007). For example, he has, on several occasions now, had trouble entering a professional team practice facility because he could not convince a gatekeeper that he was indeed a member of the NBA team. To quote a Tweet from Lin's Twitter account from September 12, 2015, "Went to the Hornets arena for 1st time and tried convincing security im a player. She said, 'what team?!?' lollll #everywhereigo #literally." Lin's status as an Asian American NBA player is viewed as so unusual, so unlikely, that security guards for his own team second-guess the possibility.

In ways very similar to those Lin has described, many of the J-League basketball players reported facing forms of subtle to overt discrimination. They often felt like they had to overcome stereotypes when playing, coaching, or even discussing basketball in mainstream environments. Both men and women J-League participants reported these kinds of experiences. In this chapter, however, I concentrate on the women's stories.

Women from the J-Leagues often enter mainstream basketball environments possessing high-level basketball skills and knowledge. Yet, they will frequently be seen as the least likely to possess these strengths. J-League women are also more likely than their male counterparts to be entering higher level playing environments, such as college or professional basketball. These are environments where the presence of Asian bodies might be most surprising or contested. Many young women also engaged with basketball in male-dominated sporting environments, perhaps emboldened by the mutual respect between men and women in the J-Leagues.

In these elite or male-dominated spaces, J-League women found that they embodied an intersection of multiple identities perceived as incongruent with basketball. They are female, racially categorized as Asian, and often perceived as smaller in stature than a typical basketball player. In the masculine, race-conscious sports world, they possess dissonant bodies. They were consistently reminded of this through interactions with those who expressed surprise or took it upon themselves to point out the reasons why the women did not fit in. As women who were accustomed to ruling the court, they now faced the challenge of representing the unlikeliest of athletes.

CHALLENGES TO THE DISSONANT BODY: DOING POWER IN BASKETBALL THROUGH MICROAGGRESSIONS

Sporting spaces are often reserved for certain types of bodies (Brown 2015) in a way that preserves essentialized notions about gender and race. Gender and racial ideologies are often confusing, contradictory, and hotly contested in other spaces, but sport remains an arena that is often falsely assumed to offer meritocratic, objective, and unfiltered information about which bodies are the most capable. The prevailing logic is that we know who is good at basketball simply by seeing who rises to the top. Very little critical thinking is applied to considering the influences of a multitude of social forces on sport achievement.

Men's basketball occupies a contemporary position in US society at the center of sport (Messner 2002). Men's college and professional basketball leagues draw large audiences and big profits. The standards and symbols of these institutions tend to resonate throughout many contexts of basketball participation. "Real" basketball is often associated solely with the men's game (Kian, Vincent, and Mondello 2008; Shakib and Dunbar 2002). The players embody hegemonic masculinity, an idealized manhood that grants legitimacy to male privileges and dominance (Connell 2005). Certain male bodies become hegemonic because they persuade themselves and others of their dominance. Sport becomes the symbolically meritocratic space where they can continue to confirm this dominance by demonstrating their superior performances and abilities. This space must then be protected—if marginalized groups begin to occupy sporting spaces as equals, it disrupts the natural, commonsense narratives about which bodies are superior.

Sport becomes a site for producing power (Foucault 1977) by normalizing the distinctions and hierarchies between men and women and between differently racialized bodies. Sport spaces often produce discourses, or the logics of power, that encourage us to place race and gender distinctions in the category of common sense. So, if large men of European and African descent are the normalized, hegemonic images that define the ideal basketball player, Asian American women are "illegible" (Puwar 2004)—they just do not make sense. There is often no need to enact rules or to be forceful in excluding groups perceived to not belong because it is in many ways more powerful to just to invoke reminders, make mention of what is supposed to be. Even better is to convince those holding the marginalized bodies that they are deficient, rare exceptions, or that they have overcome "natural" barriers to their success.

These dominant understandings about who possesses the "right" kind of body for basketball influence interactions for Asian American female players. When J-League women enter mainstream spaces and present themselves as basketball players, they often elicit reactions that represent a range of gender and racial microaggressions. No matter how subtle, unintentional, or well-meaning, these microaggressions carry strong messages: you are different; you do not belong. Although microaggressions are powerful in that they can often cause psychological harm to those on the receiving end (Sue et al. 2007), they also have another level of social power. They do the work of confirming what is normal and what is not; they pass along understandings of who belongs and who does not as if it is common sense.

Microaggressions are words and actions that produce power (Foucault 1977), as they reify the dominant images and discourses inscribed on marginalized bodies and reconfirm the space of basketball as reserved for hegemonic male bodies. Foucault (1977) argues that the discourse works to normalize relations of power. Even members of the group experiencing the exclusion or subordination will often engage in reifying the discourse because it becomes constructed as common sense (183). For Foucault, power produces ways of knowing; it gives us knowledge and information about what is acceptable or unacceptable.

In American culture, it is seen as common sense that the "best," most authentic basketball is played by muscular and extremely tall white and African American men. Asian American bodies in sport contexts are already often imagined as feminized bodies invading a highly masculine space. Asian American female bodies may be interpreted as even further outside of the range of normalcy in a competitive basketball environment, and especially in male-dominated spaces.

In many ways the discourse could be interpreted as protecting the hegemonic masculine signifiers associated with basketball. Many basketball environments become reserved for those who confirm the hegemonic masculine practice and imagery of the sport. If female or feminized bodies are permitted to enter the basketball arena on equal footing with men who fit the hegemonic ideal, this disrupts the symbolic power of basketball in its associations with hegemonic masculinity.

There is not necessarily always formal, or even de facto, exclusion, but it is important to interrogate why people often feel compelled to engage in microaggressions toward Asian American athletes. Many everyday interactions, not to mention media portrayals, perpetually call attention to Asian Americans' presence in sport as surprising, express doubt in the players' abilities, or trivialize Asian American engagement with sport—these are all ways of doing power by normalizing hegemonic male dominance in sport.

Puwar (2004) has argued that certain spaces are reserved for privileged men and that people of color and women of color in particular navigating these spaces may feel like space invaders. They will be treated in ways that communicate their outsider status, in ways that assume they are not the norm. Similar to how Deloria (2004) theorized the concept of the "unexpected," Puwar (2004) critically assesses the social actors who are assumed to own or occupy a space and how othered groups become constructed as interlopers.

Puwar's (2004) ideas are applicable to men and women of color in sporting spaces, especially those spaces that are elite or most associated with men and masculinity (Adjepong and Carrington 2014; Brown 2015). Gendered racist stereotypes that could be described as controlling images (Collins 2002) influence women of color in these sporting spaces. Adjepong and Carrington (2014) suggest that "controlling images serve to discipline black women, who are perceived to transgress on the sporting field" (170). For African American women, controlling images create a contradiction between their female bodies and the gendered racism that depicts them as more masculine and physically capable than white women. For Asian American women, the controlling images almost entirely line up in the "unathletic" camp—if the idealized athletic body is large and powerful, stereotypes of Asian American women as small and dainty are antithetical to this image. The film archetype of the female martial artist is an intriguing exception, but even these bodies are not typically depicted as tall or overly muscular. In the American imaginary, Asian American women are therefore unexpected athletes.

Our expectations, Deloria argues, are formed through power relations that have shaped the way that marginalized and oppressed groups are viewed by the dominant culture. These controlling images depict the marginalized group as different and inferior and limit opportunities for self-definition. The controlling images and discourses become enactments of power embedded in the culture. Using Foucault's definition of power, these discourses emerge as common sense, so that even those who do not benefit from the power that they create may reproduce them in interactions (Foucault 1977). In today's world, the enactment of power must live in the realm of common sense, in the quiet of "new racism" (Bonilla-Silva 2006). It often emerges in the form of microaggressions. Oftentimes very subtle words and behaviors communicate messages about belonging and difference.

THE SYMBOLIC CAPITAL OF WOMEN'S BASKETBALL: OUTSIDE THE J-LEAGUES

For a great many Japanese Americans in California, carrying the identity of "basketball player" is part of normalized, even idealized community citizenship. And being a "great basketball player" or "college basketball player" has the potential to elevate someone to community icon. Associations with basketball achievement, as discussed in chapter 4, are subcultural symbolic capital. The names of successful athletes are passed around in conversation and the athletes are featured in community publications. Athletes are invited as special guests and speakers at events, helping to both (re)create and capitalize on their subcultural celebrity.

In many mainstream contexts, however, the symbolic capital of "basketball player" is mediated by membership in ascribed social groupings of race and gender. Even an excellent women's basketball player of Asian American descent is likely fairly invisible to the wider society. If you are not Japanese American, and you picked up this book knowing nothing about Jamie Hagiya or Natalie Nakase before you began reading, it would not be very surprising given this context.

For many J-League female participants, asserting themselves as highly skilled basketball player in mainstream environments could be difficult. Outside of the J-Leagues, women's basketball talent and knowledge were no longer expected, but instead met with skepticism. All levels of players felt the need to prove themselves, starting at square one with people they met outside of the J-League community.

In addition, achieving in a mainstream basketball environment as a woman also did not always translate to symbolic capital the players could use in other contexts. The women's college basketball players were not always recognized by professors or students on their campuses. Because women's collegiate basketball is marginalized in many contexts, participation in a women's sport would probably not be considered social or symbolic capital as defined by Bourdieu because it does not necessarily facilitate access to rewards in mainstream contexts. Instead, it was much more translatable into community subcultural capital.

FEMALE × RACE × SIZE = THE TRIPLE THREAT?

In basketball, a "triple threat" is when a player with the ball assumes a stance conducive to three possible moves: a shot, drive, or pass. The goal is to be the ultimate offensive threat—capable of overcoming the defense and scoring in any number of ways. Two J-League players, Melissa and Jessica, both described three factors that created a "triple threat" to achieving recognition as a basketball player in contexts outside of the J-Leagues. Melissa explained, "I guess if I'd go to the gyms, or even at the park, I used to play at the park. One, yeah, you're Japanese. Two, you're short. Three, you're a female." Similarly, Jessica recalled, "When I bring up playing basketball when I'm at work, like I just talk to patients, if I bring up I play basketball, automatically I think they assume that I don't [play], maybe because I'm Japanese, because I'm a girl, because I'm short. I don't know what." Outsiders appear to perceive three aspects that they embody—race/ethnicity, gender, and size (short)—as incongruent with basketball. Rather than an intentional move to confuse the defense, these women present a different kind of "threat": an embodied, multifaceted challenge to societal expectations and the normalized, hegemonic imagery associated with basketball. The intersection of these three embodied traits constructs a sporting space invader (Brown 2015). Together they represent the threat of a particular body—one that is highly feminized in the cultural imagery—invading a masculine space.

Aware that several of their identities or characteristics make them an unlikely basketball player, the women are sometimes left wondering what exactly produced the response. Melissa seems to feel all three factors—her ethnicity, size, and gender—play a role in how she is treated when she plays in pickup games at the park or gym. Jessica has narrowed it down to the same three possibilities, but is unsure which of these factors is standing out to her patients. The individuals expressing surprise may not even fully understand their own reactions. Several interviewees told me that they had confronted disbelievers, asking why they did not expect them to be a basketball player, only to receive an ambiguous response: "you just don't seem like the type." When pressed, the surprised individual usually could not or would not explain further.

Microaggressions reflect underlying assumptions in our culture that are often unspoken or covert. They are often difficult to address because they are veiled as harmless or unintentional. Their power "lies in their invisibility to perpetrators and oftentimes the recipients" (Sue 2010, 6). Microaggressions can produce power, reifying oppressive discourses and reinforcing "commonsense" assumptions and stereotypes (Foucault 1977). Many of the women I interviewed quickly dismissed interactions that involved microaggressions as harmless or painted them in a positive light. Often, comments that revealed surprise or disbelief emerged out of playful dialogue. Women sometimes enjoyed or took advantage of others' expectations, because they could easily put others in their place with a few good moves on the court. Regardless of how harmless it seems, however, the discourse still creates a certain common sense about whose bodies belong in the sporting context.

"Basketball Definitely Isn't Their First Assumption"

Given the controlling images of Asian American women and the triple threat of athletic otherness, it might be predicted that any performance of athleticism on the part of Asian American women would be met with disbelief. According to the stories of my interviewees, their athleticism did commonly pique the interest of onlookers. However, a new set of negotiations occurred. Once aware of the women's athletic inclinations—if not through conversation, sometimes due to sport attire—it seems that many people felt compelled to guess a sport that seemed height-, gender-, and race-appropriate. For example, Nancy, a former college-level player and coach, finds that people can envision her as an athlete, but not as involved with basketball: "Because I don't have that look of a basketball player. So, yeah, normally you'd see people out or people you don't know and they'd say: 'You kind of look like an athlete, you know.' 'Yeah, I am.' And so the first sport they pick is volleyball. . . . 'Oh you play volleyball?' 'No.' . . . 'Or you play tennis? Or you run track or something?' 'No, basketball.' And they're like, 'Oh yeah? Really? You're too short!' . . . They never pick out basketball." Instead of asking "What sports are you involved in?" Nancy's new acquaintances seem to want to fumble through a list of sports that feel like a comfortable match with the racialized and gendered body in front of them. Then, when basketball is announced, they feel compelled to comment on Nancy's body size as way to challenge her right to claim space in the world of basketball.

The exchange seems to indicate that Asian American female athleticism evokes a degree of curiosity, but the claims to basketball create an even higher level of protectionist discourse. Nancy recollects that people have often shared with her that it was a struggle to believe that she was a collegiate basketball player and coach. This suggests that basketball has a particular symbolism difficult to reconcile with the controlling images associated with being an Asian American woman. It also suggests it is a space reserved for men associated with hegemonic masculinity, propped up by a commonsense discourse. Nancy even internalizes that she does not "have that look of a basketball player." Basketball—one of the sports at the center of men's dominance in sport (Messner 2002)—may be one of the spaces more symbolically protected from "feminized" invaders (Puwar 2004). As Asian American women are seen as hyperfeminine, people feel the need to do power to reestablish the unlikelihood of a female Asian American excelling in a masculinized sport.

Height plays an important role in this equation, but not always a logical one. Nancy remembers hearing people say "You're too short" as part of their comments, or microaggressions, about her career in basketball. However, height is generally thought of as an advantage in both volleyball and tennis, so it's far from an airtight argument. Volleyball and tennis may seem more likely because they are more comfortably associated with femininity (Hargreaves 2002). Again, it may be that people make sense of female Asian American athleticism, imaged as hyperfeminine, by attaching them to sports perceived as feminine.

Collegiate Players: Symbolic Capital, Symbolic Anomaly, or Symbolic Annihilation?

Playing college basketball is an accomplishment. US society tends to lionize men's Division I players, making them into celebrities (Adler and Adler 1991; Leonard 2014). However, for Chinese and Japanese American women who have made it to this level, they have experienced both hypervisibility, as onlookers took note of their supposed anomalous presence in basketball contexts, as well as invisibility. As women's college basketball players, they were not commonly well-known or recognized in the public sphere in the way that men's college basketball players may be.

Like Nancy, many of the other Japanese American college athletes had played the "what sport are you in" game. Megan, a

Japanese American who played for a Division III college in Southern California at the time of the interview, had several Asian Americans on her team. When I asked her if the team ever surprised anyone, she responded, "All the time! When we travel, everything other than basketball. It's like, 'Are you guys a swim team? Are you guys a volleyball—not a volleyball team, but a softball team?' I mean we get everything but basketball." For this team, wearing a warm-up suit in hotels, in restaurants, and around college campuses during their away-game trips meant a constant questioning of their status. Onlookers were often perplexed by a college basketball team with several Asian American players.

Even on their own campuses, Division I athletes in Southern California could not avoid people trying to make sense of their position on the basketball team:

> When I was walking around . . . campus, I would get stereotypes like, "You're on the gymnastics team?" Because I'm small and Asian. "You on the tennis team?" A lot of the athletes, we all have the same backpack, because we get free stuff, so you can tell the athletes from the students. And everybody's like, "Oh, what team are you on? Are you a gymnast?" "No." I was like, "I'm a basketball player," and they were like, "No, you're not." I get the whole, "No, you don't." Or if I even— when I'm dressing, I'll usually put on my clothes, and everyone's like, "Oh, you play soccer?" "No, guess again." No one has ever said basketball. It's kind of funny. When I said it, they were shocked. (Erika)

Erika felt that her size and race—"because I'm small and Asian"— led people to guess particular sports and to be "shocked" when she disclosed her position on the university basketball team. They even used language that further challenged her claims: "No, you don't." Producing power through microaggressions, many interactions involved a discourse that worked to reconfirm that Asian American women are unexpected athletes, and incomprehensible as college-level basketball players. Likewise, Kristen also played Division I basketball at one of the large universities in Southern California, and had similar experiences. She shared,

In athletics, everyone thinks I'm the manager or I do swimming? Everyone goes, "Oh, wow!" Because they expect a person—and I feel like when we go in the airports people think I'm the manager, because I'm around all these other tall, humongous people, and here I am. That's what I think. "I bet they think I'm the manager." But you kind of expect that, because I am on the team that's all black, basically, and I'm here, and people probably—there are a lot of Asians on other teams, like gymnastics and swimming and tennis. I think track has a few. So people think that I'm in one of those sports and not basketball. Basketball definitely isn't their first assumption. (Kristen)

Kristen describes two of the commonsense assumptions about basketball that she disrupts: basketball players are "tall, humongous people" and may be (without any surprise) black Americans. On a team that mostly conforms to these characteristics, she has experienced others' reactions that implicitly question her claims to a place on this team. Erika and Kristen can be on their own campus, surrounded by their team, or wearing the team gear, signaling their relationship to basketball, but still receive comments that question or even dispute their claims to basketball. Kristen had internalized these perceptions and now assumed onlookers singled her out from the rest of the team.

These interactions also permeated the academic realm. Rebecca played on a Division I championship team in California, but still had trouble getting professors to acknowledge her status as a varsity athlete: "I think in general they didn't care that much. It was a big enough school where you don't really know a lot of the professors, especially your freshman and sophomore year because you're in large classes. . . . I had a couple of professors who found out and they were sort of surprised. 'Gosh, you don't look like a basketball player.' [laughs] They didn't give me a break." For Rebecca, the implications of people not recognizing her as a college-level basketball player extended to her academics. She felt that professors were not as aware of her needs as a student-athlete, so it was more difficult to make up work when she was unable to attend class due to her sports schedule. Since her team went all the way to the championship game two years in a row, she missed a lot of classes—and yet, she could not mobilize her symbolic capital as a member of this prestigious team in the ways in which a more recognizable basketball body might have been able.

For women of Asian descent, asserting a claim to "college basketball player" was more difficult and elicited reactions of surprise or disbelief. The cultural symbolism of "college basketball player" seemed to be reserved for white and African American male bodies—other bodies making claims to this status had to be called out in some way. Asian American women's claims to this symbolic capital (Bourdieu 1984), as hyperfeminized bodies, seemed to elicit a lot of commentary and challenge. Meanwhile, the athletes were not entirely protected by the status and prestige of being on a collegiate basketball team. The typical student or professor with whom the athletes came into contact were not always aware of who was on the women's basketball team. The marginalization of women's sports meant a degree of invisibility that ironically led the athletes to constantly have to explain themselves and their status as part of everyday interactions.

These women's experiences on their own campuses not only show how "basketball player" is racialized and gendered, but also demonstrate how invisible they were on campus as scholarship women's basketball players. One could not imagine that a male scholarship player would have to answer similar questions or face doubts about his role on campus. On most campuses, women's basketball does not get the same fanfare, publicity, and media attention as men's basketball. So, the team is often subject to forms of erasure (Kane 1995) as their play is not recognized or publicized to the extent that men's basketball often is.

Microaggressions and the Asian Female Body

In contexts where Asian American players were already known as basketball players, this did not stop onlookers from focusing on their perceived paradoxical status. Often the interactions involved an almost obsessive focus on the Asian female body as small. These microaggressions worked to other these bodies, reminding the athletes and others involved in the interactions that Asian American female bodies not only were different and exotic (Le Espiritu 2008), but also did not belong on the basketball context. The focus on smallness produced power by reifying the discourse that only hegemonic male bodies could make real, authentic claims to basketball.

One environment where layers of othering occurred was in the intimacy of team relations. Most of the women described their university teammates' behavior toward them as funny or good-natured teasing, but they still carried messages about difference. A lot of the focus of the teasing involved body size. For example, Kelly, a Japanese American Division I player in Southern California, was given the nickname "Little Tokyo" by her teammates, referencing her ethnicity and the neighborhood in Los Angeles, but also calling attention to her size. Kristen, also a Japanese American Division I player in Southern California, shared that race or ethnicity came up regularly on her university team:

It's just funny, like, they push everything into the "Asian" category. One girl thought I was Chinese until last month. [laughs] And then it gets brought up for jokes. Not mean, but that's the thing they can point me out on. It's kind of—it makes me—it's funny, because I'm unique, and that's what they're gonna pick me out for. Because I have small feet. They're all like, "Your feet are so small. How do you balance?" My favorite one was—they're so weird—they're talking about if everyone on our team was a cookie, what kind of cookie would they be? So, of course I was the fortune cookie.

Although Kristen claimed these remarks are "not mean," that she can list the occasions when her race or ethnicity came up suggests that they may have stung more than she would like to admit. Microaggressions can often be seen as harmless, but they still do power and carry powerful messages about belonging.

The racial microaggressions that Kristen experienced included comments about her body size. She brought this topic up again at another point in the interview: "I have the smallest hands. I don't know what that implies. And like I said, my feet are small, so I get the smallest shoes. 'Your feet are so small! What size is that?'" From Kristen's stories, it sounded like her feet and hand size had become a reoccurring joke on the team. Teammates asked ridiculous questions like "How can you balance?" These are microaggressions that communicate that Kristen's Asian body is different or exotic—to the point of asserting that it must not function correctly.

As Asian American women are often racialized as small and dainty, the focus on body size is an engagement with these controlling images. As discussed, it also produces power about which bodies belong in sport. Height is the common "go-to" microaggression that my participants spoke about, but Kristen's experience is interesting. Since Kristen was not the shortest player on her team, her teammates seem to have taken up other parts of her body to focus on: her feet and hands. I asked Kristen why her size was a focus of team conversations when, at five foot eight, she was not that short. She rationalized that it was her "proportions," not just her height, that made her unique. Many of the college-level players I spoke with were shorter than the average collegiate women's basketball player, so calling attention to their height became an easy way to mark difference. However, Kristen's experience shows that even a somewhat larger Asian body is inscribed with smallness. If a Japanese American woman was not the shortest on the team, players found a way to still mark her as small, emphasizing and amplifying the ways that Asian American bodies are viewed as space invaders in basketball.

Overt Racism

A few J-League participants playing with women in mainstream contexts experienced even more overt racism. Diane, Chinese American, is a current college basketball coach who played in college and also for many years in the J-Leagues, Chinese Leagues, and Parks and Recreation Leagues. She commented that she did not enjoy playing in the Rec Leagues as much as the Asian Leagues because, "A lot times they don't think Asians can play. And they get kind of rude. I got 'chink.'"

In some instances, my interviewees ventured out into mainstream play not alone, but as part of an Asian American team. When Asian American women played together, they sometimes experienced negative reactions from the opposing teams or onlookers. For example, Tammy said, "When we were playing, like, intramurals in college. You know how these girls are, they're like—because we were called 'The Orient Express'—so they were kind of making fun of us. But then we beat them." Tammy also had a story about playing in a three-on-three tournament sponsored by Foot Locker: "We ended up winning and we got to the Forum. . . . We were all Japanese, actually three Japanese and one Chinese. It was pretty fun, because we got that far. We played against some pretty good people getting to that point. You had to play all this regional stuff. So, when we played at the Forum—this was when Connie Chung was big—some guy goes, 'There's Connie Chung on the court,' meaning us!" Whether playing in intramural leagues in college or in a prestigious tournament, Tammy experienced jokes at her and her teammates' expense. When Asian Americans played together in mainstream contexts, this made their race more salient to others, who sometimes responded by making racist jokes and comments about them. By ending her first story with the phrase "but then we beat them," Tammy demonstrates her pride at having the opportunity to contest the racism and stereotypes vocalized by her onlookers and competitors.

Despite these stories, other players felt that women were more accepting of diversity on the court than men were. Lisa thought it would be men, not women, who might be surprised by her athleticism: "Among women, I rarely get a reaction of surprise. I believe that we are in a time where women of all nationalities are respecting the accomplishments of other women professionally and recreationally. I have played in leagues with my colleagues who I work with at school." For Lisa, women such as her work colleagues had not treated her any differently because of her race or ethnicity. In the multicultural environment of Los Angeles, it is perhaps not surprising that some of my participants did not have any stories of discrimination, especially when playing recreationally with other women. Playing in the mainstream with men was another story.

Interaction with Men

Talking to men not connected to the J-Leagues about basketball or treading into an-all male mainstream basketball playing environment carried a great deal of risk of facing doubt or ridicule as an Asian American female basketball player. Some of this involved challenges from men at school or work. Sandra, forty-nine, and Isabel, nineteen, are a mother and daughter who play on the same SCWAU league team together. When I asked them in a joint interview about anyone being surprised by their basketball abilities, there was clearly no generation gap in their experiences. Both women experienced not only surprise, but the desire of their male peers to challenge them to a game.

ISABEL: I get it so much, nothing really stands out—all their reactions are the same. Then they want to play against me, then they challenge me but I just never have the time to play them.

SANDRA: When I was younger, when I first started working . . . some of the guys were actually surprised that I did play and so forth, but yeah, because they're just like, "No way do you play." I said, "Come on, we'll just go play." So, they're really surprised that I can make baskets. I know what a lay-up is. . . . Then I had a couple of my Caucasian friends one day, you know, had said . . . "If you guys want to join us for a pickup game, you can." We're like, "Yeah, right, okay, whatever." And then we had Asian guys, basically coed. . . . They were astounded by all these Asian girls, women, and the guys who played ball as well as we did. They just didn't think of [us] having, you know, the skill sets because you never see an Asian that much even in the men's college ball, you never see an Asian ballplayer or anything like that, but he was just like, "Oh my God!" . . . The next day at work they're like, "Oh my God, your friends can play, too—you guys just tear up the court."

When they had shared with male peers that they played basketball, Sandra and Isabel experienced similar reactions—the men at first expressed surprise and then wanted to challenge them, perhaps to confirm that they were the superior players. The challenge itself, however, could be interpreted as a challenge to these women's claims to the basketball space. Isabel did not seem as interested in meeting the challenges or proving her abilities as her mother did. Sandra was able to demonstrate to her workmates that she was not alone in her basketball ability, but knew other Asian American men and women who were equally talented. Her workmates were astounded by their abilities. It appears that instead of her colleagues producing power by beating the Asian American "interlopers," Sandra and her friends actually disrupted the discourse by playing on equal footing with the male colleagues in her office.

Male-dominated sporting spaces sometimes have particular men acting as gatekeepers. In Los Angeles, pickup basketball is so popular, there are even gyms that have hired scorekeepers and referees for ostensibly casual pickup games. Erika, a former Division I college basketball player, had this confrontation while playing as the only woman in a refereed pickup game:

One incident, actually, it was pretty brutal. Some guys can just be really jerks. . . . We're going up and down the court, and I'm just—I just decide to set a screen for my friend . . . and this guy just completely runs me over. . . . The ref goes . . . "You can't just push her to the ground." He's going off like, "Are you f-ing kidding me? She shouldn't even be out here! She shouldn't be playing! Girls shouldn't be playing with guys!" [Later] I did it again, and this time he just took his hands and shoved me. He didn't even try to guard the guy, he just moved me out of the way. So the ref called another foul, and he just stopped the whole game. He was just like, "I'm not playing anymore! I can't play against this girl. First of all, she only weighs, like, ten pounds and . . . she just shouldn't be here. She's too small." He just said everything in the book you could possibly say. I just remember that incident. He started cussing and being really nasty towards me. I didn't do anything to the guy. . . . Usually I get some talk and stuff, but he was just taking it [to another level]. I was like, "I'm here to play. It's no big deal."

In this instance, Erika was completely rejected by a male player on the opposing team to the point that he treated her roughly, both physically and verbally. In Erika's recollection of the situation, this man had brought up two things that made her unsuitable for playing basketball: being a "girl" and being "too small." It this situation, Erika was not just telling someone that she played basketball, or having fun with coworkers, but actually trying to play on equal turf with men in a male-dominated space, which likely contributed to the more dramatic reaction. She had invaded a hegemonic masculine space.

Again, smallness played a role in how the Asian American female body was interpreted as unsuitable for the sporting environment. Although Erika did not mention race or ethnicity, Kristen's experience shared earlier, where teammates seemed obsessively focused on racializing the Asian body as small, indicates that race was probably intersecting with gender and body size in interpreting Erika's body as inappropriate. The male player who shoved her and verbally protested her presence on the court likely reacted to the intersection of her embodied characteristics, each heightening the saliency of the other. Her small stature also gave her adversary something to focus on in making a case for her expulsion from the game. Body size became a tool for a male player to try to protect the playing space from a feminized body, but he did not have to name race as a factor even if it was.

BODY SIZE

By suggesting a female by race by size intersectional analysis, I am, with caveats, suggesting that body size, especially height, emerges as a form of social categorization in the basketball context. However, it's more than that—size became a very important symbol with multifaceted meaning. As described in the past section, size took on meaning in many raced and gendered ways. People seemed to assume that Asian female bodies were small, even when they were average size. Maggie stated, "I think it's weird, it does come up. Because I'm short compared to—but for like Asians we're not short, we're like average height, but compared to other ethnicities we're considered short. So it's like, 'You play basketball?' Guys, maybe who aren't Japanese, they might say, 'Oh you play basketball?' To me it's like, 'Yeah, of course.' It's like kind of weird to hear that side." Small body size has symbolic connections to women. As such, body size has been a dominant way that men have been defined as superior to women in sport (Kane 1995). Small body size also has symbolic connections to people of Asian descent (Le Espiritu 2008). Participants seemed to experience an amplification effect—they were more saliently Asian, were more noticeably female, or were perceived as smaller than they really were—because of their embodiment of the three characteristics.

For Asian Americans in mainstream contexts, physical stature emerged as a significant mediating factor in basketball-related interactions. Because height is so salient to the basketball context, it became the language and symbol for negotiating gender and racial accountability. Moreover, discourse surrounding height appeared to act as a way of controlling female Asian bodies, reaffirming their status as unexpected and sometimes excluding them from sport spaces. In this way, height played a dual role: (1) smaller stature amplified the significance of the female or Asian body; and (2) discourses surrounding height and body size provided a rhetorical strategy for explaining or justifying the trivialization or exclusion of female Asian bodies.

Seeing through Raced/Gendered Glasses: "Seeing Small"

The amplification effect (race × gender × size), informed by gendered, racist controlling images and produced through discourses about which bodies belong in elite basketball, likely causes people to "see small" when they evaluate Asian American female basketball players. This may have caused some college and professional basketball coaches to disregard J-League athletes as potential players for their teams. King (2014, 3) analyzed a story about Chinese American football player Timmy Chang as an example of "the role of expectations, stereotyping, and sincere fictions in the (in)visibility of Asian American athletes." Chang was a talented collegiate football player at the University of Hawaii, but was not selected for the 2005 NFL draft. An NFL team scout had said that Chang was too short for the NFL, but when confronted with the fact that Chang was as tall as several current NFL players in his position, "the scout reportedly answered, 'But he plays short'" (Lapchick 2006, cited in King 2014, 4). This story indicates that onlookers often "see small" when they evaluate Asian American athletes. Body size becomes a focal point around which people, including prospective coaches and decision makers, make sense of Asian American athleticism.

Both Nakase and Hagiya had dreams of pursuing a career in the WNBA. Nakase spent two years in the NWBA, a US semiprofessional league, and one year playing professionally in Germany. During her playing career, Nakase also tried out for the WNBA, but felt as if recruiters and coaches were unwilling to look at her because of her height. She said, "Part of my continuation with basketball was always . . . Is it possible? Will they just look at my size and say no?" Being as small as Nakase, who exceeds five feet by only one or two inches, may be an obstacle for anyone attempting to play at higher levels of basketball. However, the WNBA's Los Angeles Sparks in 2008 signed African American Shannon Bobbitt, who is listed as five foot two on the Sparks roster. So, height did not necessarily disqualify Nakase from joining a WNBA team. Nakase tried to prove that height was not the defining factor in basketball ability, but found that many would not give her a chance.

Many Japanese Americans experienced coaches, teammates, and the media as obsessively focused on their small stature. Although no one can say for sure what were the true thoughts and intentions of the parties involved, it is probable that height became a way to speak about and construct the Asian American player as different, giving the parties a language that was not race-based, therefore allowing them to speak about race and racial difference without ever saying the words.

Rationalizing Mainstream Reactions—Using Height

Just as mainstream coaches, players, and onlookers seemed able to focus on stature or body size, it was also a way that Japanese Americans themselves rationalized people's reactions to them and made sense of their own basketball abilities and prospects. J-League participants also seemed to "see small."

When asked if people are ever surprised about her basketball know-how, former player and current collegiate coach Danielle claims up front that her size is the reason people are surprised that she's a coach:

Well, I get this all the time, not because I'm Japanese, but because I'm short. People will say, "Are you a basketball coach? You're so short." And I want to scream because I've heard that all along. . . . I would confide in some of my friends, "You know, I'm really sick and tired of people thinking that because I'm a five-foot-two Japanese American, that I'm just a reserved person." So, I think that's why I developed this outside persona because really, if you ask some referees, I have—I talk so much trash. To them, it's funny. They're like, "That person may look quiet, but she can say some things under her breath that really get you going." My friends who really know me well. . . . I have a mouth on me. I can give it right back to people. I can get a little snarly. I get so tired of people saying that Asians are supposed to be the—there's even a book called *The Quiet American*, it's about, I think, the nisei generation. My parents would tell me, "Our generation, we were taught to be very respectful and not to talk back." But I think a lot of that has to do with our camp experience. They were told to go here, do this. But I think that image of the quiet little reserved person . . . I'm just tired of people thinking that. Like, they'll say, "Have you ever gotten a technical?" "Yes." "You?" "Why are you surprised at me and not somebody else?"

Danielle relates her size to a whole host of stereotypes people have applied to her. Her comments allude to the fact that she believes ethnicity and race also play a role, but she begins with a strong assertion: "not because I'm Japanese, but because I'm short." Perhaps because race and racism are difficult subjects to discuss, height became a more comfortable trait to focus on when discussing people's prejudices and discriminatory practices.

I asked J-League participants if anyone had ever expressed surprise that they played basketball. For those who answered in the affirmative, a common explanation was height. Madeleine, a former college player said, "First of all, the first thing they would say is, 'How tall are you?' [laughs] I'm five foot five. In the Asian Leagues I was one of the taller girls. But at the college level, I was the shortest, if not one of the shortest. That was the first reaction, my height. And I don't look like a basketball player to a lot of people." Madeleine had numerous encounters where people immediately asked about her height in relation to basketball, so she was sure that this was what made her an unlikely player, although she also says more broadly that she does not "look like a basketball player." When I asked Chelsea, a former player and a current collegiate assistant coach, if her ethnicity had ever come up when playing outside of the J-Leagues, she responded, "Not so much. More so my stature. Like, in junior high school, it was like, 'Oh, the short five-foot-two Japanese girl that plays basketball!' [laughs] But yeah, it was fun. People didn't expect that I'd play basketball. They'd always be like, in high school, 'Oh, are you on the cheering squad?' I'm like, 'No.' [laughs] 'I play basketball.' They're like, 'Oh!'" When she played basketball in college, Chelsea continued to have these experiences: "Just walking around, we had . . . some big event, and just being around athletics, I think they assumed that I was either on the cheer squad or dance team or whatnot. But I'm like, 'No, I play basketball.' So I think just by my physical appearance, people don't think that I play basketball or anything like that. I'm not six foot. I'm not super-athletic-looking." Chelsea is like many of the other Japanese American women who describe people's surprise and misidentification. However, Chelsea feels that her height is the main reason why people might react in this way, even though she called herself the "five-foot-two Japanese girl," both her ethnicity and her gender highlighted. For these women quoted above, bringing up basketball in mainstream contexts consistently meant that others questioned or expressed surprise at their affiliation with basketball. They reasoned that their size was probably the main cause behind these questions.

I have a personal anecdote that suggests that people "see small" when looking at Asian American bodies in sport in ways they may not when looking at other bodies. One day, one of my African American students shared with the discussion class I was leading that she, as one of the few African American students on campus, was often asked if she was an athlete. Like many of the college women athletes I spoke with in my research, she often got guesses—usually track or basketball. However, this student was not an athlete. Moreover, she could not have been over five foot two and was rather petite in frame. Here was a person who, because of her race, was assumed by others to be an athlete, despite her small stature and despite being a woman. And the sports that people guessed fell right along racial stereotypes, perhaps not surprisingly, since those who asked in the first place were already stereotyping her, insinuating that it was unlikely she was attending the university for academic reasons alone. In this case, my student's experience of being short and female did not necessarily discourage people from thinking she was a basketball player. Instead, her status as an African American attending a university caused people to assume that she was a college-level athlete.

Reasoning that small stature was behind any teasing or questioning they received about basketball could be a way that many of my interviewees avoided thinking about how other stereotypes may have been at play. In addition, for Asian Americans, discussion of height may be a nicer, symbolic way to express feelings and describe experiences of being from a marginalized group— both in society and in basketball. Without bringing up antiracist or feminist politics, many of my interviewees could discuss their own as well as the collective challenges that came along with being short. As discussed in chapter 4, the emergence of Japanese American women as the most visible icons of mainstream success in basketball permits, to a certain degree, a way to celebrate an exaggerated image of the group's collective identity as small.

Both participants and onlookers are able to consume (and enact) images of small Japanese Americans who are beating the odds. Interviewees connected their pride in successful players to several factors, but they often added in comments about height, indicating a sense of group identification as height-disadvantaged. In doing so, they compared themselves to an often unspoken norm: the normalized, hegemonic sporting body. As one participant, Rebecca, explained, "The reality of it is that we are physically smaller, we're shorter, but I think getting to be able to enjoy something that's not really a little person's sport, and being able to enjoy it and carry it through to the rest of your life is an accomplishment, I think." Rebecca indicates that (for a group who identifies as smaller than average) just enjoying and participating in a sport not meant for small people elicits a feeling of accomplishment. Debbie makes a similar comment: "Well I think it's just pride. You know? People assume that Japanese Americans can't play basketball and especially when you see these girls, they are so little. Some of them are barely five feet one, five feet two, and yet they are little dynamos." Debbie expresses a sense of pride at seeing Japanese American women play at the college level—she loves the way that they defy expectations, especially because they tend to be small in stature.

Participants often seemed to want to disassociate height discrimination or disadvantage from discussions of racial discrimination or racialized discourse. However, Bob, a J-League coach, spoke about what it can sometimes feel like to be the underdog: "As Asians you probably always feel like you're an underdog. Because always in the . . . society, it's always whoever is bigger, more of a controlling individual than a smaller individual. I mean when you're small, you tend to, you can either go one [way] or the other, you either have a chip on your shoulder, or you're very, what word am I looking for . . . withdrawn, a little more quieter and just kind of take the abuse, or kind of out of sight, out of mind, get lost in the shuffle." These observations about how Asian Americans are perceived and treated suggest that size and race are ideologically linked concepts. Whether it's about gender, ethnicity, race, or height, many J-League participants felt like they had something to prove. Bob shared that he enjoys coaching in the J-Leagues as a way to help young men overcome a sense of being an underdog by gaining self-esteem through basketball.

CONCLUSION

Because identity as a basketball player is laden with symbolism about race, class, and gender, it provides a useful illustration of how these intersecting oppressions based on embodied symbols can influence interactions. It is in sport, where bodies are so salient, that one can observe more clear-cut reactions to bodies that subvert dominant images.

Cultural and biological triangulations between Asian Americans, African Americans, and whites play a dominant role in the racial ideologies surrounding Japanese American participation in basketball. As African Americans are viewed as dominating the top levels of basketball (particularly men's basketball), white and Asian American bodies are viewed as less physically gifted.

It is within this context of racial comparison that most J-League participants agree with the image of the Asian "race" as physically smaller, with the groups in comparison being African Americans and whites. This self-image as short or small is reified in rhetoric about the purpose of the leagues, which are often seen as necessarily exclusive of non-Asians in order to preserve a height-controlled environment. Therefore, despite the collective action that the J-Leagues represent, providing safe spaces for Asian Americans to play basketball virtually unburdened by dominant images, the definition of the leagues themselves plays into dominant understandings of race that aid in normalizing other (white and black) male bodies as more athletic.

In mainstream environments, some J-League participants described experiences where people were surprised by or trivialized their connections to basketball. Gender and height became mediating factors for many in interpreting a person's legitimacy as a basketball player. Being small or short seemed to make women appear *more* female and Asian Americans appear *more* Asian. The increased saliency of these identities caused others to, at best, express surprise at their athleticism or to, at worst, belittle or discriminate against the player. Height also gave those interacting with Asian Americans an easy way to speak about them "not being the basketball type" and to trivialize them or exclude them (especially women) from play.

Height or "size" becomes the symbol around which race and gender are centered. Both mainstream actors (described by interviewees) and J-League participants seemed to use height as a euphemism for either or both. Thus both female bodies and Asian bodies were coded as "short bodies" and easily excluded from sport (or self-segregated into the J-Leagues) without having to talk about the politics of race and gender.

6 · CONCLUSION

"It's a Testament of What the Japanese Leagues Can Do for Young Girls"

When the nisei in California be gan to participate in a wide range of community sports in the 1920s and 1930s, they probably could not have imagined the future popularity of J-League basketball. Just as the Playground Movement (Cahn [1994] 2015) touched the lives of the early nisei generation, Title IX and the growing popularity of organized youth sports (Adler and Adler 1994) touched the lives of the sansei and yonsei generations of the past forty years, helping to bring basketball to its heightened role in the Japanese American community. Many of the organizers and participants seem unaware of the exact origins of J-League basketball or how it became so central to the community, but they see the palpable results in terms of community support and social connections and, as a result, give every effort to sustaining and growing the programs for the next generations.

The gender-inclusivity that has grown hand in hand with the J-Leagues also seems to be, in some ways, an organic progression for the community. There were some teams of women, such as the Imperials Purple, who pushed boundaries, and some leaders, such as Ed Takahashi, who hastened change within the Southern California girls' and women's leagues. Overall, however, I found no evidence of a planned social movement or even intentional vision within the J-Leagues to be forerunners in women's sport. Instead, much of the investment in women's sports was an outgrowth of the larger investment in a community activity that continues to attract community members generation after generation.

The institutions and networks that helped create college-level talent in women's basketball over the past five decades could be described as opportunistic adaptations to changing times. Even if the community cultural wealth that investment in women's basketball engenders is not necessarily the type of status or capital that is conventionally sought after, it is working for Japanese Americans.

COLLECTIVE IDENTITY
AND ENDURING COMMUNITY

The relationship between Japanese Americans and the larger US society is most affected by two issues: (1) a history of discrimination, exclusion, and incarceration based on a socially constructed racial/ethnic difference and (2) the persistent racialization of Asian Americans as small, weak, and feminine as well as foreign and unassimilable. Within this context, Japanese Americans have been active agents in creating a collective identity and an enduring community. This project demonstrates that basketball—and a strong investment in women's basketball—is a way for Japanese Americans to mobilize community resources for a project they see as beneficial for them all.

In coming together through the sport of basketball, Japanese Americans chose a perhaps unlikely path, one where girls and boys in the community shared a degree of equal footing. As both girls and boys gained training and exposure to basketball, a unique atmosphere evolved—where a range of masculinities and femininities have become congruent with athletic identities. Women's participation in basketball is rarely trivialized—instead their knowledge and skills in the game are taken for granted. As a sport institution, the J-Leagues represent patterns in gender relations that feminist sports scholars have found difficult to imagine achieving. In this sense, there is a lot to learn from what the Japanese Americans have created.

THE THREE-LEVEL ANALYSIS

This project involved a three-level of analysis, examining the J-Leagues at the level of structure, cultural symbol, and interaction (Glenn 2002; Messner 2002). Using this model, I have shown that the empowerment of female players within J-Leagues occurs through a mutually reinforcing process: the community-inclusive structure of the J-Leagues provides the spaces for girls to learn basketball; the top women go on to play at the college level, thereby providing a symbolic resource in support of Japanese American women's basketball; and the community members reinforce the trend by getting their own daughters involved, talking about the successful female players, and interacting with fellow Japanese Americans who confirm respect and investment in girls' and women's basketball.

Structure

Sport institutions commonly reify gender and racial inequality (Connell 2005; Kian, Vincent, and Mondello 2008; Messner 1988), but they also can be vulnerable to contestations that challenge these inequalities (Hartmann 2003; Messner 1988). This in-depth study of a subcultural context helps us to better understand some of the social dynamics and processes involved in the social construction of race and gender.

Many of the patterns in the J-Leagues follow mainstream gender norms, helping to reproduce larger societal patterns of gender relations. The division of labor is unequal, where men hold the majority of the leadership positions and women engage in most of the support labor. Many of the playing opportunities are sex-segregated. These are patterns that emerge in other youth recreational sports contexts (e.g., Messner 2009), reifying the belief in natural, categorical differences between the sexes (Kane 1995; Messner 2009) and reproducing structural inequalities.

However, the structure of the J-Leagues as predominantly Japanese American or Asian American does appear to provide a collective counterhegemonic resource. The J-Leagues provide a safe space where Asian Americans—both male and female—are anticipated and supported as athletes. The latent effect is a safe space for girls and women to play, and to feel a sense of normalcy about their connections to basketball. This effect reverberated outside of the community: Asian Americans, and especially Asian American women, who have participated in the J-Leagues felt that the leagues gave them the skills and the courage to play basketball in mainstream environments.

The pure expansiveness of the J-Leagues also plays a role. Williams (2002) theorizes that an abundance of sport opportunities can "agitate" a local gender pattern (gender regime) because it provides a greater number of choices for girls and women. Young women may engage with sport for any number of different motivations, and it appears that the J-Leagues do a fairly good job of offering options. As discussed in chapter 2, this has allowed participants to renegotiate the meanings around sport.

The patterns that have emerged within the J-League create a progressive opportunity structure for girls' and women's involvement in sports. The linchpin of the structure lies in the beliefs that (1) community participation is important, (2) community participation is best exercised through participation in sports (the J-Leagues), and (3) active youth participation by both sexes is the best avenue to facilitate lifelong participation in the J-Leagues. With these convictions, the J-Leagues instituted patterns (their gender regime) that are relatively progressive for a sport institution and that have helped to promote feelings of support and admiration for female co-participants. Trends toward more women coaches and greater opportunities for coed competition could represent an "agitation" of the existing division of labor and sex segregation, indicating that early and sustained opportunities for girls in sport paired with encouragement to participate may produce challenges to gender regimes as boys and girls raised in this environment become adults who help to organize and lead the J-Leagues.

Cultural Symbol

The unique gender regime in the J-Leagues is sustained by community cultural symbols, as many of the most dominant "stars" or role models for the community are women who have gained success playing basketball at the university and professional levels. These local icons become gendered symbols of ethnicity, race, and community and represent, in many ways, a counterhegemonic representation of Japanese American identity.

A review of the literature suggests that we should not be altogether surprised by the way that the Japanese American community has embraced its women athletes, particularly by *Rafu Shimpo*. Research suggests that niche ethnic- or race-based media often pay regular attention to their successful female athletes, seemingly placing more importance on racial/ethnic pride and solidarity than on reproducing aspects of hegemonic masculinity (Jamieson 2001; Paraschak 1990; Williams 1987; Yep 2009). Additional research suggests that there may be more coverage for female athletes when they represent their country in an international competition, particularly if they are more successful than men from the same country or can be depicted as embodying something positive about the values of the nation (Wensing and Bruce 2003). Japanese American women fit these descriptions in multiple ways. They are viewed as more successful than Japanese American men and often described as nice girls and ideal citizens, doing well in school and giving back to the community.

This study goes beyond content and textual analysis to understand the experiences of J-League participants in their consumption of their female basketball stars. Although racial and ethnic affiliation plays a large part in Japanese Americans' propensity to follow the progress of Japanese American athletes, the devotion toward them is also a product of the tight J-League community. Many interviewees saw the women as products of the J-League experience; they saw them as teammates, as family.

Thus, just as the inclusive structure of the J-Leagues is sustained primarily because it aids in community building, yet concurrently produces an empowering atmosphere for female athletes, the female icons can also been viewed as a resource for promoting community cohesion *and* as empowering role models. Many people in the community follow the progress of these women and see their success as reaffirming of the value of the J-Leagues and as positive images of Japanese Americans. As these women venture into mainstream play, what are the implications of their presence on major college basketball teams? How might they be challenging controlling images of Asian American women?

Interaction

The unique gender patterns in the J-Leagues are productive of and sustained by interactions between J-League participants. When Japanese Americans meet each other for the first time, it is common to break the ice by asking if they or their children play basketball and trying to find out if there might be mutual friends or acquaintances through the basketball networks. This interaction ritual that occurs among many Japanese Americans is important in reinforcing the idea that just about everyone in the community plays basketball or is connected to someone who does. The purpose of these interactions is to establish community ties, but the latent effect is an affirmation of the normalcy and acceptability of Japanese Americans playing basketball. Because of the racialization of Asian Americans as small, feminine, and more interested in education than sports, these interactions help to disrupt the controlling images about Asian Americans. Because women still face a marginalized status in sports, particularly in team sports and physical sports, these interactions also help to disrupt controlling images of women.

Sport gives salience to bodies and plays a part in symbolically "naturalizing" beliefs about racial and gender differences (Birrell and Cole 1990; Carrington and McDonald 2001). By analyzing the experiences related to me by J-League participants, one can see an illustration of how race and gender become inscribed on the body and affect the way that people hold each other accountable for enacting situational identities based on these power relations. Through these experiences, one can trace some of the processes in the social construction of gender and race.

In discussing Serena and Venus Williams, Douglas (2002) argues that imagery surrounding the two sisters' bodies becomes a symbolic boundary between them and their white opponents. The interactions many of the participants had outside of the J-Leagues suggest that there is a related, triangulated (Kim 1999) conception of Asian American bodies—and Asian American women's bodies in particular—as lacking physicality (as diminutive or "not the type"), creating a symbolic boundary between them and the game of basketball.

The J-Leagues help to contest images of Asian Americans as weak or foreign because of the connection with the physical, "all-American" game of basketball. However, participants both react to and reproduce racialization that involves a triangulation between Americans of Asian, European, and African descent. The overwhelming majority of participants view Asians as smaller than other races and therefore at a disadvantage in competition with whites and African Americans. This thought prevails even in the face of many examples of mainstream success, particularly by Japanese American women.

IMPLICATIONS: A PLACE TO PLAY

NICOLE: What do you think of all these women that made it to college in recent years?

KEITH: I think it's great. It's a testament of what the Japanese Leagues can do for young girls.

In 1998, the City of Los Angeles was sued for unequal treatment of a Parks and Recreation girls' softball league (*Baca v. City of Los Angeles*). The settlement of the case required Los Angeles to raise participation rates of girls in their athletic programs citywide. Although progress was far from perfect, the city was able to raise participation by lowering program fees for girls, raising awareness, and increasing the availability of teams (Cooky 2009). Even in an era of ever-growing athletic participation by girls, Los Angeles, like many urban environments (Sabo 2009), appears to be failing its girls in the realm of sports. Improvements in participation that occurred after the lawsuit confirm that the interest was there, but a range of structural barriers stood in the way. Despite the improvements, lingering perceptions about the lack of interest in sport among girls may continue to perpetuate gender inequality within Los Angeles Parks and Recreation (Cooky 2009). Nationwide, 69 percent of girls and 75 percent of boys participate in organized sports, but the gaps are much larger in urban areas. Among urban third- through fifth-graders, 59 percent of girls and 80 percent of boys are involved in athletics; among urban high school students, 59 percent of girls and 68 percent of boys play sports (Sabo 2009).

It is in the context of the urban environment of Los Angeles that several J-League organizations and leagues appear to provide what the Parks and Recreation department has not: a well-organized playing space where girls and women are welcome. Although the kinship and community shared by Japanese Americans may be difficult to replicate without the socioeconomic and sociohistorical circumstances that help to make the J-Leagues possible, the J-Leagues may offer some lessons on how we might envision a sport environment where gender-inclusion is possible.

Aligning Community Goals with an Ethic of Inclusion

Most Japanese Americans share a common history and sense of kinship, as well as insecurities about the future of the community, that motivate them to make use of the shared interest in basketball (across generations, among both sexes). This may be a combination of factors that would be difficult to duplicate from scratch. However, one takeaway for groups that desire stronger community ties is that these ties can be strengthened by active and inclusive engagement with sport, in men and women of all ages seeing sports as a joint enterprise in which they share equal footing.

Getting All Ages/Generations Involved

One important way that Japanese Americans cultivate J-League involvement is by encouraging all ages to play. Now this may be a chicken-or-egg question, but facilitating early and continued involvement appears to strengthen attachments to both basketball and the community. In the case of Japanese Americans, basketball helps to bridge generation gaps and strengthen families. Getting (or keeping) women involved provides role modeling for girls and boys in the community. Although sports scholars are often focused on opportunities in sport for girls at the youth level, it may be equally important to open up playing opportunities for older women so that girls can envision a future in the sport, even if just at the recreational level. Getting older women involved, however, requires having multiple types of playing opportunities.

Offering a Wide Spectrum of Playing Opportunities

Since most feminist scholars agree that there is a never-ending variety of human beings under the label of "woman," it seems illogical that anyone would look to one model for attracting girls and women to sport or for sustaining existing athletic interests. The J-Leagues offer a wide range of playing contexts, though far from perfect, including single-sex and coed and spanning different levels of skill and motivations. This helps to foster engagement with basketball for a wide spectrum of players with a variety of interests and abilities. For instance, there are some players in the J-Leagues who engage with basketball purely for the social benefits and others who do so purely for the competition (and everything in between). That J-Leagues are able to satisfy both types of players is a testament to their ability to attract and sustain interest among so many participants. This seems to be an ideal model for getting girls and women (not to mention boys and men) involved since it does not exclude certain groups of women or force them to play alongside women with mismatched abilities or goals.

FINAL THOUGHTS

In many ways the Japanese American commitment to ethnically restricted sports leagues is somewhat surprising, just as my interviewee Mitch suggests:

When you look at our Japanese American community and our history, it has been one of creating its own institutions, its own way of doing things. But then, the question . . . is, what do you do when the need for that—well, maybe it doesn't entirely go away—but it's no longer a factor. . . . There were forces from the outside that forced the people back in because there was no place for them out there. . . . "You can't play in this league. You can't use this gym. You can't participate in this program." A lot of those things are gone. . . . That's why it's interesting that so many parents today continue to stick their kids in those youth leagues. It's choice. It is not something that they have to do. It's something that they choose to do, and it's so strong that it surprises me. I don't know what it means. It intrigues me, though, that they feel so strongly about that.

Whereas at one time Japanese Americans found themselves restricted from many mainstream environments, today that is not often the case. As Fugita and O'Brien (1991) found, many Japanese Americans live the bulk of their lives outside of the Japanese American community, making close friendships with non–Japanese Americans, and at times keeping only "weak ties" to their co-ethnics. All of this suggests a high degree of acceptance and integration, especially for those in later generations. Yet, as this research project has demonstrated, it is unlikely a coincidence that sport has remained one institution that the community preserves as Japanese (or Asians) only.

As Carrington and McDonald (2001) argue, biological racism has not, as many suggest, disappeared from modern race relations. Sport, with its focus on bodies, is a place where this form of racism is most transparent. Sport is a complex web of ideologies about race and gender, all of which seem to place the white male body as the norm, while other bodies are depicted as possessing deficiencies or special abilities that require special note and consideration. Within this web, the Asian body and the female body are both symbolically excluded from physical team sports, often leading to actual exclusion or dissuasion from these sports.

The J-Leagues offer a functional solution to this exclusion, and their popularity points to the ongoing, persistent racialization of

Asian bodies, particularly in the world of sport. The J-Leagues offer physical spaces where Asian bodies are athletic bodies; they are the norm. These spaces afford protection from discrimination and provide opportunities to play that are sometimes not available in mainstream contexts. They also offer a more symbolic power: their very existence (not to mention the successful athletes they have produced) confirms the idea that Asian Americans are strong, skilled athletes. As with taiko, bringing women into this collective identity appears to work to strengthen the community (and its image) as a whole. That women can succeed in the mainstream more often than the men is a "reality" that is embraced, rather than shunned. Seeing themselves as a collective, Japanese Americans are able to take pride in anyone from the home team.

ACKNOWLEDGMENTS

First and foremost, I would like to thank each and every one of my research participants who shared her or his time and stories with me. Truly accessible heroines, Jamie Hagiya and Natalie Nakase have been especially generous over the years. I owe a debt of gratitude to all of the Japanese American leagues and tournaments and their affiliated organizations. In particular, I want to thank the Tigers Youth Club, Nisei Athletic Union, Southern California Women's Athletic Union, Little Tokyo Service Center, *Rafu Shimpo*, and Nikkei Games. A special shout-out to the San-Tai-San tournament committee—each and every person on the committee was incredibly generous with their time and energy and cheerfully allowed me to shadow them over the span of three years. Thank you also to Leland Lau, Sally Kane, Mickey Komai, and Jeff Murakami for being my early guides on this journey. I would like to thank Carol and Kevin Jue, Mike Murase, Jon Takasugi, the *Orange County Register*, and the *Rafu Shimpo* for sharing graphics and photographs for use in this book.

Over the years there have been a great number of generous colleagues who have given me advice and feedback on this research. My gratitude goes out to Kristen Barber, Andrea Bertotti-Metoyer, Suzel Bozada-Deas, Claudia Bucciferro, Melissa Fujiwara, Stacy Keogh George, Vik Gumbhir, Bill Hayes, Sharon Hays, Pierrette Hondagneu-Sotelo, Joe Johnston, Karen Kelsky, Rich King, Lon Kurashige, Danny Layne, James McKeever, Mike Messner, Al Miranne, Naghme Morlock, Lata Murti, Viet Ngyuen, Leland Saito, Evren Savri, and Sarah Stohlman Zafirau. Special thanks to Leland Saito for helping me think from new perspectives and to Lon Kurashige for suggesting the illustrative metaphor of concentric circles used in chapter 4. I would also like to single out Mike Messner to thank him for being such an amazing advisor and mentor. Mike is also a women's basketball fan and supported this project in part by accompanying me to USC women's basketball games to watch Jamie Hagiya swish three-pointers, as sometimes it requires this type of solidarity to get through the more tedious parts of the research process—ha!

The Graduate School at the University of Southern California helped to fund this research with a year of fellowship that enabled me to gather most of my interviews and a final summer dissertation grant that facilitated time to devote to writing. Gonzaga University has also been supportive through the process of writing this book—thank you especially to my department chair, Andrea Bertotti-Metoyer, for helping me find time to write and to the Dean of Arts and Sciences, Elizabeth Mermann-Joswiak, for her wise counsel. In putting the final touches on this manuscript, I had the help of research assistants who are current and former Gonzaga University undergraduates: Analea Clark, Zoe Dugdale, Zach Oxford-Romeike, Morgan Schindele, and Morgan Willie.

Many thanks to Rutgers University Press and editor Peter Mickulas. It has been a pleasure to work with the Rutgers team on this book. Thank you to Critical Issues in Sport and Society series editors Michael Messner and Douglas Hartmann for supporting this project, for creating this important series, and for all the meaningful ways you have contributed to the Sociology of Sport.

Resilience and inspiration are vital components to success, and I have access to these tools only due to the friends and family who have believed in me. I would not be where I am today without the inspiration of Valerie Cushman, who modeled an irresistible path in which one could earn a PhD studying women's basketball. Many supportive friends and "coaches" provided immeasurable support throughout the research and writing process, in particular Rebecca Rudd, Mariama Souare, and Candice Wong. I could not have completed this project without the helping hands, advice, and support of my husband, Steven Bingo, my brother Derek Willms, and my parents, Ray and Vicki Willms. Thank you also to my children, Celia and Julian, for providing an impetus for regular writing breaks.

METHODOLOGICAL APPENDIX

METHODOLOGY AND NOTES ON THE RESEARCH

On a dark Thursday night in December 2007, I drove through the back gate of a South Bay middle school and steered my car around outlying buildings to an isolated school gymnasium. I entered the brightly lit gym, and other women came in soon after. We gathered at a bench, waiting for a group of men to finish a pickup game. Immediately, I felt like I was a bit out of place. Not only was I the only non–Asian American player in the gym, but all of the other women who entered immediately found a spot on the floor and carefully removed their street shoes, replacing them with pristine court shoes. I stared down at my shabby basketball shoes, recently extracted from the back of the closet after several years of neglect. Like a rookie, I had put them on at home and worn them outside.

I was nervous. I had played basketball in high school, one year at a Division III college, and off and on since, but I was rusty and out of shape. Surely, this was a bad idea. Still, here I was, trying to forage for a few possible interviewees. So far, it had been a bit difficult to make solid contacts, but one generous individual who served on the board of a Japanese American sport organization had invited me to play in a pickup game with her and some of her teammates.

I shyly said hello to a few players, and there were some quick introductions, but by eight fifteen we were on the court and playing. Despite being a pickup game, it was high-caliber and fast-paced. Players ran a motion offense and played quality, fundamental basketball. When I could keep up, I was having the time of my life. My contact came in a few minutes later and at a half-time break officially introduced me and allowed me to explain my project. After giving my little spiel, I held up a clipboard and requested that players leave their contact information so that I could arrange an interview. I placed the clipboard on the bench. No one ran right over, and as the game progressed and players entered and exited, the single sheet of paper attached to the clipboard remained blank.

In the meantime, I became more and more exhausted. How long would these women play? When the game was finally called at ten twenty, I limped over to the bench to find that my sign-up sheet remained void of volunteers. I had been out of the game for a bit with a jammed finger, my hip was hurting, and I felt the onset of shin splints. I collapsed onto the bench, unable to move.

Then, like a dramatic transition in a movie, one of the players suddenly grabbed the clipboard and wrote down her name and number. She handed off the board to another player. Soon after, a third came over and asked to sign up. Three possible interviews!

As I thanked everyone and hobbled out of the gym, I realized that I may have been subjected to a test that night. Even following my half-time entreaty, no one was going to volunteer. Only when I stuck it out until the end, playing through two hours of fast-paced basketball with minimal breaks, had I passed the test.

Insider/Outsider

My introduction at the South Bay gym was one of those moments that both confirm and complicate the nature of an "outsider." My racial/ethnic status as a white American in many ways made me the quintessential outsider in the J-Leagues where team membership is often restricted to Japanese and Asian Americans. However, my status as a basketball player, however rusty and out of shape, helped me earn a degree of trust and camaraderie as an insider that may not have been possible if I had never played the game. Into the bargain, being a *female* athlete also allowed me access to this women-only pickup game and did not prevent me from being invited to play in a few pickup games with a group of Japanese American men. Being an athlete may have put me in a sympathetic position in the eyes of other female athletes and gave me a degree of legitimacy with my male interviewees, as well.

As much as my basketball knowledge and abilities helped to enhance my legitimacy as a researcher and as a human being (from the perspective of J-League basketball fanatics), there were some real research limitations due to my racial/ethnic background. First of all, I could not conduct participant observation as a player on an official team. Non-Asians were not allowed to play in the adult leagues if they did not play as a youth within the J-Leagues. Since I had never played in the J-Leagues before, I was shut off from this opportunity. I also, early on in my research, offered to volunteer as an assistant coach on a J-League team as part of my observations. My offers were graciously acknowledged, but I did not receive any invitations to coach. On the other hand, I was completely accepted as a volunteer on the San-Tai-San tournament planning committee, affiliated with the Little Tokyo Service Center, so different contexts elicited different degrees of community protectionism.

One issue affecting both access and rapport was that some J-League participants had felt attacked in the past by potential lawsuits and media coverage that claimed that the J-Leagues ethnicity rules were unfairly exclusionary. Because this issue is so contentious, several people whom I approached feared that I was writing an exposé on the ethnicity rules. This concern led some to stay tight-lipped and others to be especially careful when sharing information and opinions. When I sensed that this issue was on people's minds, I made a point of reassuring them that this was not the focus of my research.

Blind Spots and Power Relations

It's important to acknowledge that I live my life recognized as "white" and therefore have had different life experiences than most of the participants in my study who nearly all live their life recognized as "Asian American." Although these racial categories are socially constructed, they are real in their consequences, and different consequences can often lead to different perspectives. Specific to social research, when the researcher occupies a position as an outsider, it can lead to blind spots, particularly when the researcher belongs in any way to the dominant culture. It is all too easy to hold onto the dominant, normalized cultural lens, preventing one from fully seeing or comprehending experiences that may be different from one's own (Duneier 1999). Moreover, the power dynamics between researcher and research participant are magnified when the researcher occupies positions of status that may be experienced as dominant or oppressive by participants. Throughout my time in the field, many relationship dynamics based on status differences were in flux—I interviewed both men and women, participants who were both older and younger than me, and people from a variety of socioeconomic backgrounds. Thus, the racial/ethnic differences remained most salient. Japanese Americans are a group that has been subject to forms of state-sanctioned discrimination and attacks on their civil rights, as well as pervasive and painful racial stereotypes that often make it difficult for them to achieve a complete sense of belonging in the United States. As a white American, I can probably never fully comprehend what it feels like to navigate these waters, and it would be understandable if my participants had concerns that I may not accurately represent their experiences and perspectives.

Cognizant of these issues, I committed myself to really listening to the voices of my participants, choosing semistructured, in-depth interviews as my main method in order to share control of the interviews with interviewees (Hennink, Hutter, and Bailey 2010; Hesse-Biber 2007). Throughout the research process, including interpretation and analysis, I tried to achieve an emic, insider understanding, even while realizing that this is never fully possible (Hennink, Hutter, and Bailey 2010). In my writing, I attempted to place participants' experiences, understandings, and interpretations at center stage. I also made an effort to include many scholars of color from diverse disciplinary fields to help gain wisdom from perspectives that may have developed from experiences outside of my own.

Did issues of power and trust influence data collection? They seemed to mainly be a factor in gaining access. I had to establish myself as someone with honorable intentions, someone who really cared to listen and who did not have an agenda. As reflected in the story of the pickup basketball game, I often had to prove myself in some way to gain participants' trust. Most of my successful interview recruitment required a community member to vouch for me. Even then, participants would almost always ask for an explanation for my interest in this research before they trusted me with their experiences. For me, the most honest reason I could offer participants for my choice of research topic was my interest in USC player Jamie Hagiya. However, at times, I also shared that my fiancé (now husband) is Japanese American and that this relationship may have influenced my interest as well, even though he has never been involved in the J-Leagues. These explanations seemed to satisfy participants' curiosities and build trust. In the end, the pleasure involved in talking about the participants' life passion— in this case basketball—seemed to outweigh any trepidations about my position as an outsider.

THE METHOD

When Women Rule the Court is based on my collection and analysis of interview, observation, survey, and archival data. It is a qualitative project that delved into the lived experiences of J-League participants. My aim was to understand the emergence and popularity of several Japanese American female basketball players. However, I knew that acquiring an in-depth understanding of the community's relationship with these women would require a comprehensive study of the J-Leagues themselves and of the place of basketball in the Japanese American communities of California. I spent as much time as possible listening to stories of J-League participants and watching both the everyday and extraordinary events of J-League basketball over a period of nearly three years. The University of Southern California's Institutional Review Board granted approval for the portions of the research involving human subjects.

In-Depth Interviews

I completed in-depth, semistructured interviews, as my primary method, with sixty-five people connected in some way to J-League basketball (thirty-two women, thirty-three men/boys). The typical interview lasted about one to three hours and was audio-taped, although a small handful of interviews were shorter and two were not recorded by request of the participant. My youngest interviewee was fifteen, the oldest eighty-three. Fifty-eight of my interviewees identified as Japanese American (including those who were mixed-race), six identified as Chinese American, and one did not identify as Asian American.[1]

I recruited interview participants through several methods including volunteer and snowball sampling. Looking for volunteers, I approached people at meetings and events. I also sent recruitment emails to J-League organization leaders listed on J-League websites. I conducted snowball sampling by asking all of my participants for referrals. Although referrals helped immensely, I tried not to rely on them exclusively to avoid interviewing too narrowly, such as within a single friendship group, team, or organization. Also, referrals often led me toward leaders or exceptional people who participants thought would be most helpful. I wanted to make sure that I interviewed more everyday participants as well.

My main criterion for an interviewee was any connection (broadly defined) to Japanese American basketball in Southern California. Participants also had to be twelve or older. Toward the end of my research, I began to engage in some quota sampling, looking for participants who seemed to be underrepresented in my research on the basis of age or sex.

In addition to my interviews with leaders and everyday participants in the J-Leagues, I also used my contacts to track down as many "stars" as I could find: two men and sixteen women who played at the college level or beyond. My star interviewees include many of the elite players and coaches mentioned throughout the book: Colleen Matsuhara, Jamie Hagiya, Darin Maki, Natalie Nakase, and LeeAnne Sera, to mention just a few.

I utilized a multifaceted system for identifying and protecting the confidentiality of participants. During my research I considered the star athletes, as well as a few other prominent community members, to be public figures. I asked their permission to use their real names in future publications. In this book, participants who agreed to be identified are referenced using their full name or last name only (e.g., Jamie Hagiya or Hagiya). However, I occasionally hid the identity of these same participants with a pseudonym when I considered the subject matter potentially sensitive. In interviews and interactions with participants who were less in the public eye, I protected their confidentiality by assigning a pseudonym and removing or changing identifying information. These participants are referenced using a single given name that is a pseudonym (e.g., Laura).

After some consideration, I chose to assign pseudonyms using names that are popular in the United States. I found that sixty-three of the sixty-five interview participants in my study had a given name that more or less fit this description. I chose pseudonyms by selecting from the Social Security website a name that was popular around the time of each participant's year of birth. Two of my participants, as well as a small number of the people with whom I interacted during observations, had a Japanese given name. In order to protect their identity, I typically went with the trend of the group and assigned a pseudonym using the same Social Security naming system. In a few instances where identification was unlikely, I chose a Japanese name that seemed appropriate. I recognize that this way of renaming participants may erase some of the naming practices of the Japanese and Chinese communities of California, and that these communities' practices may differ slightly from the dominant culture reflected in the Social Security listings. However, I believe that the more typical naming practices of these communities are faithfully represented.

I designed an interview guide to help provide structure to interviews, but posed questions in a way that encouraged storytelling and dialogue. The guide included questions about the participants' personal sport history including both J-League and mainstream sport experiences. I also asked about future goals and plans for their family's involvement in basketball, their perspective on trends in the J-Leagues, and their connections to other Japanese American community institutions. Additional questions focused on the place of the J-Leagues in their life and whether following successful college-level players was part of this experience. The interviews were semistructured: I used the interview guide as a starting point, but also tried to ask a lot of follow-up questions and cater the interview to the experiences of the interviewee.

Although I did not start with a plan to have an ongoing research relationship with interviewees, I did continue the conversation, so to speak, with a handful of my participants. If requested, I shared their transcripts with them, as well as excerpts from my analysis. I invited their feedback. Although my data collection ended in the fall of 2009, this book also contains some updated information and perspectives gained from recent conversations with influential interviewees including Jamie Hagiya and Natalie Nakase.

As I collected interviews with participants, I created transcripts that I later inductively coded for themes. I coded the interviews using the software ATLAS.ti. Although this software is considered a theory-building tool, I used only its code and retrieve functions (Fielding 2002). I attached codes to particular passages within the interview transcripts and then later was able to retrieve the data by using a "single sort" (one code) or a "multiple sort" (more than one code) (Fielding 2002, 163). For example, when a participant mentioned that she enjoyed the social aspects of the J-Leagues, I could code this passage as "social." By also coding each interview according to interviewee demographics, I could also code the entire interview as "female" and "college-level player." This enabled me to retrieve transcription excerpts of all interviewees who spoke about the social aspects of the J-Leagues, or restrict my excerpts by gender or other participant characteristics.

Thematic codes helped me to discover patterns in the data. Oftentimes, it took multiple coding sessions and an iterative relationship with reading, coding, and analyzing transcripts to discover the most important themes (Hennink, Hutter, and Bailey 2010). For example, it was only in a later-stage recoding of the data that I recognized how common it was for college-level players to talk about the role of mentors and J-League basketball connections in their playing careers. This led me to develop arguments about the importance of J-League networks and mentorship in developing players for college-level play.

Participant Observation

Over the three-year span of my research, I engaged a wide variety of observations at many sites throughout the greater Los Angeles area, and a few other outposts of J-League activity. My participant observation with the Little Tokyo Service Center as a member of the San-Tai-San tournament committee was my earliest, most intense, and longest in duration. San-Tai-San ("three-on-three" in Japanese) is a basketball tournament that started in 1998 for the purpose of drawing attention to a campaign to build a recreation center in Little Tokyo. For three years, I served as a volunteer on the planning committee, getting a behind-the-scenes look at how community members orchestrate a basketball tournament and choose the marquee special guests.

My other observations were more spread out, as I tried to soak up a little of everything that the J-Leagues and the larger Japanese American community had to offer. Starting in December 2007, I began observing at J-League games and team practices. Game observations continued intermittently over the following two years. I also sat in on committee meetings for the Tigers Youth Club, Nisei Athletic Union, and Nikkei Games. I attended several tournaments and related events (2008–2009) including the Wanjettes, F.O.R., Jets/Jetts, Tigers, and Las Vegas Invitational tournaments. I also attended Nikkei Games in 2007 and 2008 and San-Tai-San/Children's Day festivities from 2006 to 2009. I attended a meeting/presentation of the Little Tokyo Historical Society featuring pre–World War II basketball players. Also during this period, I observed at high school and college games featuring Japanese American players at Marina High School, the University of Southern California, UCLA, and Chapman College. I attended a semiprofessional game featuring Natalie Nakase in San Diego. I attended a Los Angeles Sparks game against Phoenix when Phoenix had a Japanese national on their team. I played pickup basketball in two contexts: with some of the (male) staff and volunteers from the Little Tokyo Service Center (on three occasions) and with a group of women mainly from the Tigers Youth Club (on two occasions), as described earlier.

To understand the community more broadly, I observed in several contexts that were not directly related to basketball: a Nisei Week parade, a Japanese Cultural Institute carnival, an obon festival at a Westside Buddhist Church, and the Tofu Festival in Little Tokyo.

For the bulk of these observations, I created descriptive field notes, attempting to capture the rituals and interactions that were part of J-League and Japanese American community life. At other times, I observed as a way to soak up some of the local culture and make contacts with community members. I analyzed my field notes in much the same way as my transcripts, coding them in ATLAS.ti and reading them over multiple times to discover connections and themes. Most of the stories that anchor each chapter of the book emerged from my participant observations.

Survey

Because I consider myself a primarily qualitative researcher, I undertook a survey only at the solicitation of one of my interviewees. One of the board members of the SCWAU league suggested that I design a survey for the women in the league and indicated that she would also like to see the results. I crafted a survey that the board member then forwarded to all of the coaches/team leaders and, in turn, asked them to forward to their players. The survey consisted of a few demographic questions, some quantifiable questions, and then a number of qualitative questions that resembled several from my interview guide. Only seventeen SCWAU participants responded, but I was able to pull out some descriptive statistics by coding some of the short answers and counting similar responses. I coded the responses to open-ended questions in ATLAS.ti in the same fashion as I did the interview transcripts.

Archival Data/Content Analysis

Often when a researcher is conducting research through interviews and observations, it is difficult to verify some of the large-scale trends that emerge. I was curious, for instance, exactly how many women were coaching in the J-Leagues and how much coverage women's basketball was getting in *Rafu Shimpo*. These kinds of questions seemed to be best answered by conducting content analysis on texts created by the community: tournament programs and newspaper content.

Tournament Programs. Basketball tournaments started to gain momentum in the J-Leagues in the 1960s and 1970s, and according to organizers, many are growing larger every year. Tournament programs list every team participating in the tournament including the names of players and (when applicable) the coach of the team. I picked the 2006 program from the largest tournament, the Tigers Tournament, and coded each coach's name as male, female, or ambiguous. I then counted the number of women versus men coaching overall and also looked at the distribution by grade level.

Newspaper Study. In envisioning this research, I determined that much of the meaning making surrounding J-League basketball would be closely related to the negotiation of a collective ethnic identity, which Bacon (1999) argues is formed in public forums. One important community forum for participants in the J-Leagues in the Los Angeles area is the Japanese American newspaper *Rafu Shimpo*.[2] Therefore, I chose to analyze the sports pages of *Rafu Shimpo* for the entire year of 2007, corresponding to the start of my ethnographic research. Although I reference my analysis of *Rafu Shimpo* in this book, a more detailed description of the findings and method can be found in an earlier publication (Willms 2014).

STUDYING A COMMUNITY

Although my work with the community probably does not fully qualify as ethnography, I was inspired by the ideals of ethnographic research to immerse myself in as many community contexts as I could. In the end, however, I relied quite heavily on my interviewees to translate the community for me, to show me J-League basketball through their eyes. I hope that this book stands as an accurate representation of what these participants have seen and experienced, even as I have injected myself into their narratives by applying academic concepts to help interpret and explain. In the end, I gift these stories back to the J-Leagues and the Japanese American communities of California. As Asian American athletes and sport enthusiasts are often invisible or incomprehensible in the American imagination, I hope that this book plays some small role in upending the current discourses in sport that limit claims to athleticism to a dominant few. I hope the stories in these pages cause many to rethink our cultural practices that withhold respect of and investment in athletes who do not fit an idealized version of "athlete."

NOTES

INTRODUCTION

1. Title IX is an amendment to the Higher Education Act passed by the US Congress in 1972. It reads, "No person in the United States shall, on the basis of sex, be excluded from participation in, or denied the benefits of, or subjected to discrimination under any educational program or activity receiving federal aid" (Title IX of the Education Amendments of 1972, 20 USC 1681).

2. Of those who identified as "Japanese only" on the census, 60 percent of Los Angeles County residents and 67 percent of Orange County residents reported being born in the United States (2010–2014 American Community Survey).

3. For those who identified as "Japanese only," 20.2 percent of Japanese Americans in Los Angeles and 19.7 percent of Japanese Americans in Orange County were employed in this field (2010–2014 American Community Survey).

4. In Los Angeles County, the median income of a Japanese American household was $63,757 (for comparison, the median income for all households was $55,476 and for white non-Hispanics was $61,681). In Orange County, the median income of a Japanese American household was $81,640 (for comparison, the median income for all households was $74,344 and for white non-Hispanics was $78,276) (2010–2014 American Community Survey).

CHAPTER 3: "WOMEN WHO TOOK SPORTS BEYOND PLAY"

1. Early women's basketball often included rules intended to prevent overexertion due to perceptions of female frailty. In this vein, the court was split into segments and the players prevented from crossing from one area to the next. In the 1930s, the game switched from a three-court to a two-court format. In the late 1960s to early 1970s, the game format gradually changed to the full-court version we know today (McElwain 2004).

2. In the 2010 census, 4.8 percent of the US population reported being "Asian only" and an additional 0.9 percent reported being "Asian in combination with one or more other races" (2010–2014 American Community Survey).

METHODOLOGICAL APPENDIX

1. Although the leagues are traditionally Japanese American, there are a number of Chinese Americans who participate and occupy leadership positions.

2. *Rafu Shimpo* is currently the only Japanese American daily still in print. Founded in 1903, it was originally printed only in Japanese, but became bilingual in 1926. It currently maintains a circulation of approximately twenty thousand and estimates its readership to be at least twice that number. It very recently expanded its website to include more content, which may greatly increase its accessibility. It publishes daily, Tuesday through Saturday, commonly four to six pages in English and eight pages in Japanese. This study examines the English-language sports page, as the overwhelming majority of participants in the leagues do not read the Japanese-language section, which is aimed at more recent Japanese immigrants.

BIBLIOGRAPHY

Abney, Robertha. 1999. "African American Women in Sport." *Journal of Physical Education, Recreation & Dance* 70 (4): 35–38.

Acosta, R. Vivian, and Linda Jean Carpenter. 2014. "Women in Intercollegiate Sport: A Longitudinal Study—Thirty-Seven Year Update, 1977–2014." www.acostacarpenter.org.

Adjepong, Lady Anima, and Ben Carrington. 2014. "Black Female Athletes as Space Invaders." In *Routledge Handbook of Sport, Gender and Sexuality*, edited by Jennifer Hargreaves and Eric Anderson, 169–178. London: Routledge.

Adler, Patricia A., and Peter Adler. 1991. *Backboards and Blackboards: College Athletes and Role Engulfment.* New York: Columbia University Press.

———. 1994. "Social Reproduction and the Corporate Other: The Institutionalization of Afterschool Activities." *Sociological Quarterly* 35 (2): 309–328.

———. 1998. *Peer Power: Preadolescent Culture and Identity.* New Brunswick, NJ: Rutgers University Press.

Alamillo, José M. 2003. "Peloteros in Paradise: Mexican American Baseball and Oppositional Politics in Southern California, 1930–1950." *Western Historical Quarterly* 34 (2): 191–211.

Anderson, Benedict. 2006. *Imagined Communities: Reflections on the Origin and Spread of Nationalism.* New York: Verso Books.

Arnaldo, Constancio. 2016. "Manny 'Pac-Man' Pacquiao, the Transnational Fist, and the Southern California Ringside Community." In *Asian American Sporting Cultures*, edited by Stanley I. Thangaraj, Constancio R. Arnoldo, Jr., and Christina B. Chin, 102–125. New York: New York University Press.

Asian Americans Advancing Justice (AAJC). 2015. "A Community of Contrasts: Asian Americans, Native Hawaiians and Pacific Islanders in the West." http://advancingjustice-aajc.org/sites/default/files/2016–09 /AAAJ_Western_Dem_2015.pdf.

Bacon, Jean. 1999. "Constructing Collective Ethnic Identities: The Case of Second Generation Asian Indians." *Qualitative Sociology* 22 (2): 141–160.

Balderrama, Francisco E., and Richard A. Santillan. 2011. *Mexican American Baseball in Los Angeles.* Charleston, SC: Arcadia.

Banet-Weiser, Sarah. 1999. "Hoop Dreams Professional Basketball and the Politics of Race and Gender." *Journal of Sport and Social Issues* 23 (4): 403–420.

Beran, Janice A. 1985. "Playing to the Right Drummer: Girls' Basketball in Iowa, 1893–1927." *Research Quarterly for Exercise and Sport, Centennial Issue* 51: 78–85.

———. 1991. "Iowa, the Longtime 'Hot Bed' of Girls Basketball." In *A Century of Women's Basketball: From Frailty to Final Four*, edited by Joan S. Hult and Marianna Trekell, 181–204. Reston, VA: AAHPERD.

———. 2008. *From Six-on-Six to Full Court Press: A Century of Iowa Girls' Basketball.* Iowa City: University of Iowa Press.

Birrell, Susan, and Cheryl L. Cole. 1990. "Double Fault: Renee Richards and the Construction and Naturalization of Difference." *Sociology of Sport Journal* 7 (1): 1–21.

Birrell, Susan, and Mary G. McDonald, eds. 2000. *Reading Sport: Critical Essays on Power and Representation.* Boston: Northeastern University Press.

Bonilla-Silva, Eduardo. 2006. *Racism without Racists: Color-Blind Racism and the Persistence of Racial Inequality in the United States.* Lanham, MD: Rowman & Littlefield.

Bourdieu, Pierre. 1978. "Sport and Social Class." *Social Science Information* 17 (6): 819–840.

———. 1984. *Distinction: A Social Critique of the Judgement of Taste.* Cambridge, MA: Harvard University Press.

———. 1989. "Social Space and Symbolic Power." *Sociological Theory* 7 (1): 14–25.

Bourdieu, Pierre, and Loïc J. D. Wacquant. 1992. *An Invitation to Reflexive Sociology.* Chicago: University of Chicago Press.

Brown, Letisha Engracia Cardoso. 2015. "Sporting Space Invaders: Elite Bodies in Track and Field, a South African Context." *South African Review of Sociology* 46 (1): 7–24.

Bruce, Toni. 2008. "Women, Sport and the Media: A Complex Terrain." In *Outstanding Research about Women and Sport in New Zealand*, edited by Camilla Obel, Toni Bruce, and Shona Thompson, 51–71. Hamilton, New Zealand: Wilf Malcolm Institute of Educational Research.

Bruce, Toni, Mark Falcous, and Holly Thorpe. 2007. "The Mass Media and Sport." In *Sport in Aotearoa/New Zealand Society*, edited by Chris Collins and Steve Jackson, 147–169. Boston: Cengage.

Bruce, Toni, Jorid Hovden, and Pirkko Markula. 2010. *Sportswomen at the Olympics: A Global Comparison of Newspaper Coverage.* Rotterdam, Netherlands: Sense.

Bruce, Toni, and Emma Wensing. 2009. "'She's Not One of Us': Cathy Freeman and the Place of Aboriginal People in Australian National Culture." *Australian Aboriginal Studies* (2): 90–100.

Cahn, Susan K. [1994] 2015. *Coming on Strong: Gender and Sexuality in Women's Sport*. University of Illinois Press.

———. 2004. "'Cinderellas' of Sport: Black Women in Track and Field." In *Sport and the Color Line: Black Athletes and Race Relations in Twentieth-Century America*, edited by Patrick B. Miller and David K. Wiggins, 211–232. New York: Routledge.

Cain, Patricia A. 2000. "Women, Race, and Sports: Life before Title IX." *Journal of Gender, Race and Justice* 4: 337–351.

Campbell, Bobby. 2015. "Hot Sauce and White Chocolate: And1 and Ghetto Style in Basketball." *Communication Design* 3 (1): 51–61.

Carrington, Ben. 2012. "Introduction: Sport Matters." *Ethnic and Racial Studies* 35 (6): 961–970.

Carrington, Ben, and Ian McDonald. 2001. "Introduction: Race, Sport and British Society." In *"Race," Sport and British Society*, edited by Ben Carrington and Ian McDonald, 1–26. London: Routledge.

Cavallo, Dominick. 1981. *Muscles and Morals: Organized Playgrounds and Urban Reform, 1880–1920*. Philadelphia: University of Pennsylvania Press.

Chin, Christina B. 2012. "Hoops, History, and Crossing Over: Boundary Making and Community Building in Japanese American Youth Basketball Leagues." Doctoral diss., University of California, Los Angeles.

———. 2015. "'Aren't You a Little Short to Play Ball?' Japanese American Youth and Racial Microaggressions in Basketball Leagues." *Amerasia Journal* 41 (2): 47–65.

———. 2016. "'We've Got Team Spirit!' Ethnic Community Building and Japanese American Youth Basketball Leagues." *Ethnic and Racial Studies* 39: 1070–1088.

Chou, Rosalind S. 2012. *Asian American Sexual Politics: The Construction of Race, Gender, and Sexuality*. Lanham, MD: Rowman & Littlefield.

Chu, Bryan. 2008. "Asian Americans Remain Rare in Men's College Basketball: Players, Coaches Cite Race Factors." *SFGATE*, December 16. www.sfgate.com/sports/article/Asian-Americans-remain-rare-in-men-s-college-3258007.php.

Coakley, Jay. 2009. "From the Outside In: Burnout as an Organizational Issue." *Journal of Intercollegiate Sports* 2 (1): 35–41.

Collins, Patricia Hill. 2002. *Black Feminist Thought: Knowledge, Consciousness, and the Politics of Empowerment*. New York: Routledge.

Combs, Matthew Tyler, and Jeffrey Nathan Wasserstrom. 2013. "The Guard's Three Bodies: Linsanity, Celebrity and National Identity." *International Journal of the History of Sport* 30 (11): 1259–1270.

Connell, Raewyn. 2005. *Masculinities*. Berkeley: University of California Press.

Connell, Raewyn, and James W. Messerschmidt. 2005. "Hegemonic Masculinity Rethinking the Concept." *Gender & Society* 19 (6): 829–859.

Cooky, Cheryl. 2009. "'Girls Just Aren't Interested': The Social Construction of Interest in Girls' Sport." *Sociological Perspectives* 52 (2): 259–283.

Cooky, Cheryl, Michael A. Messner, and Michela Musto. 2015. "'It's Dude Time!' A Quarter Century of Excluding Women's Sports in Televised News and Highlight Shows." *Communication & Sport* 3: 261–287.

Costa, D. Margaret, Jane Adair, and Karen Jackson. 1991. "For the Good of the Community: Nisei Women's Basketball in the Thirties in Southern California." North American Society for Sport History (NASSH) Proceedings. http://www.la84foundation.org/SportsLibrary/NASSH_Proceedings/NP1991/NP1991zf.pdf.

Costello, Margaret Louise. 2009. "The Filipino Ringside Community: National Identity and the Heroic Myth of Manny Pacquiao." Master's thesis, Georgetown University.

Creef, Elena Tajima. 2004. "Another Lesson in 'How to Tell Your Friends from the Japs': The 1992 Winter Olympics Showdown between Kristi Yamaguchi of the United States and Midori Ito of Japan." In *Imaging Japanese America: The Visual Construction of Citizenship, Nation, and the Body*, 145–171. New York: New York University Press.

Culross, Mickey Hirano. 2014. "Calling All Submissions: Basketball Season Is Here and I Have a Migraine." *Rafu Shimpo*, December 10. www.rafu.com/.

Culver, Lawrence. 2010. "America's Playground: Recreation and Race." In *A Companion to Los Angeles*, edited by William Deverell and Greg Hise, 421–437. Malden, MA: Blackwell.

Dalrymple, Timothy. 2012. *Jeremy Lin: The Reason for the Linsanity*. New York: Center Street.

Daniels, Roger. 1974. *The Politics of Prejudice*. New York: Atheneum.

Davies, Wade. 2012. "How Boarding School Basketball Became Indian Basketball." In *American Indians and Popular Culture: Media, Sports, and Politics*, vol. 1, edited by Elizabeth DeLaney Hoffman, 263–78. Santa Barbara, CA: ABC-CLIO.

Deloria, Philip Joseph. 2004. *Indians in Unexpected Places*. Lawrence: University Press of Kansas.

Douglas, Delia D. 2002. "To Be Young, Gifted, Black and Female: A Meditation on the Cultural Politics at Play in Representations of Venus and Serena Williams." *Sociology of Sport Online* 5 (2): 1–16.

Dozier, W. L. 1999. "Gender, Sport, and Media." Doctoral diss., University of South Florida.

Duneier, Mitchell. 1999. *Sidewalk*. New York: Farrar, Straus and Giroux.

Eisen, George, and David Kenneth Wiggins, eds. 1995. *Ethnicity and Sport in North American History and Culture*. Santa Barbara, CA: ABC-CLIO.

Ellcessor, Elizabeth. 2012. "Tweeting@ feliciaday: Online Social Media, Convergence, and Subcultural Stardom." *Cinema Journal* 51 (2): 46–67.

Emery, Lynne Fauley, and Margaret Toohey-Costa. 1991. "Hoops and Skirts: Women's Basketball on the West Coast, 1892–1930s." In *A Century of Women's Basketball: From Frailty to Final Four*, edited by Joan S. Hult and Marianna Trekell, 137–154. Reston, VA: AAHPERD.

Fader, Mirin. 2016. "Queens of the Court: They May Be Petite, but Their Love of Basketball Is Huge." *Orange County Register*, May 3. www.ocregister.com/.

Fielding, Nigel G. 2002. "Automating the Ineffable: Qualitative Software and the Meaning of Qualitative Research." In *Qualitative Research in Action*, edited by Tim May, 161–178. London: Sage.

Figueroa, Arturo. 2003. "Community Identity and Sports: A Social History of Soccer in Salinas, California." *Culture, Society and Praxis* 2 (1): 27–32.

Foley, Douglas E. 1990. "The Great American Football Ritual: Reproducing Race, Class, and Gender Inequality." *Sociology of Sport Journal* 7 (2): 111–135.

Foucault, Michel. 1977. *Discipline and Punish*. Translated by Alan Sheridan. New York: Pantheon.

Franks, Joel S. 2010. *Crossing Sidelines, Crossing Cultures: Sport and Asian Pacific American Cultural Citizenship*. Lanham, MD: Rowman & Littlefield.

———. 2016. *Asian American Basketball: A Century of Sport, Community and Culture*. Jefferson, NC: McFarland.

Fugita, Stephen S., and David J. O'Brien. 1991. *Japanese American Ethnicity: The Persistence of Community*. Seattle: University of Washington Press.

Gardiner, Greg. 2003. "Running for Country Australian Print Media Representation of Indigenous Athletes in the 27th Olympiad." *Journal of Sport and Social Issues* 27 (3): 233–260.

Gems, Gerald R. 2013. *Sport and the Shaping of Italian-American Identity*. Syracuse, NY: Syracuse University Press.

———. 2014. "Historians Take on Ethnicity, Race, and Sport." In *A Companion to American Sport History*, edited by Steven A. Riess, 403–433. New York: John Wiley.

Glenn, Evelyn Nakano. 2002. *Unequal Freedom: How Race and Gender Shaped American Citizenship and Labor*. Cambridge, MA: Harvard University Press.

———. 2010. *Issei, Nisei, War Bride: Three Generations of Japanese American Women in Domestic Service*. Philadelphia, PA: Temple University Press.

Granovetter, Mark S. 1973. "The Strength of Weak Ties." *American Journal of Sociology* 78: 1360–1380.

———. 1982. "The Strength of Weak Ties: A Network Theory Revisited." In *Social Structure and Network Analysis*, edited by Peter V. Marsden and Nan Lin, 105–130. Beverly Hills, CA: Sage.

Grasmuck, Sherri. 2005. *Protecting Home: Class, Race, and Masculinity in Boys' Baseball*. New Brunswick, NJ: Rutgers University Press.

Grundy, Pamela. 2000. "From Amazons to Glamazons: The Rise and Fall of North Carolina Women's Basketball, 1920–1960." *Journal of American History* 87 (1): 112–146.

Hancock, Harrie Irving. 1904. *Japanese Physical Training: The System of Exercise, Diet, and General Mode of Living That Has Made the Mikado's People the Healthiest, Strongest, and Happiest Men and Women in the World*. New York: Putnam.

Hanson, Sandra L. 2005. "Hidden Dragons—Asian American Women and Sport." *Journal of Sport and Social Issues* 29 (3): 279–312.

Hargreaves, Jennifer. 1994. *Sporting Females: Critical Issues in the History and Sociology of Women's Sports*. New York: Routledge.

———. 2002. *Sporting Females: Critical Issues in the History and Sociology of Women's Sport*. New York: Routledge.

Hartmann, Douglas. 2003. *Race, Culture, and the Revolt of the Black Athlete: The 1968 Olympic Protests and Their Aftermath*. Chicago: University of Chicago Press.

Hedani, Dustin Tokuji. 2015. "Identity Ballin: J-League Basketball and Its Impact on Japanese American Identity." Master's thesis, San Francisco State University.

Hennink, Monique, Inge Hutter, and Ajay Bailey. 2010. *Qualitative Research Methods*. Thousand Oaks, CA: Sage.

Hesse-Biber, Sharlene N. 2007. "The Practice of Feminist In-Depth Interviewing." In *Feminist Research Practice: A Primer*, edited by Sharlene Nagy Hesse-Biber, 111–148. Thousand Oaks, CA: Sage.

Hesse-Biber, Sharlene N., and Patricia L. Leavy. 2007. *Feminist Research Practice: A Primer*. Thousand Oaks, CA: Sage.

Hoberman, John M. 1997. *Darwin's Athletes: How Sport Has Damaged Black America and Preserved the Myth of Race*. Boston: Houghton Mifflin Harcourt.

Hofmann, Annette R. 2008. "Between Ethnic Separation and Assimilation: German Immigrants and Their Athletic Endeavours in Their New American Home Country." *International Journal of the History of Sport* 25 (8): 993–1009.

Hult, Joan S. 1991. "The Saga of Competition: Basketball Battles and Governance Wars." In *A Century of Women's Basketball: From Frailty to Final Four*, edited by Joan S. Hult and Marianna Trekell, 223–248. Reston, VA: AAHPERD.

Innis-Jiménez, Michael D. 2009. "Beyond the Baseball Diamond and Basketball Court: Organized Leisure in Inter-war Mexican South Chicago." *International Journal of the History of Sport* 26 (7): 906–923.

Jamieson, Katherine M. 1998. "Reading Nancy Lopez: Decoding Representations of Race, Class, and Sexuality." *Sociology of Sport Journal* 15: 343–358.

———. 2001. "Reading Nancy Lopez: Decoding Representations of Race, Class, and Sexuality." In *Contemporary Issues in Sociology of Sport*, edited by Andrew Yiannakis and Merrill J. Melnick, 345–355. Champaign, IL: Human Kinetics.

Japanese American National Museum. 2014. "2014 Gala Dinner." www.janm .org/events/2014/dinner/.

Jenks, Hillary. 2008. "Urban Space, Ethnic Community, and National Belonging: The Political Landscape of Memory in Little Tokyo." *GeoJournal* 73 (3): 231–244.

Joo, Rachael, and Sameer Pandya. 2015. "On the Cultural Politics of Asian American Sports." *Amerasia Journal* 41 (2): ix–xx.

Joo, Sang Uk. 2015. "Consuming Sporting Orientals: Reading Asian American Sport Celebrities." Doctoral diss., University of Iowa.

Kagawa-Singer, Marjorie, Paul Ong, Tarry Hum, and Susan Nakaoka. 2012. "Cultivating a Cultural Home Space: The Case of Little Tokyo's Budokan of Los Angeles Project." *AAPI Nexus: Policy, Practice and Community* 10 (2): 23–36.

Kamphoff, Cindra S., and Nicole LaVoi. 2013. "Women in Positions of Power within US High School Sports." *Research Quarterly for Exercise and Sport* 84: A97.

Kane, Mary Jo. 1995. "Resistance/Transformation of the Oppositional Binary: Exposing Sport as a Continuum." *Journal of Sport and Social Issues* 19 (2): 191–218.

Kawahara, L. 2000. "Beyond the Lines: San Francisco Girls' Basketball, 1947–1967." In *More Than a Game: Sport in the Japanese American Community*, edited by Brian Niiya, 174–183. Los Angeles: Japanese American National Museum.

Kian, Edward M., John Vincent, and Michael Mondello. 2008. "Masculine Hegemonic Hoops: An Analysis of Media Coverage of March Madness." *Sociology of Sport Journal* 25 (2): 223–242.

Kietlinski, Robin. 2008. "Faster, Higher, Stronger: Gender and the Olympic Games in Twentieth Century Japan." Doctoral diss., University of Pennsylvania.

Kim, Claire Jean. 1999. "The Racial Triangulation of Asian Americans." *Politics and Society* 27 (1): 105–138.

Kim, Kyoung-yim. 2012. "Producing Korean Women Golfers on the LPGA Tour: Representing Gender, Race, Nation and Sport in a Transnational Context." Doctoral diss., University of Toronto.

King, C. Richard. 2006. "Defacements/Effacements Anti-Asian (American) Sentiment in Sport." *Journal of Sport and Social Issues* 30 (4): 340–352.

———. 2010. "Asian Americans in Unexpected Places: Sport, Racism, and the Media." In *Learning Culture through Sports: Perspectives on Society and Organized Sports,* edited by Sandra Spickard Prettyman and Brian Lampman, 174–181. Lanham, MD: Rowman & Littlefield.

———, ed. 2014. *Asian American Athletes in Sport and Society.* New York: Routledge.

King, Jamilah. 2012. "The Asian American Basketball Leagues That Helped Create Linsanity." *Colorlines,* February 21. www.colorlines.com/articles/asian-american-basketball-leagues-helped-create-linsanity.

King, Rebecca Chiyoko. 2002. "'Eligible' to Be Japanese American: Multiraciality in Basketball Leagues and Beauty Pageants." In *Contemporary Asian American Communities: Intersections and Divergences,* edited by Linda T. Vo and Rick Bonus, 120–133. Philadelphia: Temple University Press.

King-O'Riain, Rebecca Chiyoko. 2006. *Pure Beauty: Judging Race in Japanese American Beauty Pageants.* Minneapolis: University of Minnesota Press.

Knoppers, Annelies. 1992. "Explaining Male Dominance and Sex Segregation in Coaching: Three Approaches." *Quest* 44 (2): 210–227.

Komai, Chris. 2000. "The Japanese American Basketball Connection." In *More Than a Game: Sport in the Japanese American Community,* edited by Brian Niiya, 184–193. Los Angeles: Japanese American National Museum.

Konagaya, Hideyo. 2005. "Performing Manliness: Resistance and Harmony in Japanese American Taiko." In *Manly Traditions: The Folk Roots of American Masculinities,* edited by Simon T. Bronner, 134–153. Bloomington: Indiana University Press.

Koshy, Susan. 2004. *Sexual Naturalization: Asian Americans and Miscegenation.* Stanford, CA: Stanford University Press.

Kugelmass, Jack. 2007. *Jews, Sports, and the Rites of Citizenship.* Urbana: University of Illinois Press.

Kurashige, Lon. 2002. *Japanese American Celebration and Conflict: A History of Ethnic Identity and Festival, 1934–1990.* Berkeley: University of California Press.

LaVoi, Nicole M. 2009. "Occupational Sex Segregation in a Youth Soccer Organization: Females in Positions of Power." *Women in Sport and Physical Activity Journal* 18 (2): 25–37.

———. 2016. *Women in Sports Coaching.* New York: Routledge.

Le Espiritu, Yen. 2008. *Asian American Women and Men: Labor, Laws, and Love.* Lanham, MD: Rowman & Littlefield.

Lee, Johnathan, ed. 2016. *Chinese Americans: The History and Culture of a People.* Santa Barbara, CA: ABC-CLIO.

Lee, Stacey J. 1996. *Unraveling the "Model Minority" Stereotype: Listening to Asian American Youth.* New York: Teachers College Press.

Lee, Yomee. 2005. "A New Voice: Korean American Women in Sports." *International Review for the Sociology of Sport* 40 (4): 481–495.

Leitch, Will. 2012. "The Rocket." *GQ*, October 16. www.gq.com/story/jeremy -lin-gq-november-2012-cover-story.

Leonard, David J. 2014. "A Fantasy in the Garden, a Fantasy America Wants to Believe: Jeremy Lin, the NBA and Race Culture." In *Race in American Sports: Essays,* edited by James L. Conyers, Jr., 144–165. Jefferson, NC: McFarland.

Leung, Maxwell. 2013. "Jeremy Lin's Model Minority Problem." *Contexts* 12 (3): 52–56.

Levine, Peter. 1992. *Ellis Island to Ebbets Field: Sport and the American Jewish Experience.* Oxford: Oxford University Press.

Liang, Ursula. 2014. *9-Man.* Documentary film.

Liberti, Rita. 1999. "'We Were Ladies, We Just Played Basketball Like Boys': African American Womanhood and Competitive Basketball at Bennett College, 1928–1942." *Journal of Sport History* 26 (3): 567–584.

Lim, Shirley Jennifer. 2006. *A Feeling of Belonging: Asian American Women's Public Culture, 1930–1960.* New York: New York University Press.

———. 2008. "Asian American Youth Culture." *Journal of Asian American Studies* 11 (2): 211–228.

Lin, Nan. 2000. "Inequality in Social Capital." *Contemporary Sociology* 29 (6): 785–795.

Lowe, Lisa. 2016. "Afterword." In *Asian American Sporting Cultures,* edited by Stanley I. Thangaraj, Constancio R. Arnoldo, Jr., and Christina B. Chin, 247–252. New York: New York University Press.

Macartney, Suzanne, Alemayehu Bishaw, and Kayla Fontenot. 2013, February. "Poverty Rates for Selected Detailed Race and Hispanic Groups by State and Place: 2007–2011." American Community Survey Briefs. www.census .gov/prod/2013pubs/acsbr11–17.pdf.

Matsumoto, Valerie J. 2014. *City Girls: The Nisei Social World in Los Angeles, 1920–1950.* New York: Oxford University Press.

McElroy, Kathleen. 2014. "Basket Case: Framing the Intersection of 'Linsanity' and Blackness." *Howard Journal of Communications* 25 (4): 431–451.

McElwain, Max. 2004. *The Only Dance in Iowa: A History of Six-Player Girls' Basketball.* Lincoln: University of Nebraska Press.

Messner, Michael A. 1988. "Sports and Male Domination: The Female Athlete as Contested Ideological Terrain." *Sociology of Sport Journal* 5 (3): 197–211.

———. 2002. *Taking the Field: Women, Men, and Sports.* Minneapolis: University of Minnesota Press.

———. 2009. *It's All for the Kids: Gender, Families, and Youth Sports*. Berkeley: University of California Press.

———. 2012. "Reflections on Communication and Sport: On Men and Masculinities." *Communication & Sport* 1: 113–124.

Messner, Michael A., and Suzel Bozada-Deas. 2009. "Separating the Men from the Moms: The Making of Adult Gender Segregation in Youth Sports." *Gender & Society* 23 (1): 49–71.

Messner, Michael A., Margaret C. Duncan, and Nicole Willms. 2006. "This Revolution Is Not Being Televised." *Contexts* 5: 34–38.

Miller, Aaron L. 2015. "Foucauldian Theory and the Making of the Japanese Sporting Body." *Contemporary Japan* 27 (1): 13–31.

Miller, Patrick B. 1998. "The Anatomy of Scientific Racism: Racialist Responses to Black Athletic Achievement." *Journal of Sport History* 25: 119–151.

Mok, Teresa A., and David W. Chih. 2015. "The Intersection of the Asian American Model Minority Myth and Sports: The 'Linsanity' Narrative." In *Modern Societal Impacts of the Model Minority Stereotype*, edited by Nicholas Daniel Hartlep, 63. Hershey, PA: IGI Global.

Montez de Oca, Jeffrey. 2013. *Discipline and Indulgence: College Football, Media, and the American Way of Life during the Cold War*. New Brunswick, NJ: Rutgers University Press.

Murjani, Monisha. 2014. "Breaking Apart the Model Minority and Perpetual Foreigner Stereotypes: Asian Americans and Cultural Capital." *Vermont Connection* 35: 78–90.

Musto, Michela. 2014. "Athletes in the Pool, Girls and Boys on Deck: The Contextual Construction of Gender in Coed Youth Swimming." *Gender & Society* 28 (3): 359–380.

Nagel, Joane. 1994. "Constructing Ethnicity: Creating and Recreating Ethnic Identity and Culture." *Social Problems* 41 (1): 152–176.

Nakamura, Yuka. 2016. "Rethinking Identity Politics: The Multiple Attachments of an 'Exclusive' Sport Organization." *Sociology of Sport Journal* 33 (2): 146–155.

National Collegiate Athletic Association. 2010. *NCAA Student-Athlete Ethnicity Report: 1999/2000–2009/10*. www.ncaapublications.com.

Niiya, Brian, ed. 1993. *Japanese American History: An A-to-Z Reference from 1868 to the Present*. New York: Facts on File.

———, ed. 2000. *More Than a Game: Sport in the Japanese American Community*. Los Angeles: Japanese American National Museum.

Nikkei Games. 2014. "2014 Nikkei Games: 'Games for the Generations.' History." www.ocsabasketball.org/wwwNikkeigames/general/History.pdf.

Omi, Michael, and Howard Winant. 2014. *Racial Formation in the United States*. New York: Routledge.

Osajima, Keith. 1988. "Asian Americans as the Model Minority: An Analysis of the Popular Press Image in the 1960s and 1980s." In *Reflections on Shattered Windows: Promises and Prospects for Asian American Studies*, edited by Gary Okihiro, Shirley Hune, Arthur Hansen, and John Liu, 165–174. Pullman: Washington State University Press.

Paek, Hye Jin, and Hemant Shah. 2003. "Racial Ideology, Model Minorities, and the 'Not-So-Silent Partner': Stereotyping of Asian Americans in US Magazine Advertising." *Howard Journal of Communication* 14 (4): 225–243.

Paraschak, Victoria. 1990. "Organized Sport for Native Females on the Six Nations Reserve, Ontario from 1968 to 1980: A Comparison of Dominant and Emergent Sport Systems." *Canadian Journal of History of Sport* 21 (2): 70–80.

———. 1995. "Invisible but Not Absent: Aboriginal Women in Sport and Recreation." *Canadian Woman Studies* 15 (4): 71–72.

———. 1999. "Doing Race, Doing Gender: First Nations, 'Sport,' and Gender Relations." In *Sport and Gender in Canada*, edited by Philip White and Kevin Young, 153–169. Oxford: Oxford University Press.

Paraschak, Victoria, and Janice Forsyth. 2010. "Aboriginal Women 'Working' at Play: Canadian Insights." *Ethnologies* 32 (1): 157–173.

Park, Michael K. 2015. "Race, Hegemonic Masculinity, and the 'Linpossible!' An Analysis of Media Representations of Jeremy Lin." *Communication & Sport* 3 (4): 367–389.

Park, Roberta J. 1995. "Athletic Leagues and Playdays: Sports and Games for School-Aged Children in California, 1900–World War II." In *Proceedings and Newsletter—North American Society for Sport History*, 26–27. http://library.la84.org/SportsLibrary/NASSH_Proceedings/NP1995/NP1995p.pdf.

———. 2000. "Sport and Recreation among Chinese American Communities of the Pacific Coast from Time of Arrival to the 'Quiet Decade' of the 1950s." *Journal of Sport History* 27 (3): 445–480.

Pedersen, Paul Mark. 2002. "Examining Equity in Newspaper Photographs: A Content Analysis of the Print Media Photographic Coverage of Interscholastic Athletics." *International Review for the Sociology of Sport* 37 (3–4): 303–318.

Penrose, Jan. 2003. "When All the Cowboys Are Indians: The Nature of Race in All-Indian Rodeo." *Annals of the Association of American Geographers* 93 (3): 687–705.

Pescador, Juan Javier. 2004. "¡Vamos Taximaroa! Mexican/Chicano Soccer Associations and Transnational/Translocal Communities, 1967–2002." *Latino Studies* 2 (3): 352–376.

Petersen, William. 1966. "Success Story: Japanese-American Style." *New York Times Magazine*, January 9, 21.

Putnam, Robert D. 2000. *Bowling Alone: The Collapse and the Revival of American Democracy*. New York: Simon & Schuster.

Puwar, Nirmal. 2004. *Space Invaders: Race, Gender and Bodies Out of Place*. New York: Berg.

Pyke, Karen D., and Denise L. Johnson. 2003. "Asian American Women and Racialized Femininities: 'Doing' Gender across Cultural Worlds." *Gender & Society* 17 (1): 33–53.

Regalado, Samuel O. 2000. "Incarcerated Sport: Nisei Women's Softball and Athletics during Japanese American Internment." *Critique* 27: 431–444.

———. 2013. *Nikkei Baseball: Japanese American Players from Immigration and Internment to the Major Leagues*. Urbana: University of Illinois Press.

Robinson, Tracy, and Janie Victoria Ward. 1991. "'A Belief in Self Far Greater Than Anyone's Disbelief': Cultivating Resistance among African American Female Adolescents." *Women & Therapy* 11 (3–4): 87–103.

Rosaldo, Renato. 1997. "Cultural Citizenship, Inequality, and Multiculturalism." In *Latino Cultural Citizenship: Claiming Identity, Space, and Rights*, edited by William V. Flores and Rina Benmayor, 27–38. Boston: Beacon.

Sabo, Don. 2009. "The Gender Gap in Youth Sports: Too Many Urban Girls Are Being Left Behind." *Journal of Physical Education, Recreation & Dance* 80 (8): 35–40.

Saito, Leland. 2009. *The Politics of Exclusion: The Failure of Race-Neutral Policies in Urban America*. Stanford, CA: Stanford University Press.

Santillan, Richard. 2000. *Mexican Baseball Teams in the Midwest, 1916–1965: The Politics of Cultural Survival and Civil Rights*. Vol. 7. Tucson: University of Arizona, Mexican American Studies Research Center.

Schippers, Mimi. 2007. "Recovering the Feminine Other: Masculinity, Femininity, and Gender Hegemony." *Theory and Society* 36 (1): 85–102.

Sclar, Arieh. 2008. "'A Sport at Which Jews Excel': Jewish Basketball in American Society, 1900–1951." Doctoral diss., Stony Brook University.

Shakib, Sohaila, and Michele D. Dunbar. 2002. "The Social Construction of Female and Male High School Basketball Participation: Reproducing the Gender Order through a Two-Tiered Sporting Institution." *Sociological Perspectives* 45 (4): 353–378.

Silverstein, Lynn. 1996. "Full-Court Press? The New York Times' Coverage of the 1995 Women's NCAA Basketball Tournament." Paper presented at the annual meeting of the Association for Education in Journalism and Communication, Anaheim, CA. http://files.eric.ed.gov/fulltext/ED400551.pdf.

Smith, Yvonne R. 1992. "Women of Color in Society and Sport." *Quest* 44 (2): 228–250.

Spaaij, Ramn. 2011. *Sport and Social Mobility: Crossing Boundaries*. New York: Taylor & Francis.

Stodolska, Monika, and Konstantinos Alexandris. 2004. "The Role of Recreational Sport in the Adaptation of First Generation Immigrants in the United States." *Journal of Leisure Research* 36 (3): 379–413.

Sue, Derald Wing. 2010. *Microaggressions in Everyday Life: Race, Gender, and Sexual Orientation*. Hoboken, NJ: John Wiley.

Sue, Derald Wing, Christina M. Capodilupo, Kevin L. Nadal, and Gina C. Torino. 2008. "Racial Microaggressions and the Power to Define Reality." *American Psychologist* 63 (4): 277–279.

Sue, Derald Wing, Christina M. Capodilupo, Gina C. Torino, Jennifer M. Bucceri, Aisha Holder, Kevin L. Nadal, and Marta Esquilin. 2007. "Racial Microaggressions in Everyday Life: Implications for Clinical Practice." *American Psychologist* 62 (4): 271–286.

Swanson, Lisa. 2009. "Complicating the 'Soccer Mom': The Cultural Politics of Forming Class-Based Identity, Distinction, and Necessity." *Research Quarterly for Exercise and Sport* 80 (2): 345–354.

Takaki, Ronald. 1989. *Strangers from a Different Shore: A History of Asian Americans*. New York: Penguin.

Thangaraj, Stanley I. 2014. "'Liting It Up': Indo-Pak Basketball and Finding the American-ness in South Asian American Institutions." In *Asian American Athletes in Sport and Society*, edited by C. Richard King, 47–66. New York: Routledge.

———. 2015. *Desi Hoop Dreams: Pickup Basketball and the Making of Asian American Masculinity*. New York: New York University Press.

Tigers Youth Club. n.d. "History." www.tigeryouthclub.org/set_history.htm.

Trussell, Dawn E., and Susan M. Shaw. 2012. "Organized Youth Sport and Parenting in Public and Private Spaces." *Leisure Sciences* 34 (5): 377–394.

Tuan, Mia. 1999. "On Asian American Ice Queens and Multigeneration Asian Ethnics." *Amerasia Journal* 25: 181–187.

US Census Bureau. 2006–2010. "American Community Survey." www.census.gov/programs-surveys/acs/.

———. 2007–2011. "American Community Survey." www.census.gov/programs-surveys/acs/.

Vang, Chia Youyee. 2016. "Hmong Youth, American Football, and the Cultural Politics of Ethnic Sports Tournaments." In *Asian American Sporting Cultures*, edited by Stanley I. Thangaraj, Constancio R. Arnoldo, Jr., and Christina B. Chin, 199–220. New York: New York University Press.

Vavrus, Mary Douglas. 2000. "From Women of the Year to 'Soccer Moms': The Case of the Incredible Shrinking Women." *Political Communication* 17 (2): 193–213.

Vertinsky, Patricia. 1998. "'Run, Jane, Run': Central Tensions in the Current Debate about Enhancing Women's Health through Exercise." *Women & Health* 27 (4): 81–111.

Vertinsky, Patricia, and Jennifer Hargreaves. 2006. *Physical Culture, Power, and the Body.* New York: Routledge.

Villenas, Sofia, and Melissa Moreno. 2001. "To Valerse Por Si Misma between Race, Capitalism, and Patriarchy: Latina Mother-Daughter Pedagogies in North Carolina." *International Journal of Qualitative Studies in Education* 14 (5): 671–687.

Vo, Linda T., and Rick Bonus, eds. 2002. *Contemporary Asian American Communities: Intersections and Divergences.* Philadelphia: Temple University Press.

Wachs, Faye Linda. 2002. "Leveling the Playing Field: Negotiating Gendered Rules in Coed Softball." *Journal of Sport and Social Issues* 26: 300–316.

———. 2006. "'Throw Like a Girl' Doesn't Mean What It Used To: Research on Gender, Language, and Power." In *Sport, Rhetoric, and Gender*, edited by Linda K. Fuller, 43–52. New York: Springer.

Walker, Nefertiti. 2016. "Cross-Gender Coaching: Women Coaching Men." In *Women in Sports Coaching*, edited by Nicole M. LaVoi, 111–125. New York: Routledge.

Walseth, Kristin. 2008. "Bridging and Bonding Social Capital in Sport—Experiences of Young Women with an Immigrant Background." *Sport, Education and Society* 13 (1): 1–17.

Wang, Oliver. 2016. "Everybody Loves an Underdog: Learning from Linsanity." In *Asian American Sporting Cultures*, edited by Stanley I. Thangaraj, Constancio R. Arnoldo, Jr., and Christina B. Chin, 75–101. New York: New York University Press.

Ward, Janie Victoria. 1996. "Raising Resisters: The Role of Truth Telling in the Psychological Development of African American Girls." In *Urban Girls: Resisting Stereotypes, Creating Identities*, edited by Bonnie J. Leadbeater and Niobe Way, 85–99. New York: New York University Press.

Waters, Mary C. 1990. *Ethnic Options: Choosing Identities in America.* Berkeley: University of California Press.

Waugh, Isami Arifuku. 1978. "Hidden Crime and Deviance in the Japanese-American Community, 1920–1946." Doctoral diss., University of California, Berkeley.

Wenger, Etienne. 1998. *Communities of Practice: Learning, Meaning, and Identity.* Cambridge: Cambridge University Press.

Wensing, Emma Hope. 2003. "New Zealand National Identity in Print Media Representations of the 2002 Commonwealth Games." Master's thesis, University of Waikato.

Wensing, Emma Hope, and Toni Bruce. 2003. "Bending the Rules Media Representations of Gender during an International Sporting Event." *International Review for the Sociology of Sport* 38 (4): 387–396.

West, Candace, and Don H. Zimmerman. 1987. "Doing Gender." *Gender & Society* 1 (2): 125–151.

Williams, Linda Darnette. 1987. "An Analysis of American Sportswomen in Two Negro Newspapers: The *Pittsburgh Courier*, 1924–1948 and the *Chicago Defender*, 1932–1948." Doctoral diss., Ohio State University.

Williams, Linda Darnette, and Pamela J. Creedon. 1994. "Sportswomen in Black and White: Sports History from an Afro-American Perspective." In *Women, Media and Sport: Challenging Gender Values*, edited by Pamela J. Creedon, 45–66. Thousand Oaks, CA: Sage.

Williams, L. Susan. 2002. "Trying on Gender, Gender Regimes, and the Process of Becoming Women." *Gender & Society* 16: 29–52.

Willms, Nicole. 2014. "Cheering for Our Team: Coverage of Women's Basketball in a Japanese American Community Newspaper." In *Asian American Athletes in Sport and Society*, edited by C. Richard King, 67–85. New York: Routledge.

Wren, James A. 2016. "Chinese American Baseball." In *Chinese Americans: The History and Culture of a People*, edited by Johnathan Lee, 335–338. Santa Barbara, CA: ABC-CLIO.

Wrynn, Alison M. 1995. "The Recreation and Leisure Pursuits of Japanese Americans in World War II Internment Camps." In *Ethnicity and Sport in North American History and Culture*, edited by George Eisen and David Kenneth Wiggins, 117–132. Santa Barbara, CA: ABC-CLIO.

Yano, Christine Reiko. 2006. *Crowning the Nice Girl: Gender, Ethnicity, and Culture in Hawaii's Cherry Blossom Festival*. Honolulu: University of Hawaii Press.

Yep, Kathleen S. 2009. *Outside the Paint: When Basketball Ruled at the Chinese Playground*. Philadelphia: Temple University Press.

———. 2010. "Playing Rough and Tough: Chinese American Women Basketball Players in the 1930s and 1940s." *Frontiers* 31 (1): 123–141.

———. 2012. "Peddling Sport: Liberal Multiculturalism and the Racial Triangulation of Blackness, Chineseness and Native American-ness in Professional Basketball." *Ethnic and Racial Studies* 35 (6): 971–987.

Yoo, David, and Konrad Ng. 2012. "#Linsanity." *Amerasia Journal* 38 (3): 129–132.

Yorkey, Mike. 2012. *Linspired: The Remarkable Rise of Jeremy Lin*. Grand Rapids, MI: Zondervan.

Yosso, Tara J. 2005. "Whose Culture Has Capital? A Critical Race Theory Discussion of Community Cultural Wealth." *Race Ethnicity and Education* 8 (1): 69–91.

Zieff, Susan G. 2000. "From Badminton to the Bolero: Sport and Recreation in San Francisco's Chinatown, 1895–1950." *Journal of Sport History* 27 (1): 1–29.

Zinn, Maxine Baca, and Bonnie Thorton Dill. 2003. "Theorizing Difference from Multiracial Feminism." In *Reconstructing Gender: A Multicultural Anthology*, edited by Estelle Disch, 81–90. Boston: University of Massachusetts Press.

Zirin, Dave. 2012. "Jeremy Lin: Taking the Weight." *Nation* 294 (12): 24–25.

INDEX

ABOUT THE AUTHOR

NICOLE WILLMS is an assistant professor at Gonzaga University in the Department of Sociology. Her research focuses on gender, race, and class in American sports. In addition to her work on Japanese American basketball, she is also examining the negotiation of gendered space on school playgrounds and the discourses surrounding women's basketball. At Gonzaga, she enjoys mentoring sociology students in the undergraduate research program.